THE PLAN OF ST GALL

IN BRIEF

Haec tibi dulcissime fili cozb̄te de posicione officinarum paucis exemplata direxi · quibus sollertiam exerceas tuā meamq · deuotionē utcumq · cognoscas · qua tuae bonae uolun tati satisfacere me segnem non inueniri confido · Ne suspiceris autem me haec ideo elaborasse · quod uos putemus nr̄is indigere magisteriis · sed potius ob amorē dei tibi soli ꝑscrutinanda pinxisse amicabili fr̄nitatis intuitu crede · Uale in xp̄o semꝑ memor nri am̄.

For thee, my sweetest son Gozbertus, have I drawn out this briefly annotated copy of the layout of the monastic buildings, with which you may exercise your ingenuity and recognize my devotion, whereby I trust you do not find me slow to satisfy your wishes. Do not imagine that I have undertaken this task supposing you to stand in need of our instructions, but rather believe that out of love of God and in the friendly zeal of brotherhood I have depicted this for you alone to scrutinize. Farewell in Christ, always mindful of us, Amen.

*

The salutation, "my sweetest son", implies that the writer of the note of transmittal was of higher rank than the receiver.

This dedicatory inscription of the Plan of St Gall is illustrated on page 67.

SPECIAL ACKNOWLEDGMENT: *Ten years ago, in 1972, the University of California was privileged to participate in forging an important cultural link between the peoples of Switzerland and the United States. Through efforts of Pro Helvetia and Mr. Luc Boissonnas, its director, and the University Art Museum, Berkeley, and its director Peter Selz, now Professor of Art History, Berkeley, the first major exhibition of the paintings of Ferdinand Hodler was mounted in this country. The exhibition "The Plan of St Gall" forms a new link between this University and the nation of Switzerland.*

We thank Professor Roger Stally, Trinity College, Dublin, and Professor Rosemary Cramp, University of Durham, as well as Mr. Sean McCrum of the Douglas Hyde Gallery, Trinity College, and Mr. J. R. Kilburn of the Bede Monastery Museum, Jarrow, for helping to launch the St Gall exhibit in Ireland and in England.

Many hands and minds touched the St Gall project long before either this book or the exhibit were formed. With the late Hans Bessler and the support of the Historical Society of St Gall, Dr. Msgr. Johannes Duft (then head of the Stiftsbibliothek of St Gall and official guardian of the Plan) made possible, in 1952, publication of a magnificent eight color facsimile of the Plan of St Gall. The facsimile made the Plan available for intensive measurement studies that could not be carried out on the fragile parchment.

Professor Wolfgang Braunfels gave a motivating impulse to Walter Horn and Ernest Born when he charged them with a twofold task for the Council of Europe Exposition "Charlemagne," convened in Aachen in 1965. They were to provide architectural drawings for a new model of the Plan's buildings, and also a summary of current knowledge about the Plan. Because of complex historical questions and the controversial nature of many issues connected with it, the second task could not be fulfilled at Aachen. Professor Braunfels' challenge eventually resulted in the three-volume work, THE PLAN OF ST GALL, *published by the University of California Press in 1979.*

THE PLAN OF St GALL IN BRIEF

by

LORNA PRICE

An overview based on the 3-volume work by WALTER HORN and ERNEST BORN including selected facsimile illustrations in color and black and white, and also a Note on Architectural Scale Models, with illustrations in color of the Reconstruction Scale Model of the Monastery of the PLAN of St GALL, as interpreted by Horn and Born, and crafted in basswood by Carl Bertil Lund.

UNIVERSITY OF CALIFORNIA PRESS BERKELEY LOS ANGELES LONDON

1982

UNIVERSITY OF CALIFORNIA PRESS

Berkeley and Los Angeles, California

UNIVERSITY OF CALIFORNIA PRESS, Ltd

London, England

LIBRARY OF CONGRESS CATALOGUE CARD NUMBER 82-70215

INTERNATIONAL STANDARD BOOK NUMBER

0-520-04736-2 [CLOTH]

0-520-04334-0 [PAPER]

MONOGRAM *Drawing from a silver coin, somewhat enlarged. Boundless imagination and invention are displayed in the arrangement of letters comprising the monogram that dates to the second period of Carolingian coinage. It appears on the obverse of the coin and spells KAROLUS (as illustrated) or KARLUS (in Period I the spelling is CAROLUS).*

The same freedom seen in graphic and sculptural design in coins of Period II is paralleled by radical transformations of this period in concepts of minting money—changes which created a new monetary system for Europe for long afterward. The coinage system reforms established under Charlemagne constitute the most important in the monetary history of Europe.

CONTENTS

ILLUSTRATIONS*

* *Unless otherwise identified, portions of the Plan of St Gall are reproduced after the Löpfe-Benz facsimile of 1952. "Authors' reconstruction" indicates research drawings by Horn and Born. These illustrations were first reproduced in* The Plan of St Gall, *University of California Press, Berkeley, 1979.*

ILLUSTRATIONS

LAON. Gospel Book (mid-9th cent.)
Bibliothèque Municipale, MS 63, fol 26.
SCHOOL OF TOURS
Drawn capital letters from an incipit page. ca. 1.75 x original size.

FOREWORD
& ACKNOWLEDGMENTS

by LORNA PRICE

THE PLAN OF ST GALL represents an ideal architectural scheme that was formed as part of an effort to guide Benedictine monastic planning in the Age of Charlemagne. The Plan portrays a great church surrounded by buildings of a monastic community designed to serve some 270 souls, both monks and laymen. Need for such a scheme was likely recognized, as the authors of the study of the Plan believe, in the context of two synods held in the Aachen palace of Louis the Pious in the years 816 and 817. Among the primary goals of these synods was regulation of all aspects of Benedictine monastic life.

The Plan of St Gall preserves a sophisticated ideal of an architecture and of a community. Conceived in enthusiasm, it nonetheless gave rise to controversy from the outset. Even at the time the original scheme was developed, the imperial court was stirred by disagreement over the desirable size of an abbey church. At 300 feet, the church of the Plan reflects the vision of men who, having served under Charlemagne, were accustomed to thinking in heroic terms. But the reform and moderation already in the air eventually prevailed, with profound and hurtful effect upon the scheme embodied in the Plan.*

The Plan of St Gall was traced on parchment between the years 820-830 from a lost original. It is a work of great beauty and rationality. Professor Wolfgang Braunfels has described the condition and purpose of this remarkable document in words that the Plan's originators might themselves have chosen:

> *The Plan itself is a work of art of the highest order. It draws upon old customs and serves old ideals. In styling it a "near utopian concept," we want to stress the fact that it is an architectural entity whose outer order most nearly reflects its inner order, and whose laws govern the aesthetic organization of even the smallest buildings and gardens. It was to result in an organism within which the Rule of Saint Benedict could be lived in the most rational manner . . . . It was a self-contained and completely rationalized monastic entity.*‡

The Plan depicts buildings assembled in an architecturally coherent and brilliantly arranged composition, superbly delineated. It is annotated by a wealth of explanatory legends, of which nearly forty are composed, with scholastic elegance, in meter; these define the function and furnishings of each of its structures. But because it is a complete plan–and because it is a drawing–the Plan of St Gall is a unique architectural entity in the vast array of early medieval records that abound with verbal descriptions of monastic life and architecture.

ON OCCASION the architecture of monastic communities was described by abbots who recorded details of their own building campaigns, or perhaps delegated monks to observe building activities conducted elsewhere. But the records of those who reported in writing their own programs, or those of other abbeys, generally were framed by men mainly preoccupied with affairs other than architecture. Such commentators may have been teachers, scholars, experts in liturgy or the conduct of religious services. But the

* These ideas are explained more fully below, pp. 12-17.

‡ *The Plan of St Gall,* University of California Press, Berkeley 1979, vol. I, p. xxi.

brevity and imprecision of their observations suggest that few could have laid claim to being engaged chiefly in the exacting concerns of architecture. Thus, modern scholarly efforts to reconstruct visually what these early observers transmitted in only verbal accounts confront insurmountable barriers.

But the Plan of St Gall is the creation of an architect's mind. It is a drawing and as such, annotations notwithstanding, it communicates eloquently by nonverbal means. Its buildings are positioned with awareness of specific functional interrelationships; their graphic expression is succinct, economical. The entire Plan reveals an intelligence focussed upon architecture of a high and complex order, and heightened by aesthetic sensibilities rare in any age.

The Plan of St Gall is composed of forty ground plans. These delineate numerous structures as well as a few gardens, an orchard, some lines indicating fences or walls, a road. Some details are readily identified: beds, fireplaces, privies, animal stalls, benches and tables, altars in the church, barrels in the cellar. For hundreds of years, however, certain features of the Plan remained obscure. Where were the stairways necessary for access between first and second stories? Could the scale of the Plan be identified, and if so, was it applied consistently thoughout the drawing? What purpose was served by the mysterious "*testu*", a square symbol drawn in the center of each guest and service building? Had they been built, what would these structures have looked like? These questions, and many others, have been raised since 1844 when modern studies of the Plan began to reveal its many facets—studies often marked by colorful and diverse arguments.

This book attempts to suggest the complexity of the Plan of St Gall as well as its astonishing vitality. Its intent is to engage the reader in the energy of the Plan, even if it is seen as no more than an arresting graphic image. Although some of its subtleties are esoteric, the Plan was not conceived for esoteric reasons. Rather, it is a tool intended to inform those whose metiers were stone and mortar, timber and packed earth, as well as education and the salvation of souls.

WHAT WE CAME TO REFER TO as "the St Gall project" in Berkeley—in fact the most comprehensive scrutiny of the Plan ever undertaken—began in the 1950s. Walter Horn and Ernest Born had for some time been investigating the origins of the three-aisled timber hall when, perhaps inevitably, they turned their attention to questions concerning the architectural forms of the buildings of the Plan. Their intensive studies of vernacular architecture in Northern Europe (which, they note, "is a universally neglected field") eventually helped solve the riddle of the design and construction of the Plan's guest and service buildings. This preoccupation proved to be inseparable from a consideration of the controversial issue of the Plan's scale, a problem for which they achieved an elegant and definitive solution.

These early studies were advanced in the 1960s, when architectural historian Horn and architect Born were commissioned to provide a new reconstruction model of the buildings of the Plan of St Gall for the Council of Europe exposition, "Charlemagne." It was convened in Aachen for the purpose of reviewing and evaluating the then-current state of information and research about the Age of Charlemagne. One of their tasks was to demonstrate, in the model, resolutions of controversies that interpretation of the Plan had generated among scholars in the nineteenth century.

Research for the Aachen model eventually accumulated such a wealth of new information about building in the Carolingian era that Horn and Born decided to collaborate in writing a book. Their remarkable work, entitled *The Plan of St Gall,* was published in three volumes by the University of California Press on Christmas Day in 1979.

Produced to exacting standards, *The Plan of St Gall* has frequently been cited as an exemplar of the bookmaker's craft. Although generous subvention, and the authors' determination, kept costs as low as feasible while maintaining their quality, the books when issued were still expensive—of a quality that usually attains publication only through subscription in advance of commitment to publish. But price notwithstanding, *The Plan of St Gall* went out of print in less than a year.* It was not just collectors who snapped up these books; the edition of 2500 had no exclusive appeal for the antiquarian. Rather, they were acquired by readers with wide-ranging interests, whose minds were captivated by the scope of the study, whose hands and eyes delighted in the execution of the books, and whose long patience in awaiting their publication was, we like to think, amply rewarded.

All during the 1970s, while work at the Press was going forward on the publication project, the Plan continued to work upon the imaginations of others who had contact with it. In 1972 the Regents of the University of California, recognizing the importance of the Aachen model as a research tool, and encouraged by Peter Selz, then director of the University Art Museum, decided to commission a duplicate of it for the University. Construction of the second model by Siegfried Karschunke, who had made the previous one, was unfortunately halted at an early stage by his death.

Not until 1974 did work resume on the University model. By that time an entirely new conception of it had been envisioned by Horn and Born. Rather than recreate the detailed timber-structure rendering of Aachen, they commissioned Carl Bertil Lund to make an abstract, solid-volume ensemble of the buildings at the scale of the Plan: 1/16″ equals 1′; he also made some larger, timber-structure models of certain buildings at the scale 1/8″ equals 1′. This model represented their most recent research, some of it new even since the Aachen exposition.

Lund's new model was seen in this country by Professor Florens Deuchler of the University of Geneva; he is also an officer of Pro Helvetia, an organization devoted to the arts and culture of Switzerland. Encouraged by Deuchler and Dr. Christoph Eggenberger, Pro Helvetia executive officer for exhibitions and a distinguished scholar, the board of Pro Helvetia, led by Director Luc Boissonnas, commissioned a similar model. They then proposed that it be presented in the context of an international traveling exhibition in order to gain the widest possible audience for it.

* The books received eight major awards for scholarship, bookmaking, and typography. In 1982 the authors received a medal from the American Institute of Architects, given to individuals or organizations for specific projects related to architecture. Reprinting of the volumes is under consideration.

& ACKNOWLEDGMENTS

Thus the model discussed and illustrated below, pages 94-99, came to be constructed and eventually displayed in the matrix of the exhibit that inspired the form and content of the present book.

The research conducted by Horn and Born brought resolution to many old theories about the Plan of St Gall, and proposed many new ones in an exhilirating infusion of insights developed through long study. Their work, *The Plan of St Gall,* has been called "one of those herioc enterprises of medieval architectural history," for they have recreated not only the architecture of the document but the life of the era from which it sprang. One eloquent appreciation states that the books provide "as brilliant a paradigm of 'total history' as we are likely to see. . . . Horn and Born have given us a new appreciation of the meaning of western humanism. They have also given us a fresh insight into the question of the psalmist: 'What is man that you are mindful of him? . . . You have made him a little less than the angels.' "*

Over the centuries communities founded upon common bonds and beliefs have appeared, then vanished. The Plan of St Gall is a testament of a manner of life and thought that has seldom attained lasting reality in human experience. The irony at its core—it is a noble artifact of a great monument never built as conceived—is not lost upon us. Yet, despite failure and disappointment the quest for a more nearly perfect order expressed by hand, mind, and spirit continues to address a need deeply felt in human affairs. Therefore the Plan of St Gall retains its complex vitality long after one might have expected social change and technologies to render its content obsolete, or at least naive. Today we are far from the era in which church and state were inseparable instruments, symbols for all human endeavor. But in the face of grave extremes of social condition, overspecialization, limited resources, the exemplar of the self-sufficient community reappears as an idea worthy of consideration once again.

But first and last, the Plan is a drawing. Elegant, accomplished, rational, filled with the integrity of its purpose and making, it remains unaccountably aloof, somewhat mysterious. Despite its insistence upon pragmatic values, it soars. The opportunity to frame this presentation challenged us to seek out these qualities of the Plan, to convey some of the excitement surely felt by its makers and just as surely part of it today. This book offers a brief excursion to the heart of the Plan of St Gall. It is dedicated to the document that, with its heritage from Antiquity and its millennial age, survives as a quintessentially human statement.

OUR WORK on *The Plan of St Gall,* then our work on the exhibition treatment of it, and then this book to complement the exhibition, are efforts supported by many persons who responded to the challenge of understanding an extraordinary artifact of human inspiration.

The special character of each facet of the St Gall project owes to the efforts of Pro Helvetia, Zürich, led by its president, Professor Roland Ruffieux of the universities of Lausanne and Fribourg. Luc Boissonnas, Director of Pro Helvetia, Dr. Christoph Eggenberger, its learned exhibitions officer, and Professor Florens Deuchler, University of Geneva and an officer of Pro Helvetia, worked tirelessly to bring this presentation to maturity. The Consulate General of Switzerland in San Francisco often served as intermediary and has maintained lively interest in the project.

At the Berkeley campus of the University of California, Chancellor Ira Michael Heyman, Vice Chancellor Roderick B. Park, and Assistant Chancellor Glen H. Grant participated in bringing the University of California and the people of Switzerland into this unique collaboration. We are all beneficiaries of their imagination and diplomacy.

The University Art Museum, Berkeley, has been involved with the St Gall project and committed to its exhibition aspect for a decade. Director James Elliott, Assistant Director Ronald Egherman, and a skilled staff organized and effectively mounted a complex and unusual exhibition that dissolves conventional boundaries of history, art, architecture, literature, and design. Numerous problems of presentation were resolved with resource and ingenuity. Cecilia Franklin, former Museum Business Manager, provided intelligent liaison with University officials and departments. The Museum is circulating the North American tour of the exhibition, while Pro Helvetia concurrently directs a tour in Ireland and Great Britain, as well as one in other languages throughout Europe.

Emeritus Professor Walter Horn, University of California, offered unflagging encouragement, critical insight, and the enthusiasm that has distinguished his long career. He was instrumental in initiating the European exhibit tour at Trinity College, Dublin, and then at the Bede Monastery Museum, Jarrow. Ernest Born, FAIA, NA, who designed the three volumes of *The Plan of St Gall,* the exhibit ensemble, and this book, worked unceasingly—as he has done for nearly fifteen years—to make each worthy of its sponsors' support. My personal debt to their wisdom, learning, and examples can never be repaid.

William J. McClung, Sponsoring Editor, University of California Press, is close to this book. His imagination inspired its format; his commitment inspired its makers. Czeslaw Jan Grycz, Production Manager, provided the capable and energetic attention on which we have come to depend in the production of this and many other fine volumes.

We hope to have rewarded in some small part the loyalty and support of Dr. Franklin Murphy and Miss Mary M. Davis, respectively President and Executive Vice President of the Samuel H. Kress Foundation during the St Gall project. The Herbert E. Fletcher Granite Research and Technology Fund, West Chelmsford, Massachusetts, the Doris and Harold Zellerbach Fund, and the Zellerbach Family Fund, San Francisco, also brought generous support and assistance that made *The Plan of St Gall* a superior accomplishment of American university press publishing.

* Bennet D. Hill, in *The American Historical Review,* 88:1 (Feb. 1981), 108-109.

PLAN OF ST GALL

Drawn on parchment, the Plan of St Gall is a superbly executed and carefully annotated 9th century delineation of a paradigmatic Carolingian monastery. It is the most accomplished architectural manifestation of the Age of Charlemagne and a great achievement in Western community planning.
A Swiss national treasure, the Plan has survived in its original home, the former monastery of St Gall, for nearly 1200 years.
Efforts to reproduce an image of the Plan by lithography or engraving had met with only limited success until the present century. In 1952, the Firma E. Löpfe-Benz, under the auspices of the Historical Association of the Canton of St Gall, produced a facsimile of the Plan by means of 8-color offset lithography. This printer's masterpiece inaugurated a new era of study, making an accurate Plan accessible for the first time to all who sought to explore its intricacies.

✡

the plan measures about 44 inches, 112cm, between asterisks (shown here 1 : 768, one quarter original size)

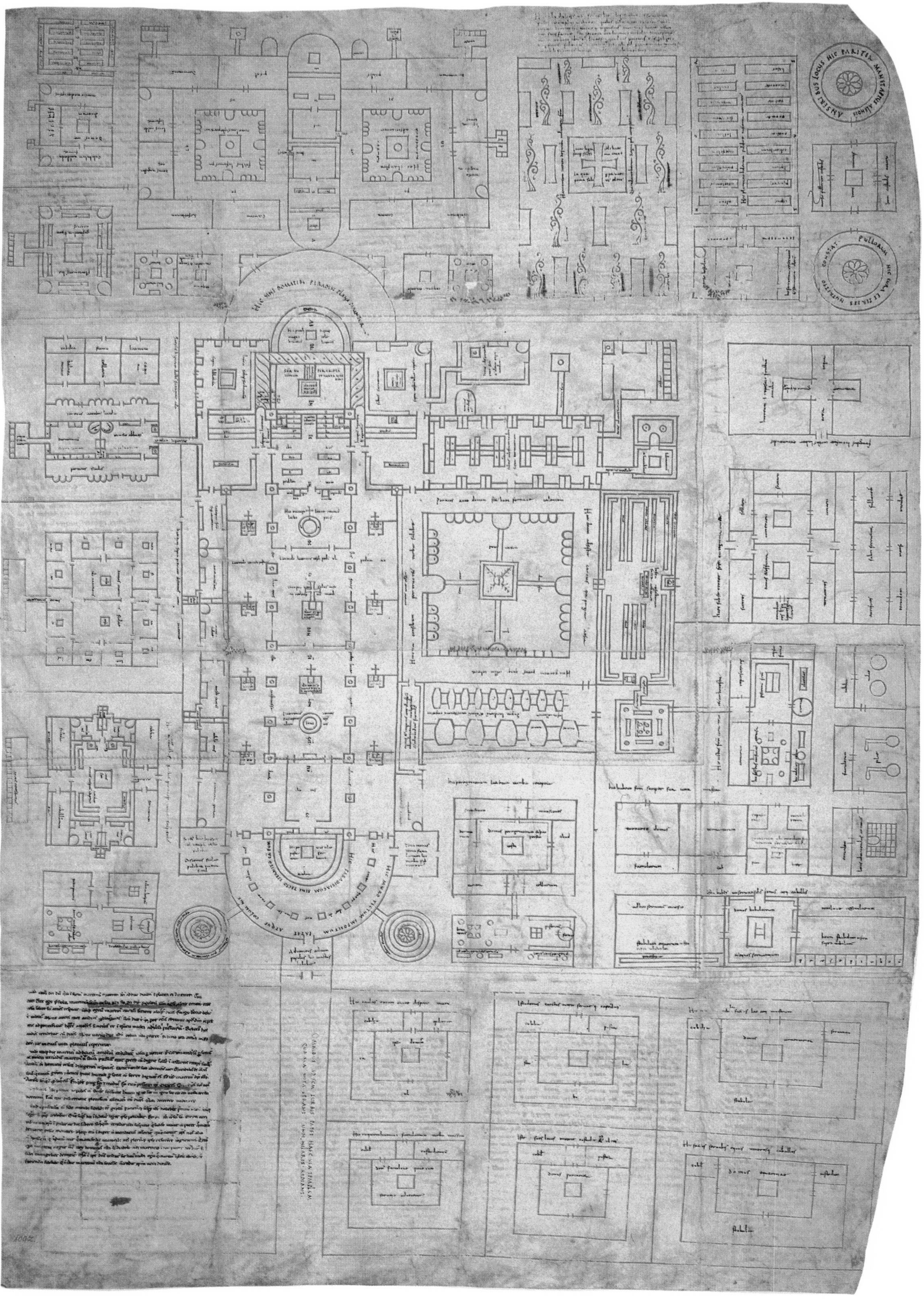

✡

THE PLAN OF ST. GALL DRAWN ON PARCHMENT IN RED AND BLACK. LIFE OF ST. MARTIN, LOWER LEFT

STIFTSBIBLIOTHEK, ST. GALL

THE MANUSCRIPT

KNOWN AS THE PLAN OF ST GALL WAS COPIED BETWEEN 820-830 A.D. from a lost original. It depicts a Benedictine monastery to shelter the work, study, and prayer of some 270 souls, over 110 of them monks. Although Charlemagne had urged adoption of Benedictine custom in Frankish monasteries, its acceptance was neither universal nor undisputed. This part of his vision for unity in civil and church affairs was attained by his son and successor, Louis the Pious, who determined to free Frankish monastic life from a wide confusion of practices in sole favor of the Rule of St. Benedict.

The St Gall monastery was founded ca. 612 by the Irish monk Gallus. Falling ill, he had left St Columban's mission to live in a retreat by the Steinach. At this site a small monastery eventually formed. In 747 its abbot, Otmar, was required to convert this community to Benedictine ways. He designated buildings for common dining, sleeping, and an infirmary and hospice. But greedy neighbors unlawfully alienated the abbey's lands and it ceased to prosper. In 816 Gozbert arrived as abbot to find the monks' spiritual life at low ebb. Through vigorous litigation he reclaimed the abbey's estates and restored its failed fortunes. By 830 he was ready to refurbish the superannuated buildings of the old settlement. For this purpose he requested the guidance of the Plan of St Gall, the document created as an instrument of policy to inform and regulate monastic planning throughout the Frankish empire.

We know the Plan was traced; one of its legends explicitly states it was a copy ("*exemplata*"),* and it lacks underdrawing. Characteristic hands of two scribes who wrote its 340 legends identify its origin in the scriptorium of Reichenau. We know Gozbert referred to the Plan to build a church. The parchment's astonishing survival owes to its having been conserved in the great monastic library of St Gall; it did not perish when those books were temporarily evacuated to Reichenau in 926 for fear of sack by Magyars. Hereafter, certainties fade.

Toward the end of the 12th century a monk of St Gall took up a large parchment composed of five smaller sheets sewn together. One side bore outlines of an architectural scheme. Perhaps this nameless man knew the Plan's importance to his monastery, for he did not cut it apart. Methodically folding it into a book-sized sequence of 14 pages, he then wrote a Life of St Martin on its blank verso. Needing one more page, he erased lines of a large building in the northwest corner of the Plan and finished his work. In the year 1461, this document was catalogued as a Life of St Martin, "with a depiction of the houses of his monastery." Thus, its original meaning forgotten, the Plan of St Gall vanished.

Not until 1604 did the Plan reappear, when Henricus Canisius published its inscriptions for their literary interest. He believed the drawing to be no more than the site "as it looked in the time of Abbot Gozbert," whom he correctly identified. By this chance the Plan of St Gall re-entered history in its own right, some 800 years after its making.

* See dedicatory inscription, page i

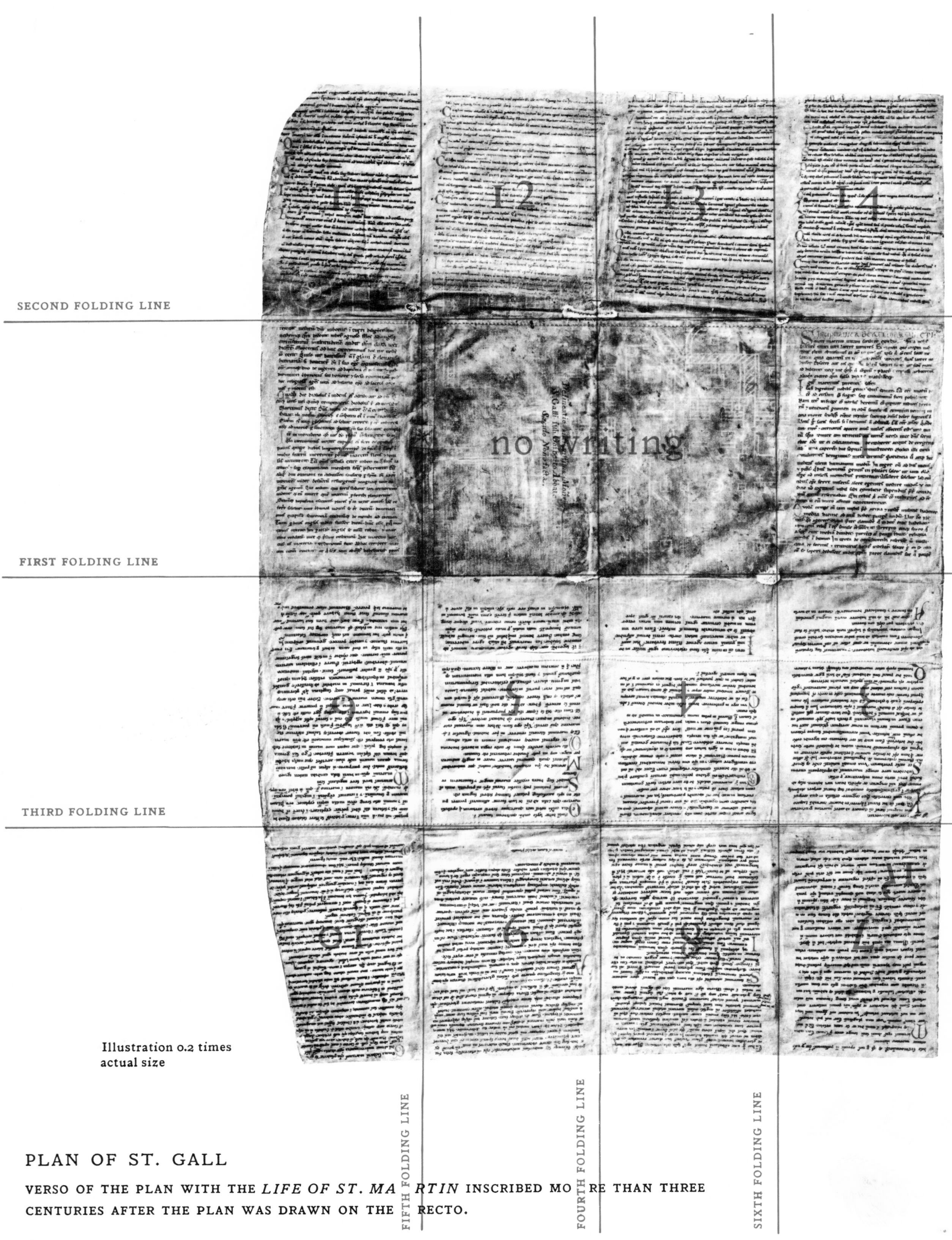

Illustration 0.2 times actual size

PLAN OF ST. GALL

VERSO OF THE PLAN WITH THE *LIFE OF ST. MARTIN* INSCRIBED MORE THAN THREE CENTURIES AFTER THE PLAN WAS DRAWN ON THE RECTO.

The first fold divided the parchment into two equal areas. The 2nd & 3rd foldings were then made to accommodate to the first fold.
For ease in folding the outer rows X and Y were made slightly shorter than the two center rows.

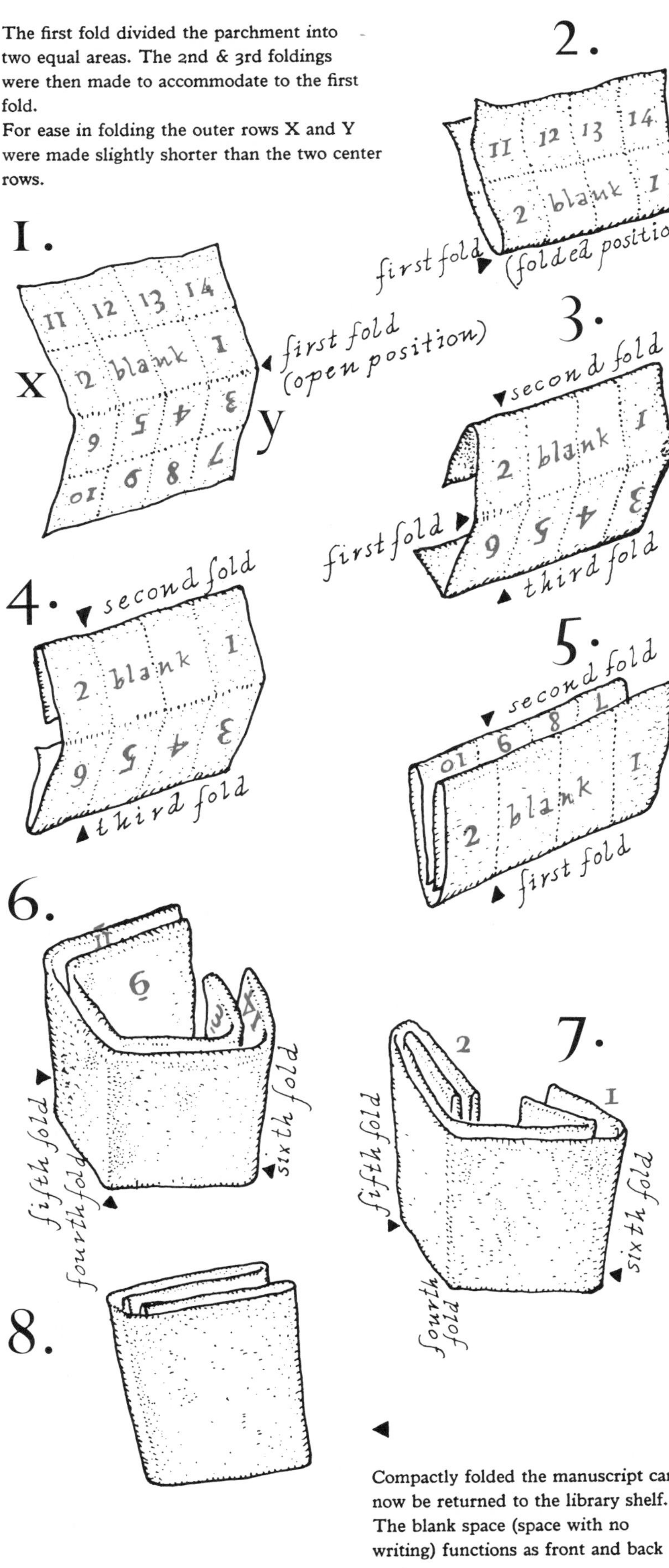

Compactly folded the manuscript can now be returned to the library shelf. The blank space (space with no writing) functions as front and back cover.

THE PLAN OF ST. GALL

THE *LIFE OF ST. MARTIN* AND THE FOLDING OF THE PARCHMENT IN RELATION TO THE READING SEQUENCE

1.*C*

THE UNFOLDING PROCEDURE AND READING SEQUENCE

The scribe planned the LIFE OF ST. MARTIN *to be easily read with the pages following each other in numerical order from left to right. The reader, on taking the manuscript from the shelf, had in hand a "package" as shown in fig. 1, diagram 8. Laying the* LIFE *on the table, the reader opened the package. Before him, in normal reading position, he saw page 1 on the left and page 2 on the right:*

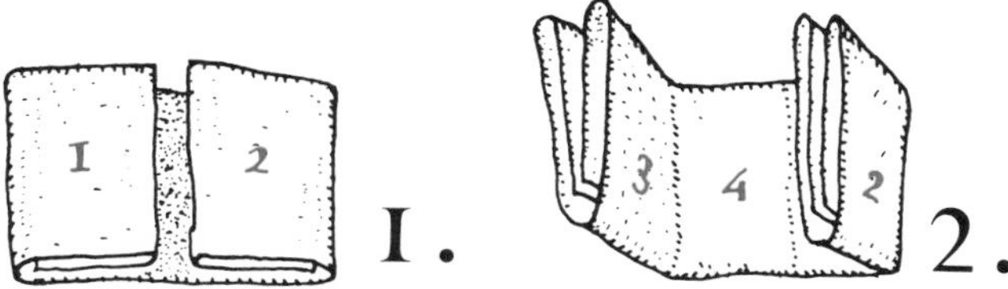

After reading pages 1 and 2, page 1 was turned backwards (on fold line 4) to the left, and page 2 was turned to the right (on fold line 5). The reader then saw a rectangle like this:

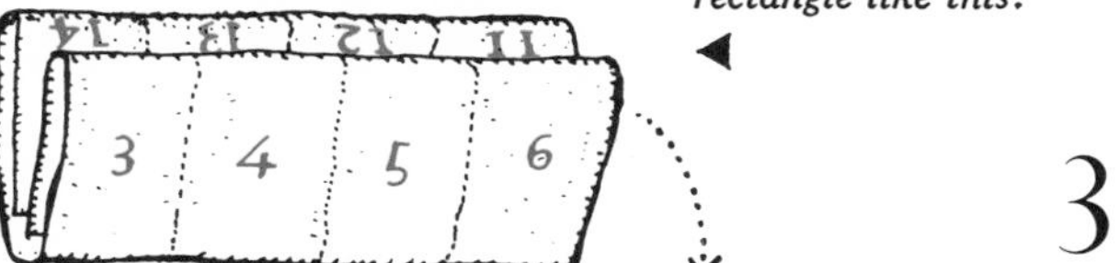

The row of pages 3, 4, 5, 6, was brought toward the reader and laid flat on the table. This is what he saw—pages 7, 8, 9, 10, in reading sequence left to right:

So far the page numbers flowed in normal sequence, left to right. Page 11, however, was clearly in view but upside down. The parchment was rotated 180 degrees to permit the upside-down pages to be read.

After reading the sequence of pages 11, 12, 13, 14, left to right, in fig. 5, the parchment was rotated back to the position shown in fig. 4. There was more to be read; 14 was not the last page of the LIFE OF ST. MARTIN.

At this stage, the reader lifted the lower row of pages, 7, 8, 9, 10 (on fold line 3), toward him and placed the parchment face down on the table. This is what he saw:

In the lower left corner, on the back of page 7, in reading position and clearly in view, was the last page of the LIFE OF ST. MARTIN, *page 15.*
On the remainder of the parchment, intact and without erasure, was displayed Haito's Plan of St. Gall: a graphic configuration, a senseless geometric abstraction. Three centuries after its conception and delineation, it was neither with meaning nor historical significance to a reader of the LIFE OF ST. MARTIN, *until its discovery or rediscovery in 1604 by Henricus Canisius*
We can be grateful that the LIFE OF ST. MARTIN *was not treated to conventional bookbinding techniques composed of cut leaves, folded and sewn into signatures.*

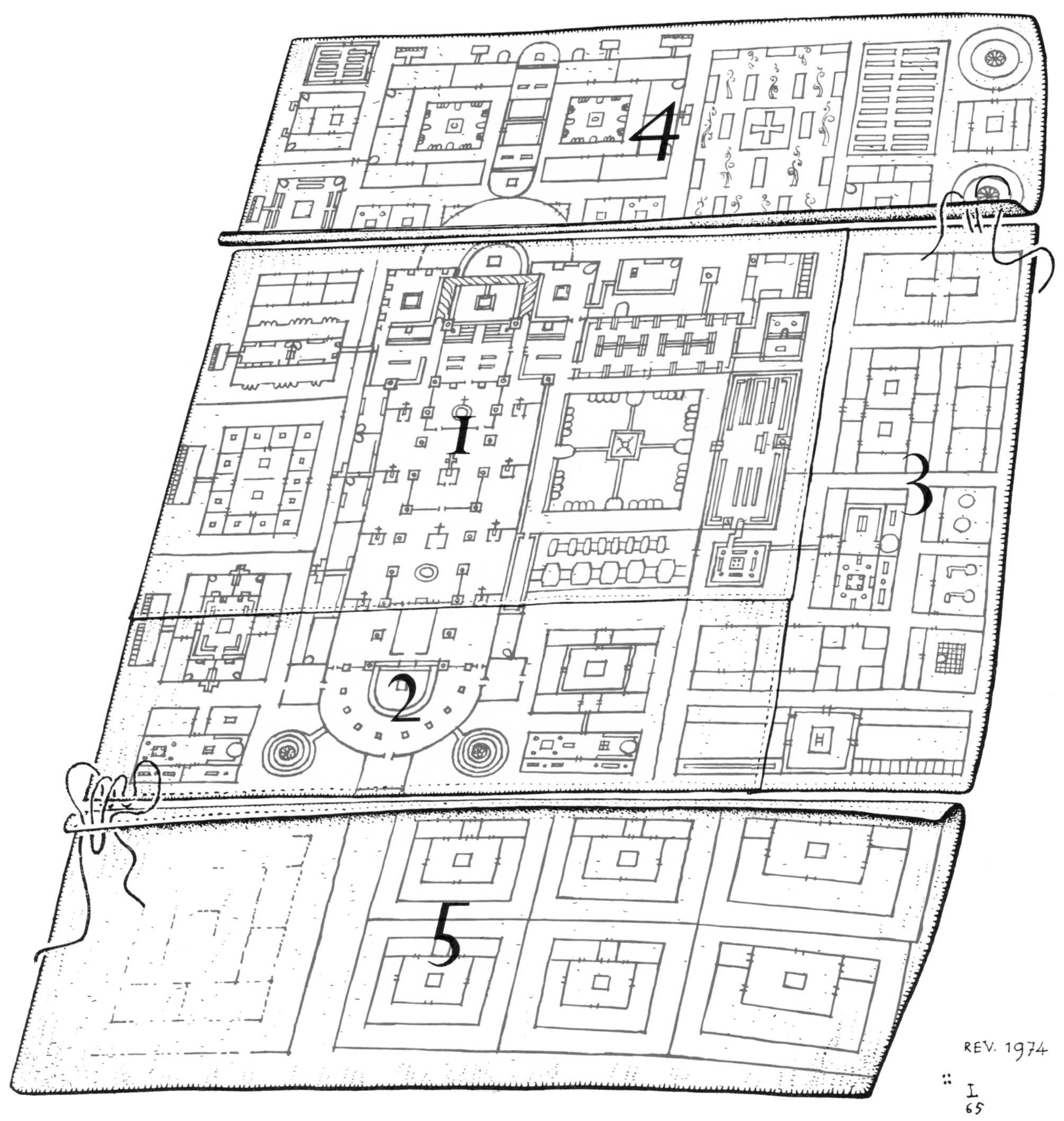

THE PLAN OF ST. GALL

ASSEMBLY OF THE PLAN FROM 5 SEPARATE PIECES

THE PLAN OF ST. GALL

The drawing above illustrates how the large skin upon which the Plan is drawn is composed of an aggregate of five separate pieces of calfskin which, after being sewn together, form a drawing surface 113 cm high × 78 cm wide, a size impossible to obtain from the hide of a single animal. Our interpretation of the manner in which these skins were sewn together is given in the analysis of details reproduced and annotated on the pages that follow.

SOME QUESTIONS

AND PROBLEMS HAVE INTRIGUED STUDENTS OF THE PLAN OF ST GALL since, in 1844, scholars first began to piece together its many puzzles. The most urgent of these issues is that of scale. Was the delineation of the monastery complex an architectural diagram intended only to show an overall scheme and the relationship of its parts? Or were the various plans depicted on the parchment drawn in proportional relationship to structures envisioned by their maker? In short: was the Plan drawn to scale? And if so, to what scale? Five legends of the Plan state measurement in feet, but discrepancies occur among two of them and the graphic portrayal of parts of the church. Does this circumstance indicate that the drawing contains more than one scale? Or was it not drawn to scale? Or are the legends in error?

The Plan of St Gall contains a wealth of visual and verbal particulars normally seen in a drawing made for a particular site and intent. These coexist in odd variance with certain conventional omissions and ambiguities of rendering which give the drawing a high degree of abstraction. Does this delineation technique indicate a reasoned quest for larger purpose than a specific building campaign? Was that purpose to create an instrument of guidance—an ideal or prototypal scheme?

What of the appearance of the Plan's guest and service structures? Did they descend from the Roman atrium house? Or did they adhere to vernacular building traditions of the North? These are the central questions. Without answers any attempt to visually reconstruct the Plan's buildings could be no more than conjecture.

These issues are discussed briefly on pp. 12f, 20f, and 75f.

*

IN 1844 Ferdinand Keller of Zürich published the first monographic study of the Plan, including as a novelty his reconstruction of its buildings. He had also intended to issue a lithographic image of the Plan at full scale but the stone broke; it was replaced by a small one accommodating an image only 4/5 the size of the original document. On this reduced image the Plan's inscriptions were imposed at actual size. In this curious form the Plan first became generally accessible to modern scholars.

IN 1848 the English scholar Robert Willis issued an enlarged edition of Keller's text. Willis called attention to the incompatibility of measurement information among some of the Plan's explanatory legends. He concluded that the Plan was not drawn to a consistent scale, a view that governed scholarly thinking for over a century. He also pointed out that the "courtyard houses" of Keller's interpretation conflicted with information in some inscriptions of the Plan's guest and service buildings. But he did not question this interpretation for most of the other buildings. Willis was also the first to make a rendering of the Plan in modern architectural idiom.

INTRODUCTION

THE

PLAN OF ST GALL *emerged at the height of a search for cultural unity that struck through the whole of Carolingian life. The Plan stood in some degree as both agent and result of a quest uniquely intensive in Western history. It was part of a web of intellectual, political, and religious life that briefly appeared as a close-woven tapestry under Charlemagne, and left behind images of dramatic potency to the future life of Europe and the West.*

The common thread of that tapestry lay in the emergence and establishment of Christianity in the West. Recognized by Emperor Constantine in 325 A.D. *as a leading religion of the Roman state, the new belief had to be guarded against attempts of the state to interpret it only for political ends, and against any tendency to weaken it through internal splits (by such heresies as Arianism, Donatism, Pelagianism, and the growing diversity of monastic observance).*

The church accomplished its defense in two ways: through institution of national synods to hold in check doctrinal differences, and through development of an administrative structure parallel to that of the Roman state. By this means Christianity could step as a traditional force into the breach created by the collapse of Roman secular power.

This transition was hard won. Unity of the church was shattered during the barbarian invasions of Rome, by the fact that the Germanic conquerors were either pagan or adherents of Arianism. Three centuries were needed to quiet the claims of other forms of faith in favor of a common creed.

A great turning point came with the conversion ca. 496 of the Frankish king Clovis to the

Dolphin and trident are attributes of the violent and unpredictable Poseidon, Greek sea deity (Roman: Neptune), protector of all waters, patron of navigators, horse lover, and bestower of fertility. During the worst of the persecutions, the Christian community of the Roman Empire was forced into hiding. Meeting covertly to worship and to proselytize, these early Christians adopted a number of signs and symbols from accepted pagan religions, in order to make their presence known to others of the faith, yet without betraying themselves to their oppressors. Poseidon's trident, usually employed to summon tempest and earthquake, stands for the Holy Trinity; the dolphin, like the fish, stands for Christ.

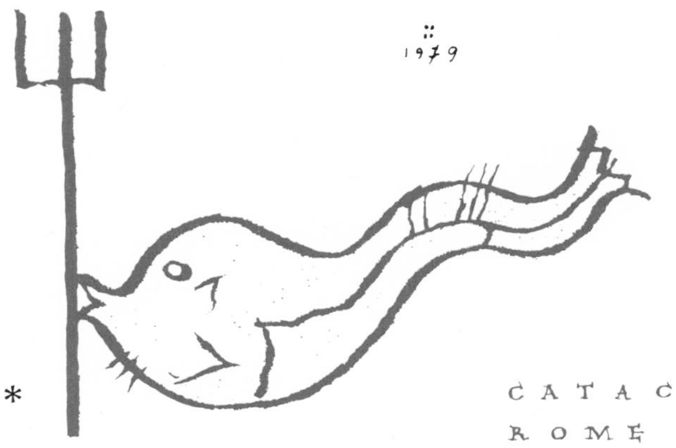

1979

*

CATACOMB PRISCILLA ROME 375

orthodox faith. As a result it was adopted by all pagan and Arian nations that fell under the sway of the Franks. As Frankish power grew, church and state once more began to draw together. The growth of this unity was expressed in a series of alliances that changed the face of the world.

Under Charles Martel, a Frankish statesman of highest caliber, this emerging world was rescued from the threat of being overrun by Moslems in 732. Frankish rulers of Martel's house delivered the papal see from the prospect of submission to the Lombards. The alliance of church with state was formally recognized when Pope Stephen II in 754 annointed Pepin king of the Franks in Paris. It attained fullest expression in the year 800 when Charlemagne allowed himself to be crowned Emperor of the Romans by Pope Leo III in Rome. In this manner there came into existence a new IMPERIUM CHRISTIANUM *that had its center not in Rome, but in the transalpine kingdom of the Franks.*

The reality was brief. The Carolingian empire, left to lesser scions of a great house, broke apart after the death of its founder. But Charlemagne's ideal survived to become an important force in the shaping of Europe. Like the concept of empire itself, the scheme transmitted to us in the Plan of St Gall survived the collapse of the power which first nurtured it and left a permanent imprint on monastic planning for centuries to come.

Adapted from *The Plan of St Gall* by Horn and Born (University of California Press, Berkeley), 1979, vol. III, p. 201

* DOLPHIN WITH TRIDENT
from an inscription in Priscilla Catacomb, Rome A.D. 375
Redrawn from Nordenfalk,
Die Spätantiken Zierbuckstaben, Stockholm 1970

ORIGINS

IN THE COURSE OF COMPLEX EXPANSION THE ROMAN EMPIRE CAME TO BE INVADED BY A HOST OF FOREIGN RELIGIONS, Christianity among them. Their initial acceptance brought confusion to the polity of the Roman gods; when Christians refused to sacrifice at the emperor's altar the state, unable to tolerate this affront, instituted the rigorous persecutions of the 2nd and 3rd centuries. Nevertheless Christianity continued to be practiced and spread throughout the empire, slowly supplanting the shattered pantheon.

Ironically, Christian adherence to one God eventually resolved Rome's metaphysical dilemma. Issued by Constantine, the Edict of Milan gave Christianity legal status in 313; by 381 Theodosius had made the orthodox Nicene Creed sole religion of the Roman state.

For the new faith consequences of acceptance were severe. As the church acquired an administrative structure as elaborate as that of the state, it lost the inspired purity of Christ's original teachings. To recapture that quality became the goal of a fanatical movement that emerged in the Nitrian desert and the Thebaid of Egypt, propounded by men seeking mystical union with God. They severed their ties with society in order to fast, meditate, and practice self-mortification.

These hermit saints of the desert acquired followers. The followers coalesced into monastic communities which grew in variety and influence, gaining strength and numbers by energetic proselytizing. As they traveled they bore with them what remained of Classical learning, and the growing body of patristic writings.

This movement swept the Roman empire like wildfire in two bold arcs. One swung east as far as Persia and Arabia; the other westward into Italy, Gaul, and the unconquered lands of Ireland and Scotland. All this came to pass in about 250 years.

In the late 6th century monks led by St Columban introduced Irish monasticism to the continent, now held by barbarian peoples and split by political and religious dissent. Their southward path was soon crossed by the diffusion northward of the Benedictine monastic philosophy emanating from Rome. Affirmed in the north by the Synod of Whitby, 664,

KILOMETERS
FOUNDERS OF EARLY MONACHISM
IN CHRONOLOGICAL ORDER
1 Founders of Eremetic Life in Egypt
ANTHONY 251/2–356/7 AMMUN †c. 350 MACARIUS †c. 394
2 Founder of Coenobitic Life in Egypt
PACHOMIUS 292–346 founds nine monasteries, vicinity of TABENNISI
3 Diffusion in the Near East
HILARION c. 291–371 founds GAZA in 329
EUSTATHIUS c. 300–377 founds SEBASTE in 340
BASIL 329/31–379 founds ANNESI in 360
ISAAC FROM SYRIA in CONSTANTINOPLE since 381
4 Transmission to Italy and Gaul
ATHANASIUS c. 295–373 transplants monachism to Rome, 339
MARTIN 316/17–397 founds LIGUGÉ in 361; MARMOUTIER in 375,
center of monastic diffusion SOUTH OF THE LOIRE
HONORATUS †423 founds monastery of LERINS in 400–410
CASSIAN c. 360–420/25 founds ST. VICTOR OF MARSEILLES in 415 which together
with Lerins becomes a center of diffusion of eremetic and coenobitic
monachism in the Rhone Valley and northern Gaul
CONTINUE ABOVE AT RIGHT
5 From Gaul to Ireland, thence to Scotland
PATRICK 385–461, educated in AUXERRE, brings eremetic forms of monachism
to Ireland in 432; founds ARMAGH in 444
COMGALL c. 516–601 founds BANGOR in 555 or 559
COLUMBA †651 founds IONA in 563
AIDAN †651 founds LINDISFARNE in 635
6 From Ireland to Gaul
COLUMBAN c. 543–615 founds LUXEUIL in 590; ST. GALL & BOBBIO in 612, and
numerous monastries in France of mixed Irish-Benedictine custom
7 Benedictine Monachism: Its Origin and Northward Spread
BENEDICT c. 480–547 founds MONTE CASSINO in 520. Located in ROME from
590 onward, it becomes a center of Benedictine conversion for Italy
AUGUSTIN †604 lands on Thanet Island, Kent, in 597; founds CANTERBURY,
a center of conversion for Kent
BENEDICT BISCOP 628–689/90 founds MONKWEARMOUTH in 665/66 and JARROW in 671/72,
centers of conversion of Northumbria
8 Benedictine Conquest of Frisia, Hesse, Thuringia and Bavaria
WILLIBRORD †739, enters FRISIA in 690; founds ECHTERNACH in 698
WINFRID-BONIFATIUS 672/75–754 founds FULDA in 746, and reorganizes the
entire Frankish church EAST OF THE RHINE
9 Benedictine Victory in Frankish Kingdom West of the Rhine
CHRODEGANG OF METZ †766
FULRAD OF ST. DENIS †784, with Bonifatius, exerts strong influence in
framing decisive synodal legislation (CONSILIUM GERMANICUM 743; SYNODS of ESTINNES
and SOISSONS 744; SYNODS of AACHEN 816 & 817) and the culmination of Benedictine Rule
REBAIS-EN-BRIE
STABLO-MALMÉDY
CORBIE
LIMOGES-SALIGNAC
BESANCON
WELTENBURG
Columba, IONA 563
559 BANGOR Comgall
444 ARMAGH Patricius
Aidan 635 LINDISFARNE
JARROW 671-72
MONKWEARM'TH 665-6
WHITBY 664
YORK
THANET
Augustinus to CANTERBURY 595
Columbanus to Luxeuil
FRISIA 690 Willibrord
Bonifatius
FULDA 746
ECHTERNACH
TOURS-MARMOUTIER 372
Martinus founds LIGUGÉ 361 first monastery in Gaul
AUXERRE
610 LUXEUIL Columbanus
ST. GALL 612
BOBBIO
GALLINARIA
MARSEILLE 415 Cassianus
410 LERINS Honoratus
ROME 580-90
MONTE CASSINO 520 Benedictus
339 Athanasius to Rome
381 CONSTANTINOPLE Isaac from Syria
Isaac
360 ANNESI Basileios
340 SEBASTE Eustathius
Epiphanios
SYRIA
JERUSALEM
BETHLEHEM
326-420
Hieronymus
Hilarion GAZA 329
BABYLONIA
320-330 NITRIA-SCETIS
Cradle of eremetic monachism Antonius, Macarius, Ammon
MON. ANTONII
In 289 St. Anthony went into total isolation for 20 years in an abandoned fort. He died age 105 years
THEBAID
Cradle of coenobitic monachism Pachomios founds 9 monasteries for men, 2 for women between 320 & 327
TABENNISI 320-25
ABYSSINIA
ARABIA
1:20,000,000
1977
MILES

ORIGIN AND DIFFUSION OF MONASTIC LIFE IN LATE ANTIQUITY AND THE EARLY MIDDLE AGES, 4TH–9TH CENTURIES

Benedictine Rule was then propagated by Sts Willibrord and Boniface in England, Gaul, and Germany. Supported by the popes and the expanding power of superior Frankish rulers, Benedictine custom became the accepted Rule in the West. Thus the foundations were laid for a new Rome in which, for a brief period of Western life, the institutions of church and state worked mutually to support rather than to compete with one another.

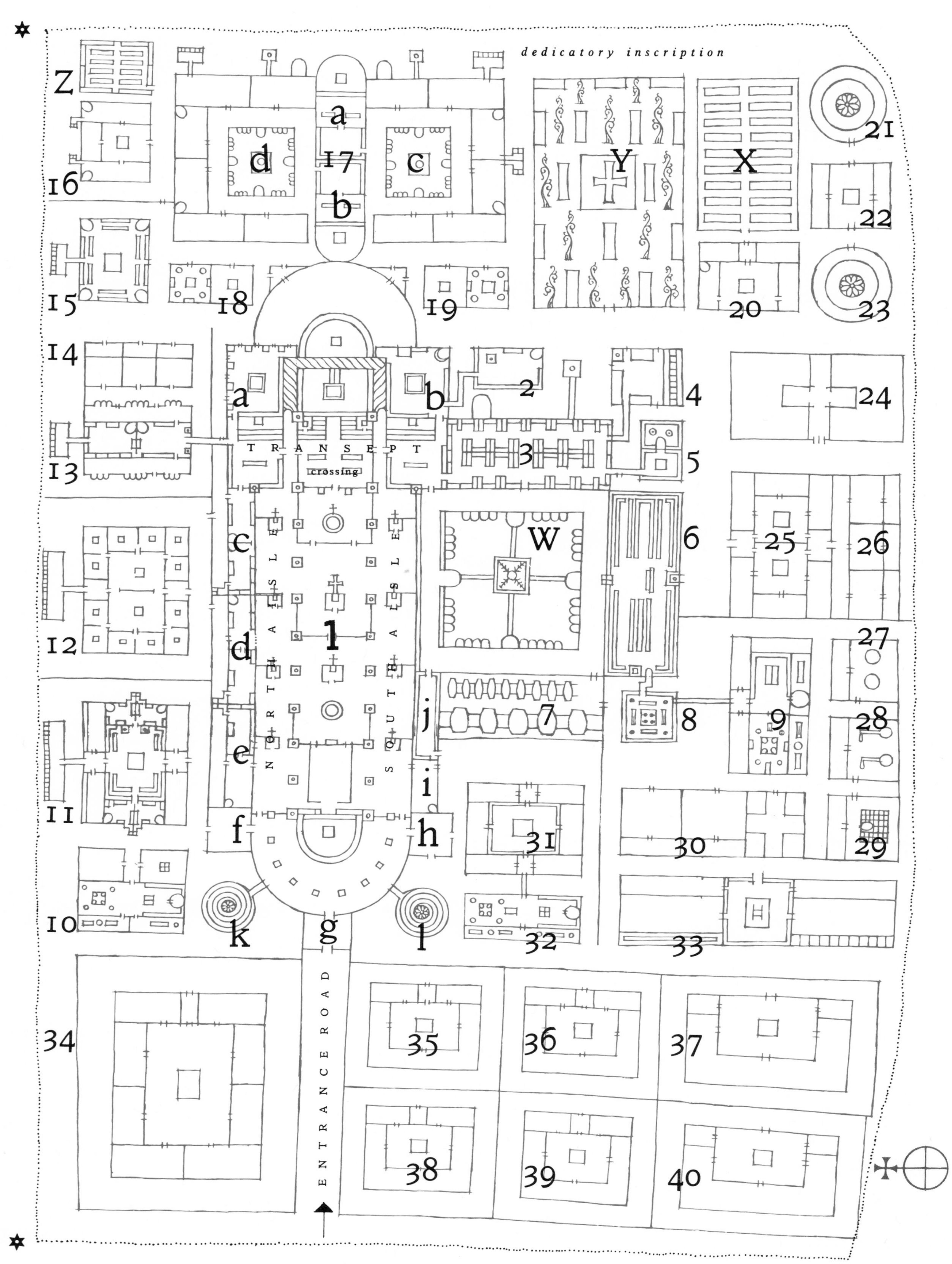

PLAN OF ST GALL WITH BUILDINGS IDENTIFIED BY NUMBERS KEYED TO INDEX ▶

INDEX

TO BUILDING NUMBERS OF THE PLAN

1. Church
   - a. Scriptorium below, Library above
   - b. Sacristy below, Vestry above
   - c. Lodging for Visiting Monks
   - d. Lodging of Master of the Outer School
   - e. Porter's Lodging
   - f. Porch giving access to House for Distinguished Guests and to Outer School
   - g. Porch for reception of all visitors
   - h. Porch giving access to Hospice for Pilgrims and Paupers and to servants' and herdsmen's quarters
   - i. Lodging of Master of the Hospice for Pilgrims and Paupers
   - j. Monks' Parlor
   - k. Tower of St. Michael
   - l. Tower of St. Gabriel
2. Annex for Preparation of Holy Bread and Holy Oil
3. Monks' Dormitory above, Warming Room below
4. Monks' Privy
5. Monks' Laundry and Bath House
6. Monks' Refectory below, Vestiary above
7. Monks' Cellar below, Larder above
8. Monks' Kitchen
9. Monks' Bake and Brew House
10. Kitchen, Bake, and Brew House for Distinguished Guests
11. House for Distinguished Guests
12. Outer School
13. Abbot's House
14. Abbot's Kitchen, Cellar, and Bath House
15. House for Bloodletting
16. House of the Physicians
17. Novitiate and Infirmary
    - a. Chapel for the Novices
    - b. Chapel for the Sick
    - c. Cloister of the Novices
    - d. Cloister of the Sick
18. Kitchen and Bath for the Sick
19. Kitchen and Bath for the Novices
20. House of the Gardener
21. Goosehouse
22. House of the Fowlkeepers
23. Henhouse
24. Granary
25. Great Collective Workshop
26. Annex of the Great Collective Workshop
27. Mill
28. Mortar
29. Drying Kiln
30. House of Coopers and Wheelwrights, and Brewers' Granary
31. Hospice for Pilgrims and Paupers
32. Kitchen, Bake and Brew House for Pilgrims and Paupers
33. House for Horses and Oxen and Their Keepers
34. House for the Vassals and Knights who travel in the Emperor's Following (identification not certain)
35. House for Sheep and Shepherds
36. House for Goats and Goatherds
37. House for Cows and Cowherds
38. House for Servants of Outlying Estates and for Servants Travelling with the Emperor's Court (not certain; cf. No. 34)
39. House for Swine and Swineherds
40. House for Brood Mares and Foals and Their Keepers

W. Monks' Cloister Yard
X. Monks' Vegetable Garden
Y. Monks' Cemetery and Orchard
Z. Medicinal Herb Garden

DRAWING

DRAWING COMMUNICATES THROUGH PERCEPTION OF IMAGES man makes to express purposes—rational, symbolic, magical, religious—that require the transcending of words. Even without its numerous legends the Plan of St Gall attests systematic order, rational intent. Along with paradigmatic purpose and utilitarian function this drawing also embodies and communicates pervasive hieratic values.

The ancient study of numerology entered Christian symbolism in the form of sacred numbers associated with Scripture and liturgy: 3, 7, 10, 12, and most important, 40. The value 40, omnipresent in the Plan, is the measure in feet of the liturgically significant crossing square where nave and transept intersect. In the site it appears in multiples ascending from 40: 40, 80, 160, 320, 640; and descending: 40, 20, 10, 5, 2½.*

This puzzling sequence is unrelated to metric usage. But sequential doubling and halving of a given value to plan space was common in ancient measurement practices. Based on the hieratic value 40, this geometric progression, applied to the Plan in terms of the Carolingian foot yields the construction scale: 1/16 inch in the drawing equals 1 foot on the ground or, 1:192. Superimposed on the drawing, the 40-foot grid reveals the ambience of a pattern of squares governing the organization of the entire site. Both church length and column intervals are integrated with the 40-foot squares, carrying modularity of the church into its elevations, an aesthetic condition in architecture then without precedent in the West (see pages 80-83).

Descent from 40 to 2½ feet reveals the basic module of the Plan. This small increment describes structures, interior furnishings, garden paths, all delineated on the Plan. Five legends conspicuously state measure on the Plan. The church is to be 200 feet long, nave 40 and aisles 20 feet wide, nave columns 12 feet apart, piers in the western apse 10 feet apart. The grid of squares demonstrates that 3 of these instructions support the fact that the drawing actually portrays a church about 300 feet long, apse to apse. What of the remaining 2 legends? While Charlemagne had encouraged great church building programs despite monastic protest that they were unduly burdensome, his successor Louis the Pious reversed this policy. In 816-817 the synods of Aachen reformed monastic practice and programs. It is surmised that the church of the Plan was then shortened to 200 feet, preserving the value 40 in crossing square and nave width, but reducing nave arcades from 20 to 12 feet. Subsequent corrections to the unaltered drawing were made by annotation. The surviving Plan thus records an architectural concept of innovative integrity, as well as the unelucidated conflict between a drawing and the words that describe it.

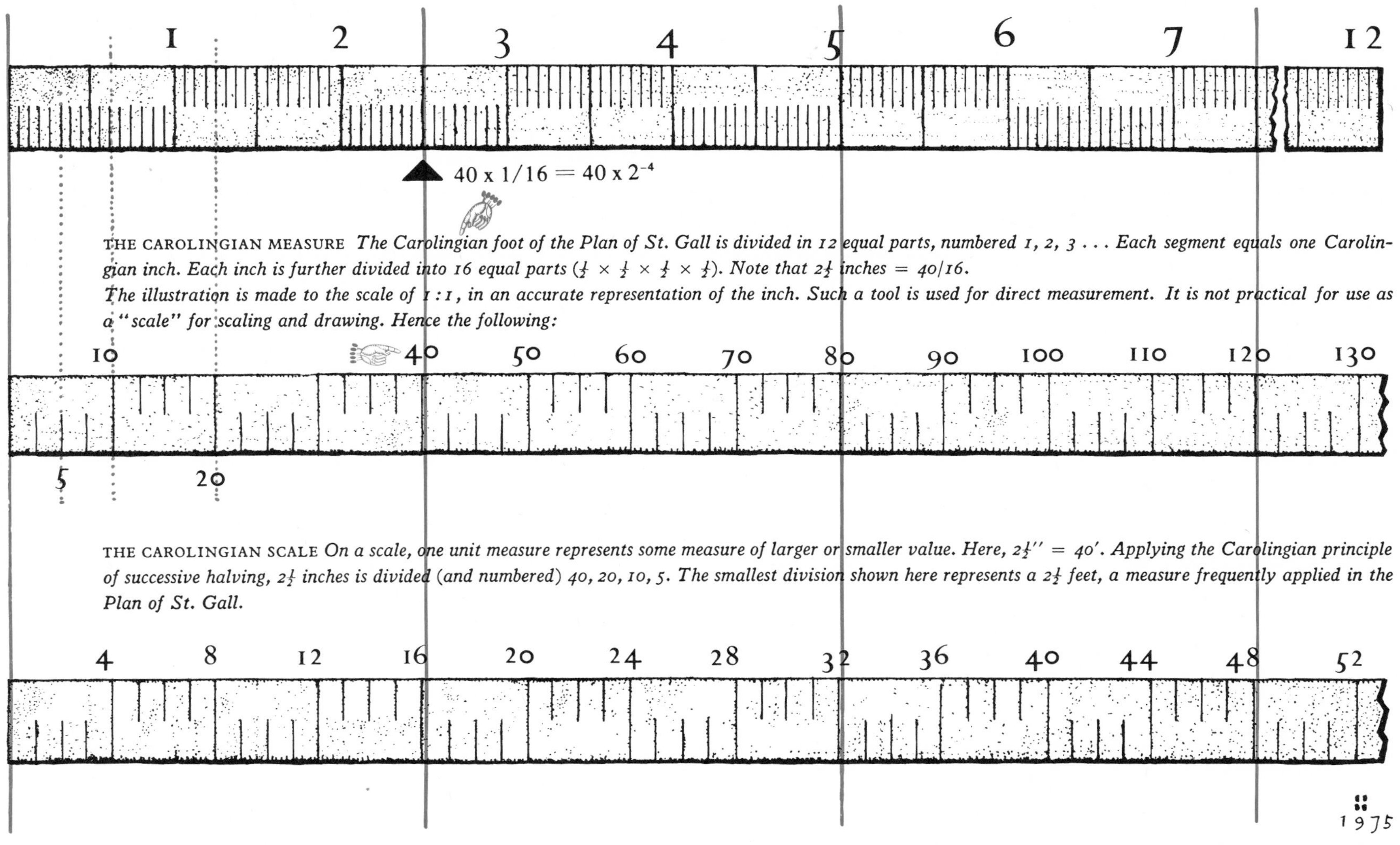

THE CAROLINGIAN MEASURE *The Carolingian foot of the Plan of St. Gall is divided in 12 equal parts, numbered 1, 2, 3 . . . Each segment equals one Carolingian inch. Each inch is further divided into 16 equal parts (½ × ½ × ½ × ½). Note that 2½ inches = 40/16.*
The illustration is made to the scale of 1:1, in an accurate representation of the inch. Such a tool is used for direct measurement. It is not practical for use as a "scale" for scaling and drawing. Hence the following:

THE CAROLINGIAN SCALE *On a scale, one unit measure represents some measure of larger or smaller value. Here, 2½″ = 40′. Applying the Carolingian principle of successive halving, 2½ inches is divided (and numbered) 40, 20, 10, 5. The smallest division shown here represents a 2½ feet, a measure frequently applied in the Plan of St. Gall.*

THE CAROLINGIAN SCALE ADAPTED TO THE NOTION OF MODULE *The same scale and graduations as above, but with divisions reading not as feet, but as multiples of 2½ feet. Other multiples convenient to the draftsman could be constructed to suit his needs. The concept of scale as an aspect of, and as opposed to measure, was clearly understood.*

THE CAROLINGIAN MEASURE AND SCALE USED IN DESIGNING THE PLAN

On the basis of the calculations listed below we compute the length of the foot used in designing the Plan to have these equivalents:

In English and U.S. standard measure: 1′ ⅝″.

In metric measure: 32.07cm

This computation can only be understood as an approximation of the real Carolingian foot that the draftsman of the Plan himself used. The computation must be corrected, first by the diminution in size to which the parchment was subjected through shrinkage throughout the ages of its existence, and second, minor distortions caused by shrinkage of photographic elements in development, or of the paper on which the facsimile was printed, during drying.

Our computation of the "foot of the Plan" as reflected in the Löpfe-Benz facsimile is based on an analysis of the longest clearly measurable dimension shown on the drawing, namely the span extending from the center of the arcade columns that stand at the entrance wall of the church to the center of the columns that form the easternmost boundary of the crossing square. This span encompasses five and one-half 40-foot squares and consequently represents a length of 220 "Plan feet". Owing to uneven shrinkage or irregularities in the drawing this distance varies slightly depending on whether it is measured along the axis of the northern, or of the southern row of nave arcades. Using an engine-divided scale of good manufacture with 16 divisions to the inch based on the U.S. standard foot (identical with the British standard foot) we arrive at the following figures:

$\frac{231 + 232}{2}$ = *average value = 231.5 units (measure on south row = 232 units of 1/16 inch, measure on north row = 231 units)*

$\frac{231.5}{220}$ = *1.05227 feet—12⅝ inches—32.067 cm* *[computation: 12 inches = 30.480 cm.*

This is the measure of the foot of the Plan. *⅝ inch = 1.587 cm*
32.067 cm]

✡

* See illustrations and captions, pages 14-15.

DIAGRAM I

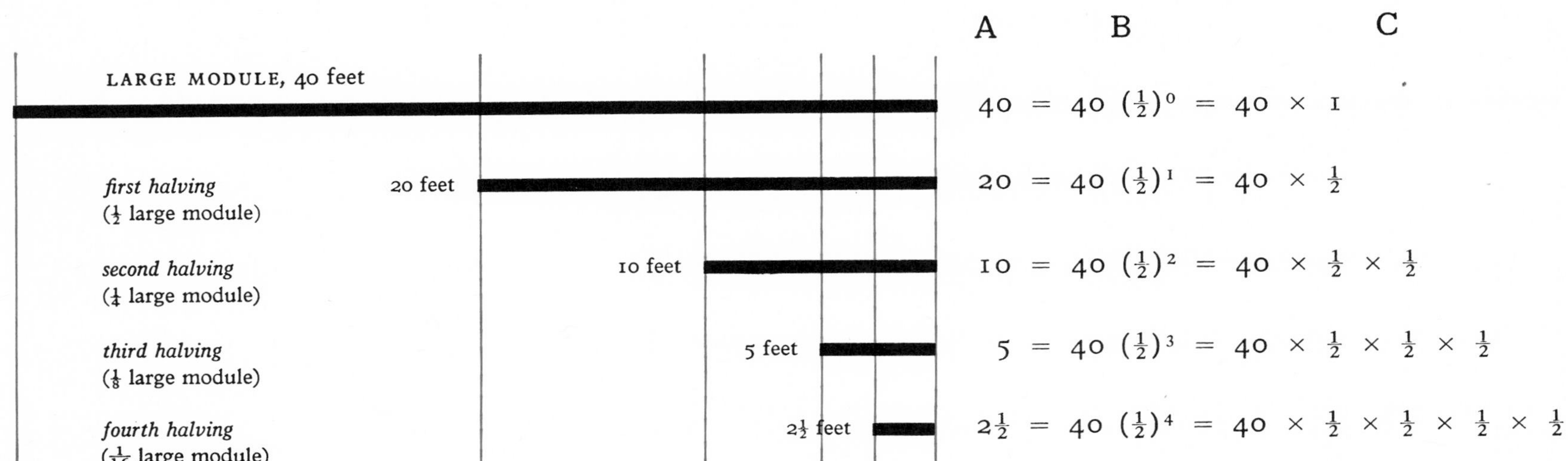

The standard module, 2½ feet, is obtained by successively halving the large module (40 feet) four times. The value of the exponent, column B, indicates the number of times that the number 40 has been halved. The procedure shown here that yields successively smaller units of measurement, decreasing from 40 feet to 2½ feet by successive halving is "reversible," and is reversible by the same pattern of geometric progression shown here, but in the "opposite" direction yielding progressively larger values.

Thus larger modules, multiples of 40 feet, such as 160 feet and 640 feet, are evolved from the same standard module and using the same pattern of development. This is illustrated on the opposite page in Diagram II.

In Diagram II one can visualize the grand symmetry of the scheme of measures by which the design of the Plan was ordered and controlled. For example, 640 is symmetrically disposed with respect to 2½ about the sacred number 40 taken as a pivot or point of origin. In the pattern of such a formula, the infinitely great and the infinitely small participate with equal significance, in a scheme, it seemed, of divine order. The crossing square, four equal sides each of 40 feet, indeed defined a holy space.

✡

THE SEQUENCE OF PROGRESSIVE DICHOTOMY USED IN THE SCHEME OF MEASUREMENTS EMPLOYED IN THE DESIGN AND DRAWING OF THE PLAN

Forty, the number of greatest value in the series of NUMERI SACRI, *was chosen by the designer of the Plan of St. Gall as that dimension in feet for the crossing square of the Church, the holy space unsurpassed in meaning and felicity to all inhabitants of the monastery.*

It was clearly discernible from tracing drafts, in our study of the Plan, that 160 feet, four times forty, was the major module of the Plan.

This is the largest measure which is a common multiple of the Plan. Four units of this module, or 640 feet, is the length of the Plan, and three units of this module, or 480 feet, is the width of the Plan.

The reason that the 160-foot module, four times the 40-foot dimension of the crossing square, was chosen as a module may be understood by perusing DIAGRAMS *I and II, giving attention to the numerical sequences in columns A, B, C, in each figure.* DIAGRAM *I portrays a progression of halving starting with the 40-foot module and* DESCENDING *to 2½ feet.* DIAGRAM *II starts out with the 40-foot module, extends the geometric series in the opposite upward direction by doubling.*

The values obtained by doubling, from 40 to 160, correspond at each level of ascent, to the smaller values obtained by the descent from 40 to 2½ feet. The bar elements of DIAGRAM *II illustrate the progression graphically: however, it is Column B that cogently reveals the homogeneity of the numerical relationships as a scheme that established the intrinsic pattern of measurements used in the Plan of St. Gall.* ▶

DIAGRAM II

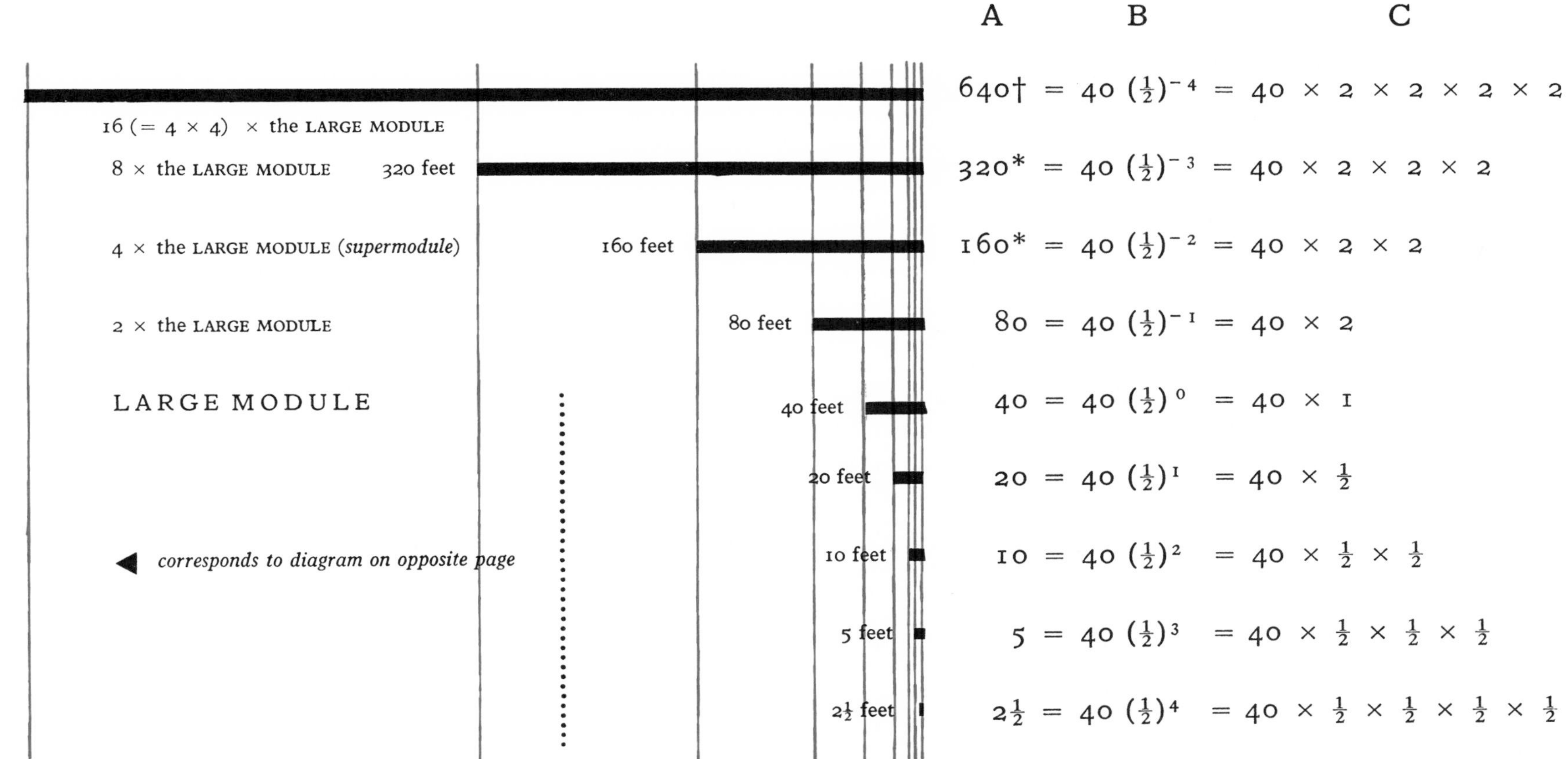

† 640 is the "height" or east–west dimension of the Plan

* 480 feet, the "width," or north–south dimension of the Plan, is an element in this geometric progression. It is derived by taking the sum of the two elements of the progression 320 & 160, or 3 × 160. With sacred numbers 3 and 4 as multipliers and 160 as a multiplicand, 480 and 640 emerge as the dimensions, in feet, of the Plan.

THE SUPERMODULE, 160 FEET, ITS DERIVATIVES, 640 FEET AND 480 FEET, AND ITS RELATIONSHIP TO THE LARGE MODULE

We noticed that, out of the sacred number 40, the values of 2½, 10, 40, 160, 640 are generated by exponential values of 4, 2, 0, −2, −4. Although the more sophisticated notation of Column B was probably not common knowledge in the 9th century, the notation of Column C was understandable. There is no magic in this simple observation. But it is apparent that the multiplier 4, operating on 40 and yielding 160 was not chosen by caprice. A module less than 40 facilitated the arduous work of design.

The number 480, 3 times 160, is not one of the natural steps of the progression between 2½ and 40, as shown in DIAGRAM *II. This strongly suggests that the* CAUSA PRIMA *of the dimension system of the Plan was the longitudinal axis of the Plan of the Church, extended to east and west to satisfy designing a plan of paradigmatic significance and future influence. The axis of the Church was extended one module of 160 feet to the east (of the front line of the altar of St. Paul) and one module of 160 feet to the west of the entrance to the covered walk of the west paradise. This established the length of the Plan, four modules of 160 feet or 640 feet. One module of 160 feet north of the axis and two modules of 160 feet south of the axis gives three modules of 160, or 480 feet, the width of the Plan. That the dimensions of the Plan are in the proportion of 3 to 4 was more than good theology. The numbers 3, 4, and 5 are the key to accurate construction of a rectangle in land surveying and in building construction.*

E. B.

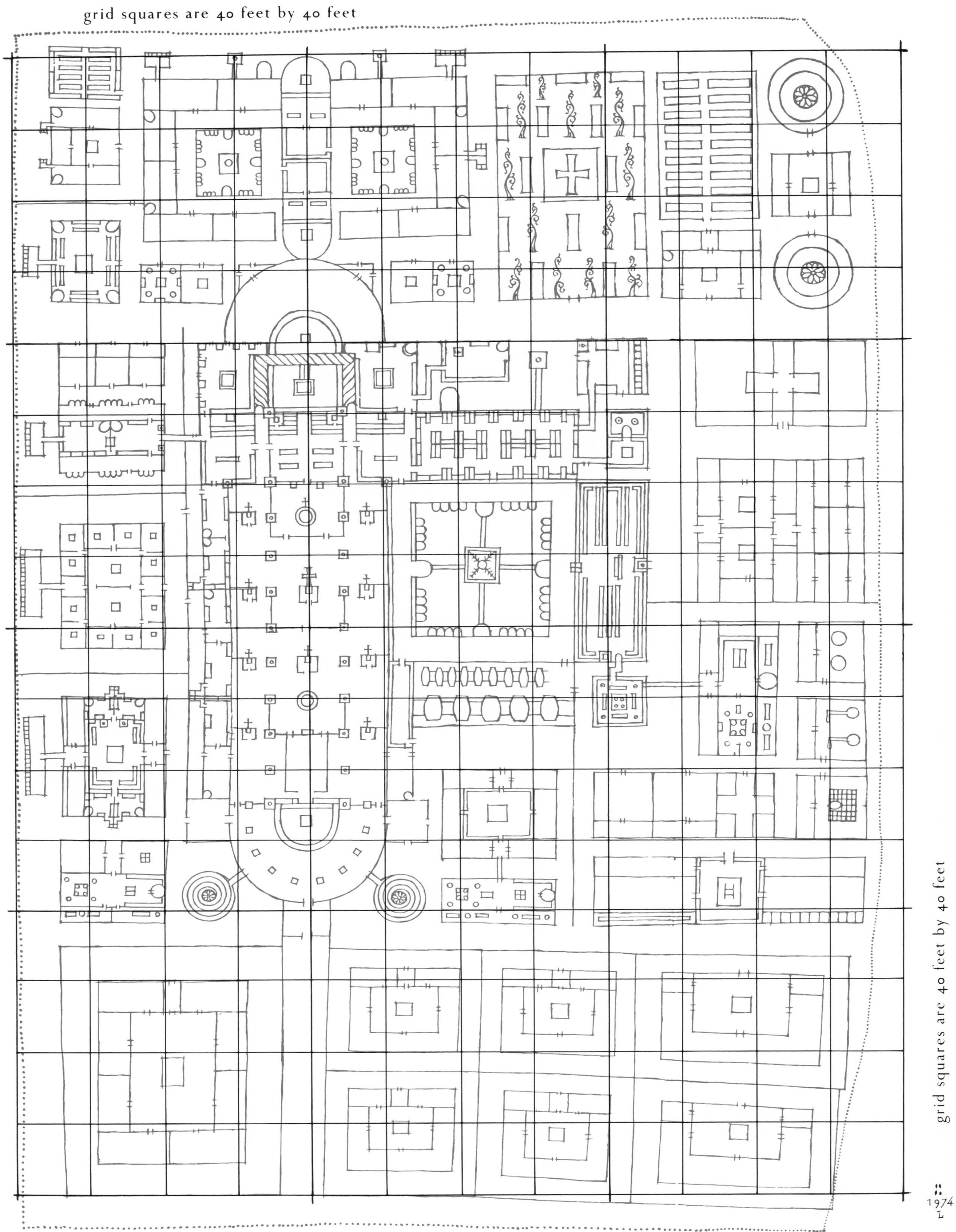

DRAWING

grid squares are 40 feet by 40 feet

grid squares are 40 feet by 40 feet

SCALE 1:768

(¼ original size)

1974
L

PLAN OF ST GALL: SHOWING 40 FOOT MODULE SUPERIMPOSED UPON THE ENTIRE SITE OF THE MONASTERY

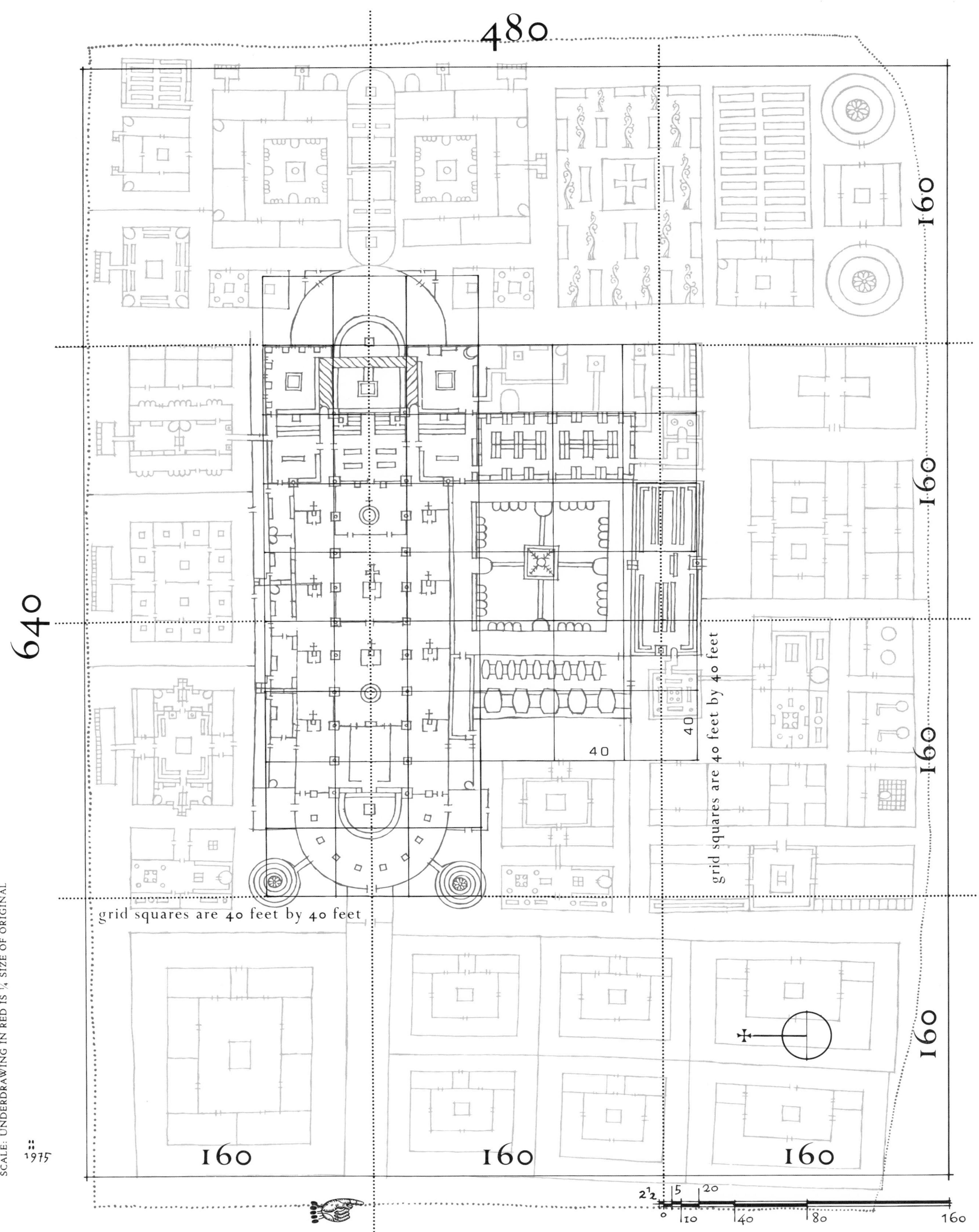

PLAN OF ST. GALL: ONE LINE OF A GRID, 160 FOOT MODULE, FIXED THE CHURCH AXIS

SERVICES

THE MONASTERY COMPLEX OF THE PLAN CONTAINS TWO WORLDS. WITHIN THE CHURCH AND ITS adjacent structures monks devoted themselves to the *Opus Dei*—liturgy and prayer, the work of God. Facilities to tend the ill, train novices, and pursue studies were arranged in the site to preserve monastic seclusion. Ordered by the canonical hours, the monks' lives were defended from outside distraction and excessive manual labor by a large lay work force integral to the community but architecturally detached from the monastic precincts of church and cloister. On the Plan workers are housed to the south and west of the church and claustral ranges, in buildings distinctly different from them in shape and historical antecedents.

The monastic world met the secular world guardedly at the porter's gate, or in the parlor where monks could receive visitors, or in the abbot's house. The abbot or his delegate mediated between these two spheres. For the monastery had worldly commitments: the Christian duty to succor the poor and shelter pilgrims; the political charge to educate sons of nobles and entertain noble travelers; the military obligation to provide the emperor with men from its estates, arms from its workshops, and mounts from its stables in time of war.

To the south and southwest, the site is devoted to industrial pursuits, agriculture, and animal husbandry, revealing dependence of the cloistered life upon those performing the *Opus Manuum*—the work of hands. Tended by the monastery's laymen, the gardens, granaries, workshops, water-powered grindstones and mortars, and livestock barns did not make the community wholly self-sufficient. Diverse goods—cloth, metals, beeswax—were supplied from outside sources.

The year's provisioning came largely from the abbey's manorial estates managed by tenants who, given protection and the right to live on the land and till it, were required to tithe both harvest and labor to their monastic overlords.

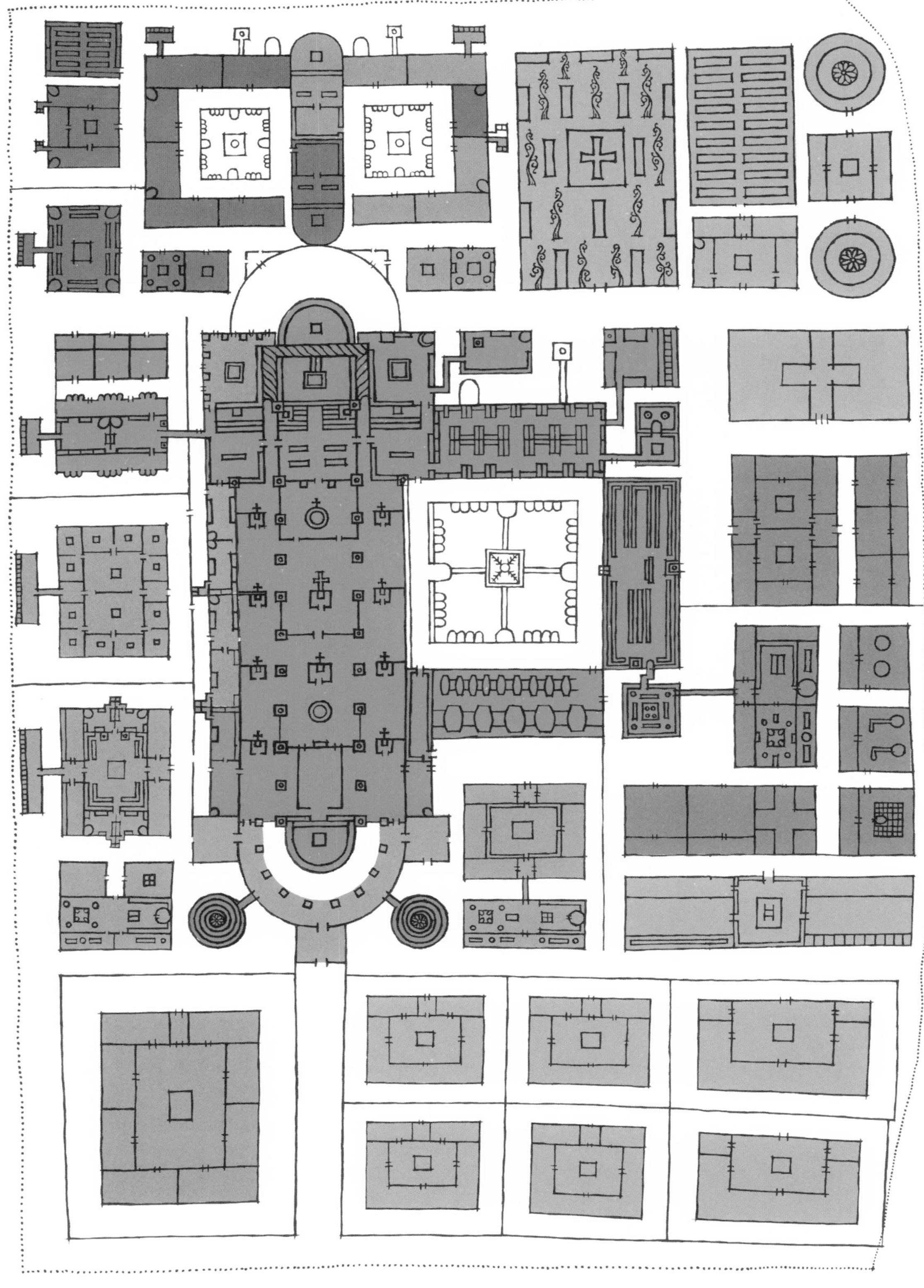

LEGEND

HEALTH, MEDICINE

EDUCATION: Public, Novices

RECEPTION: Nobles, Pilgrims, Paupers

CHURCH & DEPENDENCIES

AGRICULTURE: Pomology, Vegetables, Animal Husbandry

CRAFTS, MILLING, BAKING

DIAGRAM III

PLAN OF ST GALL

ORGANIZATION OF SERVICE FACILITIES

THE RULE OF ST. BENEDICT recognizes both charity and manual labor to be important attributes of monastic life, but neither could be allowed to overshadow worship, meditation, and study. The Plan's organization demonstrates how closely integrated with these goals life within the monastic community might be, both ideally and in reality.

Travelers approached the church from its entrance road. Visitors were largely confined to the northwest segment of the site on either side of the church's western apse. Here their admission to quarters and to the church was easily managed; their separate kitchens and diets assured that monks need not be distracted from their own pursuits within the cloister walls. Livestock barns, from which animals and herdsmen came and went daily, are all in the southwest portion of the tract. The effect was to create a band in which daily passage to and from the community was confined across its western end.

Facilities in the southern segment are devoted to crafts and activities directly associated with maintaining life in the cloister. Here monks themselves might work or supervise others, but still remain isolated from other traffic. East of the livestock barns specialized crafts were pursued by coopers and wheelwrights—near the cellar where barrels were required, near the barns where wheeled carts were used and could be stored. Brewer's granary, mill, mortar, and drying kiln are located near the cellar and monks' kitchen. In the southeast corner fowl pens, garden and orchard, and granary are located in recognition of their potential interdependent use.

In the northeast corner physicians, the ill, and novices occupied an area carefully segregated from outside contact. Here the abbot might come at will, but no one entered without his permission and knowledge. The abbot's house is the link between inner and outer worlds of the monastery, and is strategically located to give access to both. The duties of the abbot are discussed on p. 38.

PLAN 3/16 ORIGINAL PLAN, 1:1024

CHURCH

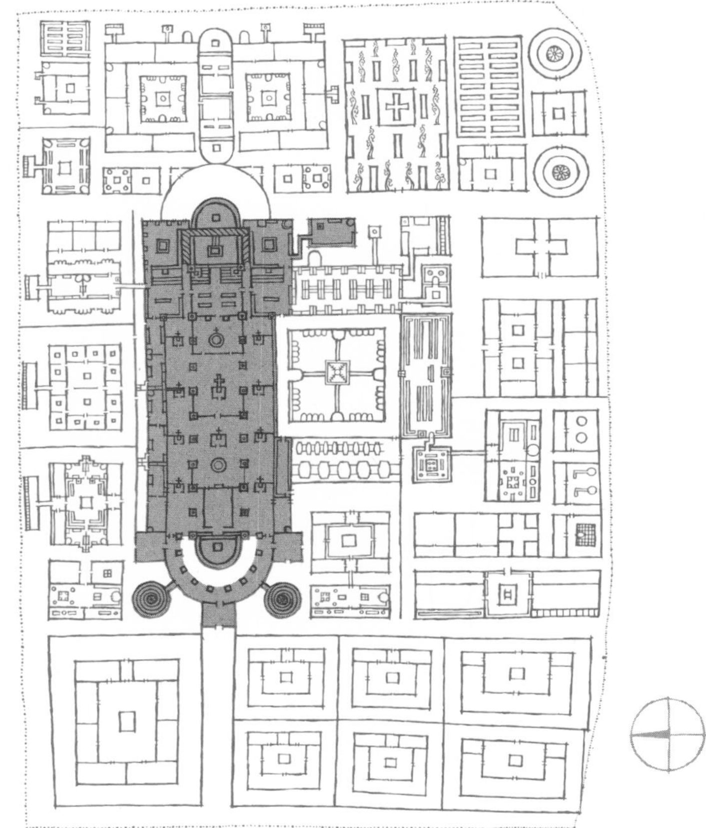

Site plan

AMONG THE MAIN ACCOMPLISHMENTS OF THE CAROLINGIAN renaissance was the revival of the T-shaped basilica of Rome. Its most powerful expression was embodied in 4 monumental churches 300 or more feet long: the cathedral of Cologne, the abbey churches of Fulda and Hersfeld; and the church of the Plan of St Gall. These grandiose structures formed part of an expression of increasingly close alliance between the Frankish empire and the see of Rome. In their early Christian prototypes, spatial relationships of nave, transept, and aisles were arbitrary. In reviving this basilican scheme, Carolingian architects reshaped it by introducing an innovative geometric rational into its dimensional planning.

Early Christian metropolitan churches initially contained but one altar served by a few priests; nave and aisles were ceded to throngs of the pious. By contrast the church of the Plan reflects centuries of elaboration in liturgy and monastic life. In it altars with screens and barriers proliferate, separating worshippers; only 1/6 of its area was accessible to serfs, pilgrims, or guests. This attempt to reflect state policy by building churches of metropolitan size in small monastic settlements proved a heroic, but economically and spiritually debatable undertaking. The church of the Plan, never built as drawn, was shortened to express retrenchment in favor of liturgical discipline, at sacrifice of symbolic values embodied in daring and ingenious architectural planning (pages 12-17).

PLAN OF ST. GALL. CHURCH INTERIOR. VIEW TOWARD EAST APSE

AUTHORS' INTERPRETATION

The Church of the Plan—its interior appearance here recreated by Ernest Born—was never built. Yet being conceived, it became a historical reality, and our reconstruction for that reason, if correct in its principal lines, is a significant contribution to the visual history of medieval architecture. The underlying compositional scheme (nave, two aisles and transept) is Early Christian. But none of the great metropolitan basilicas of the West had arcades so wide and high, or proportions so rationally coordinated with a spatial master value, by the alignment of the columnar interstices with the 40-foot module of the crossing square.

CHURCH

PLAN OF ST GALL

Aisled and cruciform in layout, the Church of the Plan has apses at each end, eastern and western paradises, and two detached round towers flanking its entrance. Apart from length, the most remarkable feature of the layout is that it is based on a system of squares—"square schematism"—carried out with a logic and consistency unmatched in any other Carolingian church except perhaps Hildebold's cathedral at Cologne (built after 800 A.D.).
The Church of the Plan measures 300 feet from apse to apse. Nave and transept are 40 feet wide; their intersection, the crossing square, forms a unit of measure central to the Plan's identity. A 40-foot modular grid superimposed on the Plan (page 16) reveals an architectural consciousness of the highest order. Symbolic and liturgical values (discussed, page 12) are embodied not only in layout and dimensions of the Church, but of the entire site.
Written in CAPITALIS RUSTICA *(widely spaced, reading East-West down the center of the nave) the following inscription appears:*

AB ORIENTE IN OCCIDENTE LONGIT. PED. .CC.
FROM EAST TO WEST THE LENGTH IS 200 FEET

This instruction to shorten the Church of the Plan destroyed its maker's vision of a unique and powerful architectural statement framed to address all of Christendom, by means of one of the most moving and profoundly shaping forces devised by man,— the art of building.

SHOWN ½ ORIGINAL SIZE. 1:384

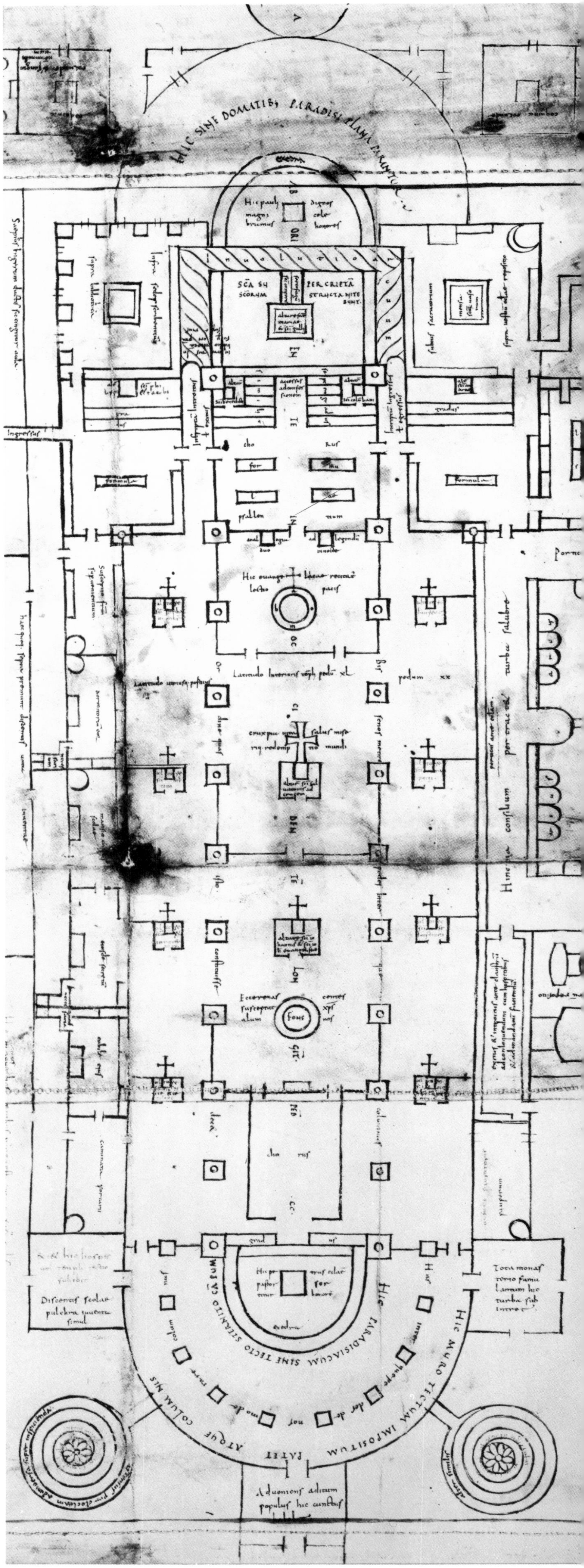

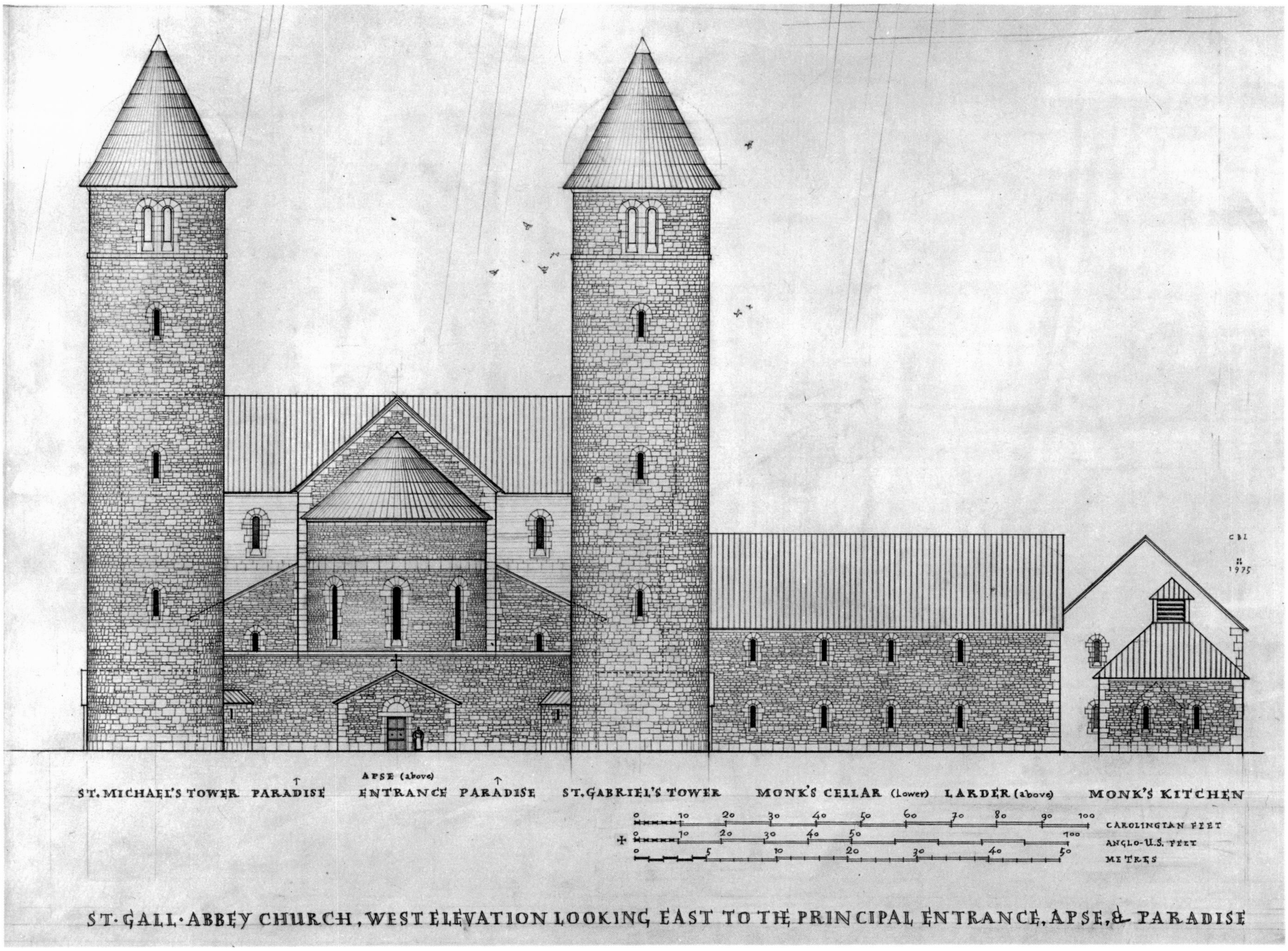

ST. MICHAEL'S TOWER PARADISE APSE (above) ENTRANCE PARADISE ST. GABRIEL'S TOWER MONK'S CELLAR (lower) LARDER (above) MONK'S KITCHEN

CAROLINGIAN FEET
ANGLO-U.S. FEET
METRES

ST·GALL·ABBEY CHURCH, WEST ELEVATION LOOKING EAST TO THE PRINCIPAL ENTRANCE, APSE, & PARADISE

1/32″ = foot [1:384]

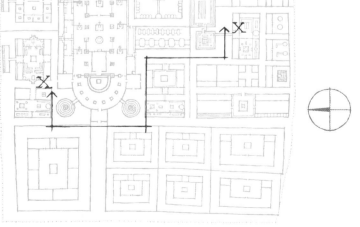

PLAN OF ST. GALL. CHURCH SEEN FROM THE WEST LOOKING EAST

AUTHORS' INTERPRETATION [after the model displayed at Aachen in 1965]. ELEVATION TAKEN ON SECTION X–X

This is the only example of a Carolingian church with detached circular towers. The motif is unique and does not appear in later medieval architecture. Explanatory titles denote that its towers carried at the top of one the altar of Michael, of the other, the altar of Gabriel. There is no indication of the presence of bells, and, because of the distance from the high altar, their sound in any case could not have been coordinated with the liturgy. Gabriel and Michael are the celestial guardians representing forces of light against those of darkness and evil. The towers have no practical function, but symbolically might announce from afar to travellers (and at close range almost threateningly) that they approach a Fortress of God.

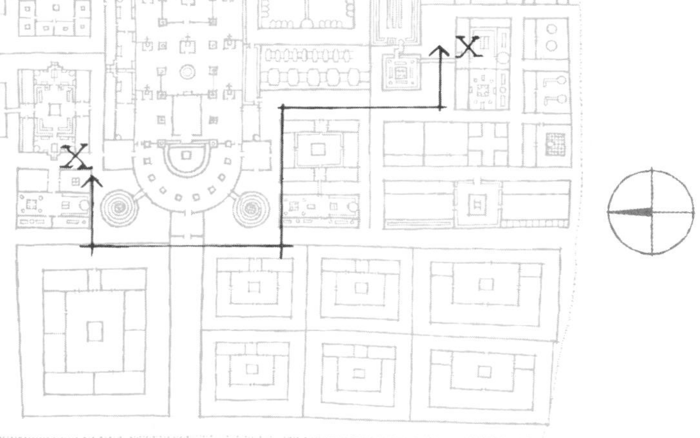

THE MONKS' CLOISTER

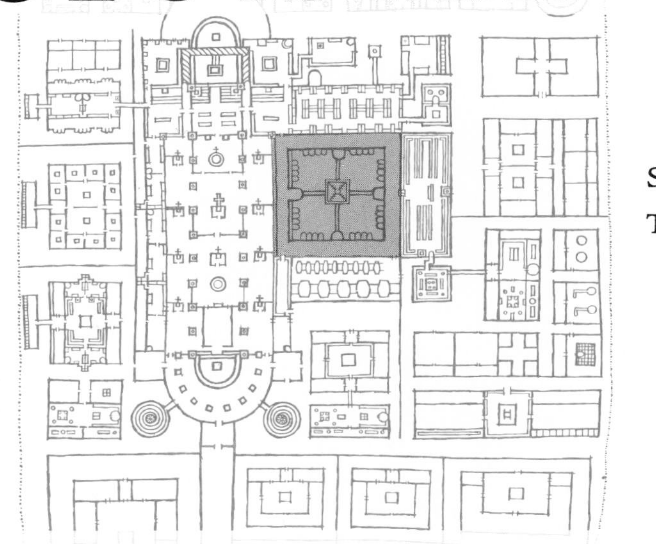

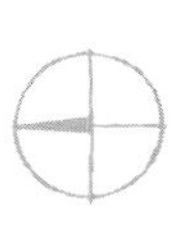

SITE PLAN
The monks' cloister

ST BENEDICT desired that the claustral complex contain "all necessary things . . . water mill, garden, various crafts . . . so that the monks may not be compelled to wander outside it." This arrangement required a host of secular workmen close at hand to assure the monks' provisioning and maintenance. Thus the need arose for an inner enclosure to isolate monks from laymen, yet allowing the latter to live close to the brothers, as their tasks required. The cloister solved this problem by creating a monastery within the monastery.

The monks' cloister of the Plan is an open yard 100 feet square, as stipulated by a 9th-century commentator on the Rule of St Benedict. Its arcaded walks give access to the surrounding buildings. Arcades drawn in elevation communicate the conceptual intent of construction design. The north walk, broader than the rest, was used as a chapter house for daily meetings, and contained 2 benches.

Three double-storied structures enclose the cloister: warming room and dormintory (east); refectory and vestiary (south); cellar and larder (west). The draftsman delineates only the levels with critical capacity, where the drawing must provide maximum guidance. Those not shown are identified by inscription; stairwell access is omitted.* The Plan is thus kept free of excessive detail. The 2½-foot module is applied meticulously in layout of furnishings, beds, benches, tables and barrels. Roots of the medieval cloister are found in the open galleried courts of Roman palaces and imperial fora. A few early Near Eastern cloisters, surrounded by monks' dwellings, were attached directly to the church, but for centuries this location was exceptional. Neither square shape, nor attachment to the southern flank of the church, nor the impenetrable architectural surround of the cloister predate the ascendancy, in the West, of Benedictine monastic custom and its highly organized communal life.

*An omission understandable in a prototypal plan; resolution of a detail (stairway) would be determined by the particular conditions encountered at each monastery site.

size of original drawing in color 51 x 53 cm

PLAN OF ST. GALL. MONKS' CLOISTER, THE CHURCH AND ADJACENT BUILDINGS

When St. Cuthbert built himself a hermitage on Farne Island, where he spent the last eleven years of his life in solitary retreat, he surrounded his living space "with a wall higher than a man standing upright," and further increased its relative height "by cutting away the living rock so that the pious inhabitant could see nothing except the sky from his dwelling, thus restraining both the lust of the eyes and the thoughts and lifting the whole bent of his mind to higher things" (BEDE, *ed. Colgrave, 1940, 214–17*). *The Plan of St. Gall achieves a like effect for an entire community in the sophisticated layout of the cloister with its egress and ingress governed by a body of rigid laws, the open inner court being the monks' only access to nature and sun—a controlled and ordered island of nature with judiciously selected and carefully tended plants:* PARADISUS CLAUSTRALIS.

THE MONKS' CLOISTER

MONK'S CLOISTER, CELLAR, KITCHEN, REFECTORY, LAUNDRY & BATH HOUSE, DORMITORY, LATRINE
MONASTERY, ST. GALL

PLAN OF ST. GALL. PRINCIPAL CLAUSTRAL STRUCTURES & THE MONKS' CLOISTER

CUTAWAY PERSPECTIVE. AUTHORS' INTERPRETATION

Three double-storied masonry buildings solidly enclosing an open yard are attached to the southern flank of the Church, and are connected at ground level by the covered arcaded walks of the cloister. The east structure contains the Warming Room, below, and the Monks' Dormitory, above. From its southern gable wall an exit leads to the Monks' Privy on the upper level, and at ground level another leads to their Laundry and Bathhouse. The south structure contains on ground level the Monks' Refectory and above it their Vestiary. From its western gable wall an exit leads to the Monks' Kitchen at ground level. The west structure contains on ground level the cellar, and above it, the Larder.

On the Plan itself, although the Dormitory layout is actually drawn on ground level, an inscription makes clear that it is to be located in the second story.

The Plan does not show any stairs between floors. We make no attempt here to correct this shortcoming by supplying features to which the designer himself chose to make no committment. By suppressing stairs he not only was able to keep his design uncluttered, but also emphasized that wherever, in the process of construction, stairs were to be installed they should be located so as not to interfere with arrangements which he considered to be of more vital concern: Dormitory bed layout, Refectory bench and table layout, Cellar barrel layout—all worked out with great care, in full consideration of the number of monks to be served by these respective structures, and the volume of wine and beer to be stored.

Not disregard, but rather a choice between details of primary and secondary importance, induced the designer to suppress stairs. In so choosing he arrived with depth of technical insight and wise restraint at a solution, at once ingeniously simple and equally sophisticated, to the special task facing him: namely, assembling on a single drafted plan all essential information needed to construct the forty-odd buildings of which a paradigmatic monastery of his period was to be composed.

PLAN OF ST. GALL. REFECTORY. INTERIOR VIEW LOOKING EASTWARD

AUTHORS' RECONSTRUCTION

The entrance to the Refectory from the south cloister walk, left middle ground, centers on the north wall directly opposite the reader's pulpit, which centers on the south wall. Beneath the pulpit stands the table for visiting monks.

The abbot's table centers on the east wall, a commanding position from which he surveys the community of which he is the ruler, ever mindful of his office and the trust reposing in him as abbot, father, in accordance with the admonition of St. Benedict, founder of the Order. Here with twelve brothers on his right and twelve on his left, the abbot, with the rest of the community at tables ranged around the rooms, eats in silence. As the mortal body partakes of earthly food, the reader from his pulpit brings spiritual sustenance of sacred writings, articulated in a voice that is heard throughout the great space.

The Refectory is illustrated with masonry-built walls. To reconstruct a space of that size as stone-vaulted in the Carolingian period would be anachronistic. The illustration shows a wood-structured ceiling.

We interpret the measure of the Refectory on the facsimile Plan to be 40 feet wide (16 standard modules). With allowance made for wall thickness, it would have been unlikely to exeed about 37½ feet internal measure, or 15 standard modules—no mean span, yet quite feasible to bridge by a timbered ceiling. The length, east to west, articulates with the cloister east-west dimension, 100 feet. Allowing for wall thickness, it is taken as 95 feet, or 38 standard modules, which conveniently resolves to seven bays: a center bay of 5 modules, with three bays of 5½ modules on each side of the center bay. Thus six bays of 5½ modules plus one bay of 5 modules (= 95 feet) is the basis for our reconstruction of the interior perspective.

Considering that the girder and beam system carried the monks' Vestiary on the upper level, we include curved timber struts supported on monolithic masonry corbels deeply embedded in the long side walls. This scheme gives an unsupported center span of about 17 feet, with two side spans, each less than 10 feet, spans of such modest length as to be commonplace and to offer no structural problems. Seven windows in the south wall, one in each bay, give abundant direct sunlight throughout the year. On the north wall the six windows that open on the cloister shelter are somewhat less effective than those on the south. A system of wood girders, beams, purlins, supporting a plank wood floor, invites the use of painting, particularly on the planks, purlins, and beams. Color thus used has amazing power to bring brightness and lift to a ceiling. With dark evenings and dark mornings of a northern winter, painted color was a simple, but effective, mode to gain light and cheer. All this, conjectural for a building never constructed, is an interpretation.

E. B.

* *the original drawing in carbon pencil measures 20.25 × 30.50 inches (51.5 × 77.5 cm)*

NOVITIATE & INFIRMARY

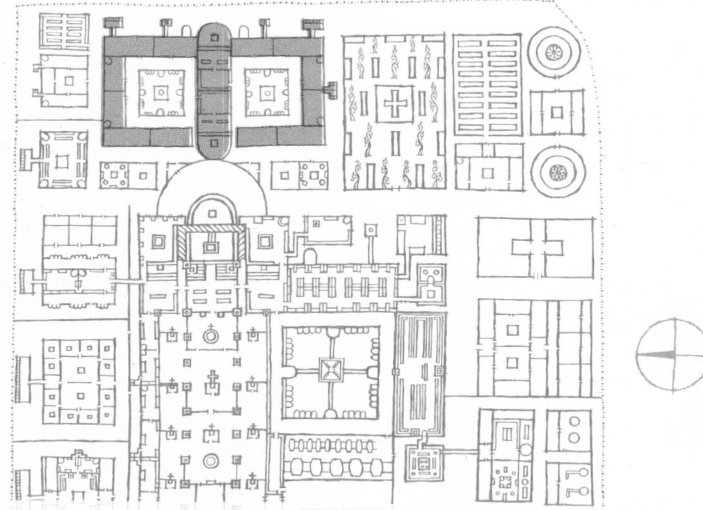

THE MOST POWERFULLY CLASSICAL ELEMENT OF THE PLAN and unique in Carolingian architecture, this complex is inspired by the axial bisymmetry of Roman imperial architecture. The novitiate and infirmary of the Plan of St Gall are housed in separate but identical quarters. A church 110 feet long, double-apsed, of masonry, and axially aligned with the large church, is partitioned transversely into two chapels. On its north and south flanks, identical architectural facilities enclose twin cloisters. It is an elegant, ingenious solution to the need for separation of novices and the ill from each other as well as from the main body of monks.

Differing needs of diet, education, bathing, and medical care prompted this division. Stringencies of monastic life were mitigated for the young and the ill, who were allowed meat and more frequent baths. Their quarters, like the monks', were warmed by hypocausts.

Novices were of two types: oblates, offered to the monastery by their parents; and *pulsantes* ("knockers") who, after initial discouragement, were admitted at their own request. Novices might include very young boys to adolescents. The goals of their lives being drastically different, they were educated separately from sons of nobles training in the outer school, and were instructed in their future duties by a master and several assistants who lived with them. Mildly ill boys kept to the novitiate sick ward and did not mingle with their seriously indisposed elders in the infirmary.

The infirmary housed the dying, critically ill, and convalescent monks, as well as some permanent residents enfeebled by chronic illness or old age. A master and perhaps two or three other monks attended their needs, prepared their meals, and celebrated Mass with them. In this quiet corner of the site, convalescent and novice found activities suited to returning strength, and the recreation St Benedict deemed appropriate for boys. Here learning and healing went forward in the embrace of the larger community.

See also HEALTH SERVICES, pages 32-37.

size of original drawing in color 46.5 x 73 cm

PLAN OF ST. GALL. AIR VIEW OF NOVITIATE AND INFIRMARY

AUTHORS' INTERPRETATION

This drawing is after the reconstruction model of the buildings of the Plan made for the exhibition KARL DER GROSSE, *in Aachen, 1965. Besides the Monastery Church the building complex which accommodates the claustral compounds of the Novitiate and Infirmary, in consummate symmetry on either side of the dominant mass of a double-apsed Church, is the largest single building shown in the Plan. Its layout, wholly unrelated to the vernacular tradition of the North, is one of the finest products of the Carolingian renascence—a concept perhaps inspired by the layout of the Constantinian aula at Trier or Roman imperial summer residences, such as Konz and Kloosterberg. Its classicism could be defined as an architectural counterpart of some of the finest and most classicising manuscripts of the so-called Palace School, such as the famous Aachen or Vienna treasure Gospels, whose evangelists, portrayed in senatorial robes and seated in open landscapes, cannot be stylistically derived from the preceding Hiberno-Saxon schools of illumination, but are a revival of an illusionistic Roman tradition that had been lost in the shuffle of the Great Migrations.*

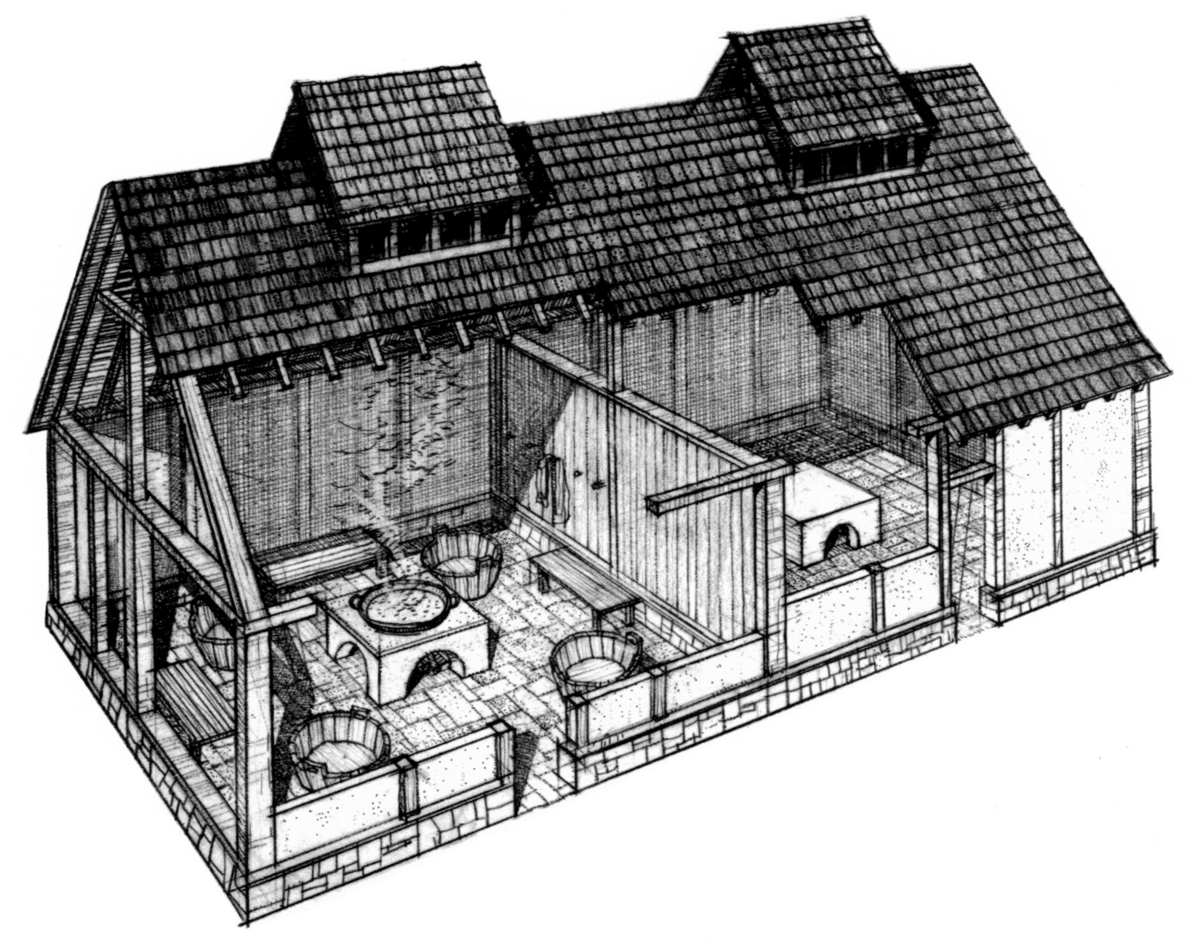

PLAN OF ST. GALL. KITCHEN & BATHHOUSE OF NOVITIATE AND INFIRMARY

AUTHORS' INTERPRETATION

Because of their different diets and remoteness from the Monks' Kitchen and Bathhouse, the planner provided the ill with a kitchen-bath building adjacent to the infirmary, and a similiar kitchen-bath building for the novices symmetrically located on the south. The Plan, in this part, reveals remarkable responsiveness to administration, practical convenience, and professional care. The walls could have been of masonry where we show timber construction.

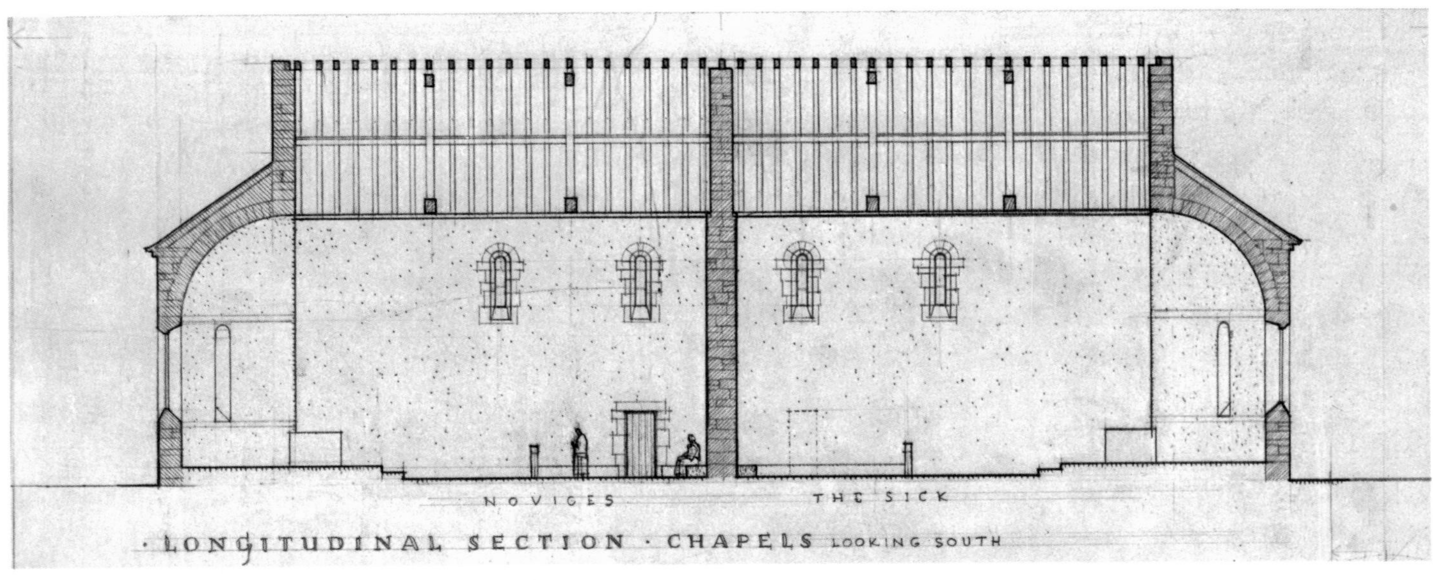

LONGITUDINAL SECTION THROUGH CHAPELS LOOKING SOUTH

PLAN OF ST. GALL. CHAPEL OF NOVITIATE AND CHAPEL OF INFIRMARY AUTHORS' INTERPRETATION

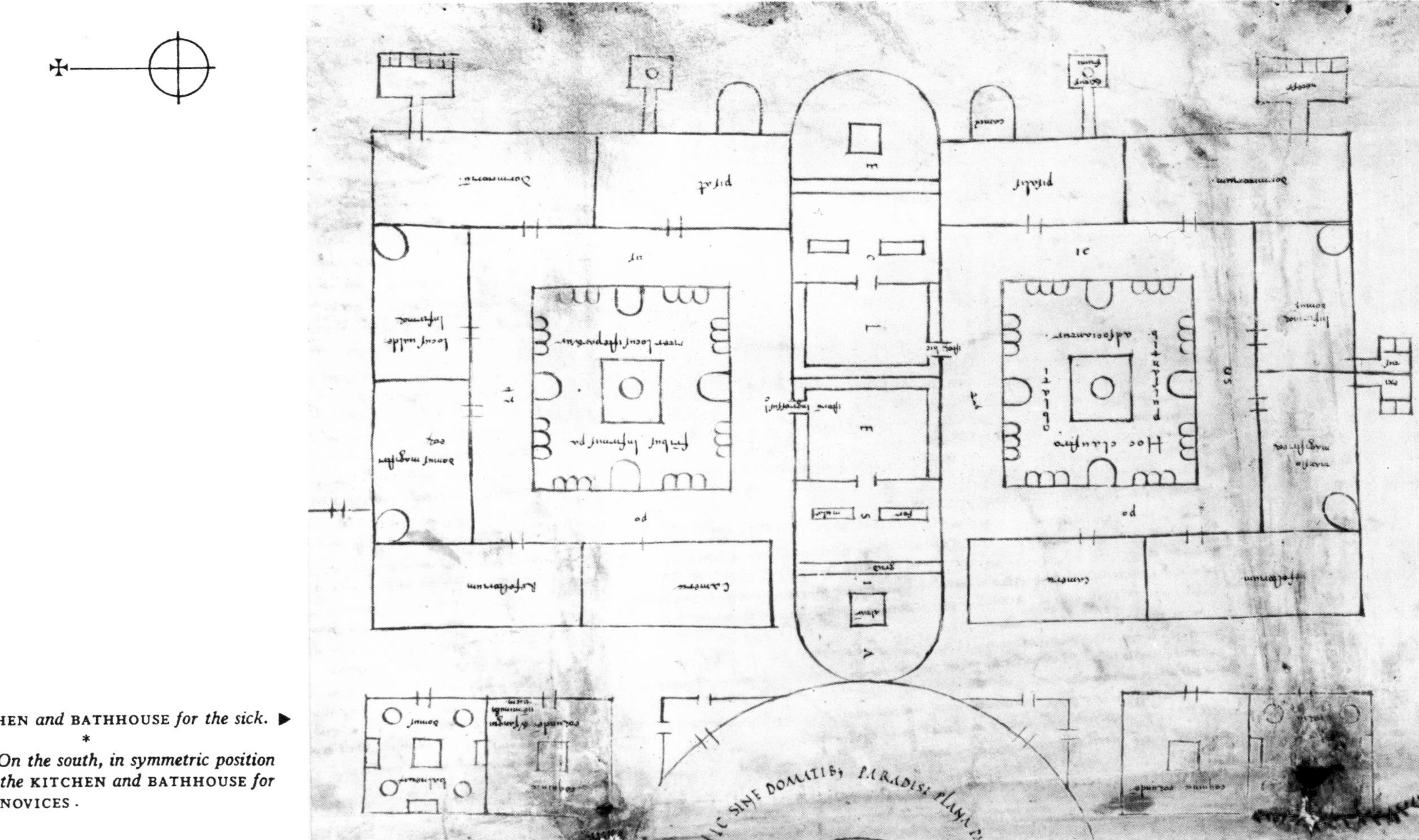

The KITCHEN *and* BATHHOUSE *for the sick.* ▶
*
On the south, in symmetric position on the Plan is the KITCHEN *and* BATHHOUSE *for* NOVICES.

PLAN OF ST. GALL. NOVITIATE AND INFIRMARY WITH KITCHENS & BATHHOUSES

SHOWN ½ ORIGINAL SIZE (1:384)

Right: the Novitiate; left: the Infirmary, each a smaller replica of the Cloister of the Monks. These facilities flank a double-apsed church, internally divided by a median transverse wall into two separate chapels: one for the Novices (facing east), the other for the ill (facing west). The layout is more Roman in spirit than any other building on the Plan, and is without antecedent in either Early Christian or early medieval architecture. It has its roots instead in Roman imperial audience halls and luxurious Roman villas.

17

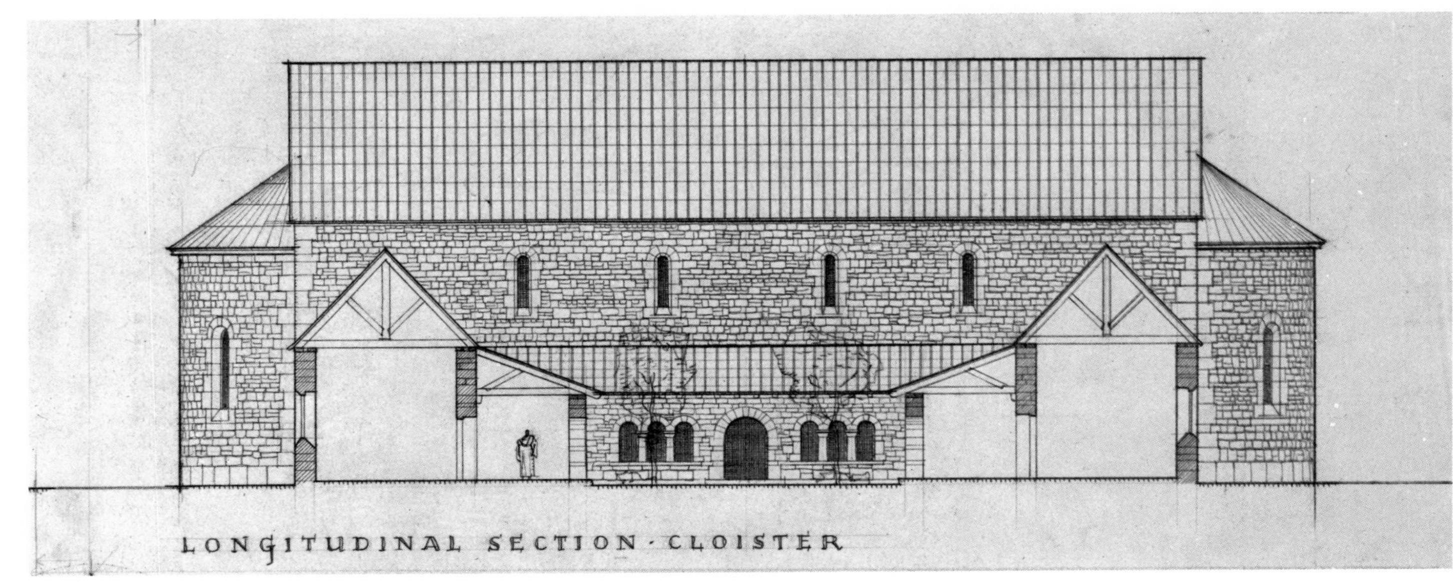

LONGITUDINAL ELEVATION OF CHAPELS AND SECTION (EAST-WEST) THROUGH CLOISTER

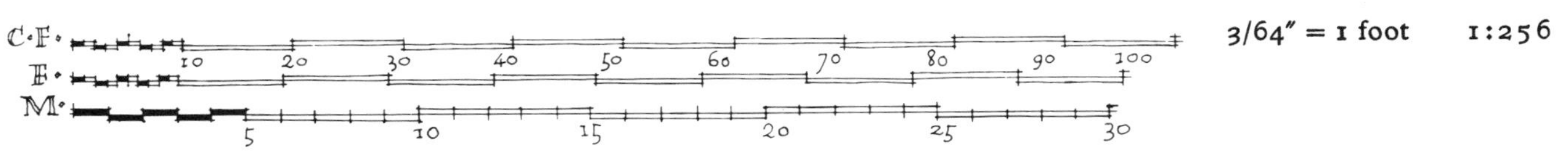

3/64″ = 1 foot 1:256

HEALTH SERVICES

Sed et vos alloquor fratres egregios, qui humani corporis salutem sedula curiositate tractatis, et confugientibus ad loca sanctorum officia beatae pietatis impeditis, tristes passionibus alienis, de periclitantibus maesti, susceptorum dolore confixi, et in alienis calamitatibus merore proprio semper attoniti; ut, sicut artis vestrae peritia docet, languentibus sincero studio serviatis, ab illo mercedem recepturi, a quo possunt pro temporalibus aeterna retribui . . .

I salute you, distinguished brothers, who with sedulous care look after the health of the human body and perform the function of blessed piety for those who flee to the shrine of holy men—you who are sad at the sufferings of others, sorrowful for those who are in danger, grieved at the pain of those who are received, and always distressed with personal sorrow at the misfortunes of others . . .

Cassiodorus*, *Institutiones,* chap. 31

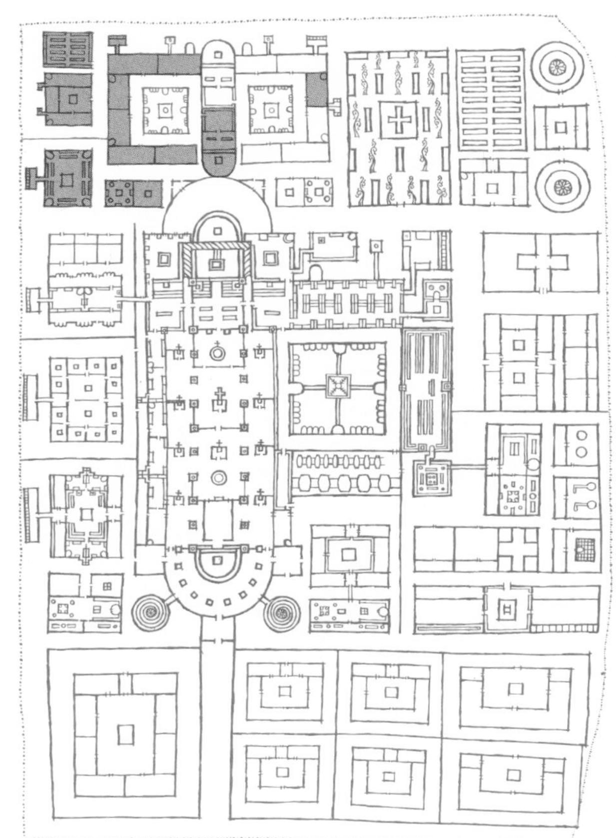

BEFORE ALL THINGS AND ABOVE ALL THINGS LET CARE BE TAKEN OF THE SICK, said St Benedict‡, and went on to counsel the ill to "not provoke their brethren with unreasonable demands." In response to this charge the Plan embodies, in the northeast corner, one of the loftiest humanitarian ideals by devoting nearly 1/10 of the monastic site to health facilities: infirmary complex, house for physicians with pharmacy and sick ward, house for bleeding, 2 bathhouses, and a medicinal herb garden.

The Rule of St Benedict does not specifically address the status of physicians. Nevertheless study and practice of healing was an honorable pursuit of monastic learning. Not an official, the physician's title was given to a monk possessing healing skills; laymen also might practice, as was the case in Adalhard's abbey of Corbie.

A certain fatalism pervaded medieval medicine. "Do not place your hopes in herbs, nor trust to human counsel," advised Cassiodorus Senator in the 6th century. "The Lord grants life to men and makes them sound." This belief conditioned medieval therapeutic intervention. Pharmacopeia derived largely from herbs, on the Plan of St Gall grown in the medicinal herb

concluded on page 34

* Cassiodorus ca. 490-ca. 585
‡ St Benedict *476-†543

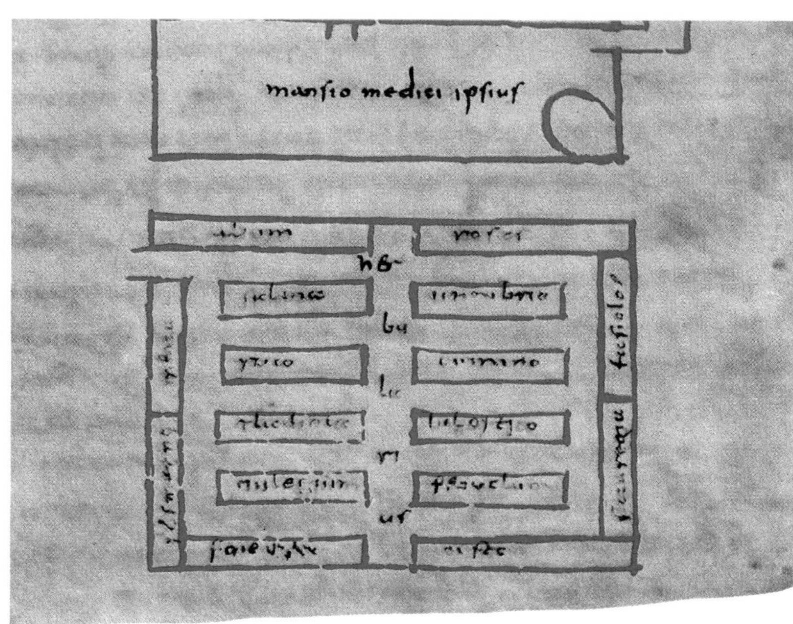

PLAN OF ST. GALL. MEDICINAL HERB GARDEN

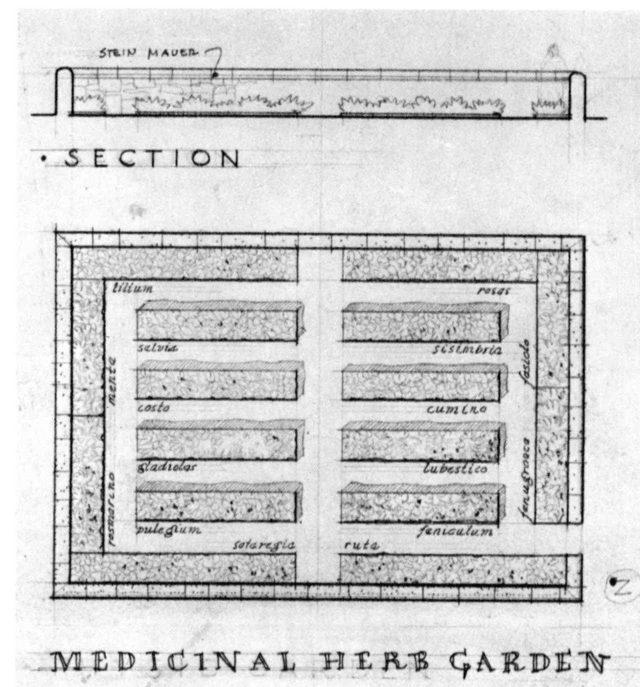

AUTHORS' INTERPRETATION

SCALE: $\frac{1}{16}$ INCH EQUALS 1 FOOT [1:192]

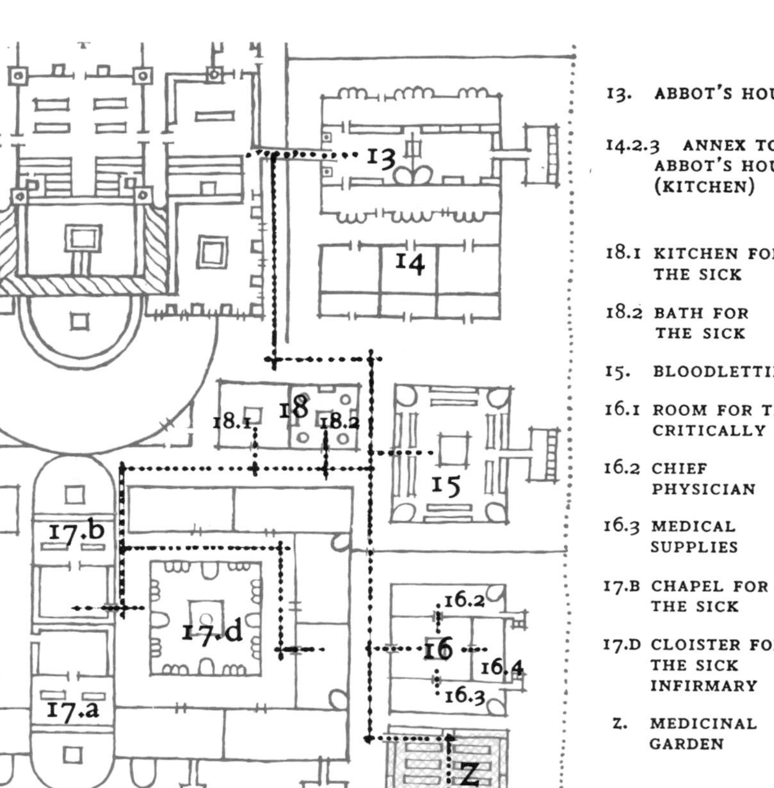

13. ABBOT'S HOUSE
14.2.3 ANNEX TO ABBOT'S HOUSE (KITCHEN)
18.1 KITCHEN FOR THE SICK
18.2 BATH FOR THE SICK
15. BLOODLETTING
16.1 ROOM FOR THE CRITICALLY ILL
16.2 CHIEF PHYSICIAN
16.3 MEDICAL SUPPLIES
17.B CHAPEL FOR THE SICK
17.D CLOISTER FOR THE SICK INFIRMARY
Z. MEDICINAL GARDEN

PLOT PLAN

SHOWING RELATIONSHIP OF HEALTH & MEDICAL FACILITIES

The plot plan suggests two traffic patterns within the Infirmary areas. Moving north, monks and serfs needing medical attention could leave the Church after services and report to whichever medical facility they were assigned. The Monks' Infirmary was available only to regular monks; the House for Bloodletting was probably used by both monks and serfs. The critically ill were lodged with the physicians; probably serfs or other laymen with minor infirmities were treated where they lodged.

Moving southward on the site, the physicians might make daily rounds: conducting or overseeing bloodletting; at the bath and kitchen for the ill recommending therapy and special diet, supplies for which might be sent for from the small stock of luxuries afforded the Abbot in his own nearby kitchen; thence reporting directly to the Abbot himself (as was their charge and his own) concerning the ill, recommending further treatment for some, or swifter cures for suspected malingerers. At mid-point in this course the physicians could stop in the Chapel and Cloister for the Ill to advise recuperating brothers.

It would be an oversight to regard these economies of movement and communication as happy accidents; on the contrary, a high degree of skill and consciousness in such matters helped the Benedictines eventually to influence the affairs of Carolingian Europe, and gave the Plan of St. Gall its unique stature as an architectural plan.

PLAN OF ST. GALL. MEDICINAL HERB GARDEN

The herbs to be cultivated in this small garden are selected for their medicinal properties. Their renascence each spring under the care of man, after the plants had either died altogether or only back to their roots during winter, has been described by Walahfrid Strabo in an account of great poetic beauty (HORTULUS) *as a recurring manifestation of the forces of life imparted to nature by Divine creation.*

The physicians cared directly for the critically ill and for those to be bled; their chief duties in addition were making medicines, and prescribing courses of treatment that might be administered by others. From the nearby garden they could pluck fresh the plants needed to compound the poultices, purges, infusions, and simples that were the main concerns of pharmacy in the 9th century.

PLANT LIST

lilium LILY, *rosas* [garden] ROSE, *fasiolo* CLIMBING BEAN, *sata regia* PEPPERWORT, *costa* COSTMARY, *fena greca* GREEK HAY, *rosmarino* ROSEMARY, *menta* MINT, *saluia* SAGE, *ruta* RUE, *gladiola* IRIS, *pulegium* PENNYROYAL, *sisimbria* WATER CRESS, *cumino* CUMIN, *lubestico* LOVAGE, *feniculum* FENNEL

15

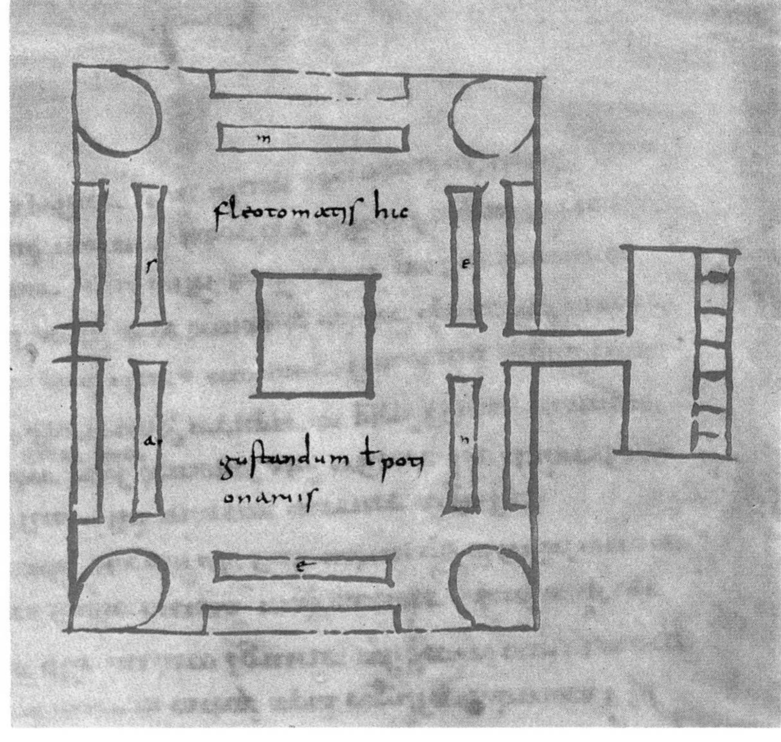

PLAN OF ST. GALL. HOUSE FOR BLOODLETTING

A SAVORY SAUCE FOR SEASONING *

Fish which are fatty by nature, like salmon, eels, shad *(alase)*, sardines, or herring, are caught, and this mixture is made from them and from dried fragrant herbs and salt: a very solid and well-pitched vat is prepared, holding three or four *modii,* and dry fragrant herbs are taken from both the garden and the field, for instance, anise, coriander, fennel, parsley, pepperwort, endive, rue, mint, watercress, privet, pennyroyal, thyme, marjoram, betony, agrimony. And the first row is strewn from these in the bottom of the vat. Then the second row is made of the fish: whole if they are small, and cut to bits if large. Above this a third row of salt two fingers high is added, and the vat should be filled to the top in this manner, with three rows of herbs, fish, and salt alternating each over the other. Then it should be covered with a lid and left so for seven days. And when this period is past, for twelve days straight the mixture should be stirred every day clear to the bottom with a wooden paddle shaped like an oar. After this the liquid that has flowed out of the mixture is collected, and in this way a liquid or sauce [?; *omogarum*] is made from it. Two *sesters* of this liquid are taken and mixed with two half *sesters* of good wine. Then four bunches [*manipuli*] apiece of dry herbs are thrown into this mixture, to wit, anise and coriander and pepperwort; also a fistful of fenugreek seed is added, and thirty or forty grains of pepper spices, three pennyweights (?) of costmary, likewise of cinnamon, likewise of cloves. These should be pulverized and mixed with the same liquid; then this mixture is to be cooked in an iron or bronze pot until it boils down to the measure of one *sester*. But before it is cooked down, a half pound [*libram semissem*] of skimmed honey should be added to the same. And when it is fully cooked in the manner of a drink [*more potionum*] it should be strained through a bag until it is clear. And it should be poured hot into a bag, strained and cooled and kept in a well-pitched bowl for seasoning viands. ‡

In the Middle Ages bleeding was used to remedy almost every known disease, to such excess that public opinion eventually turned against the procedure. It is, even today, used as a cure for a small number of pathological conditions where other means fail—but nowhere, now, to the extent of justifying the construction of special houses for bleeding. The Plan of St. Gall reveals with unique precision the appearance of this extinct species of house in the 9th century.

* Recipe quotation, after *Mitteilungen der antiquarischen Gesellschaft,* Zürich, XXI, No. 6; Bikel, 1914, 99-100.

‡ The time and exertion given to culinary preparations and procedures in medieval times, as evidenced here, seems almost unbelievable and of dubious palatability. Chacun à son goût.

continued from page 32

garden. From these simple plants physicians compounded infusions, poultices, and purges, all standard treatments. The monastic library at St Gall held texts by Galen, Dioscurides, Hippocrates, and several studies by abbots who were gifted healers.

The house for bleeding and purging is a unique feature of the Plan. It records a facility that became extinct. Although St Benedict is silent about it, by the 7th century bleeding was widely used in monastic medicine to cure a variety of real or imaginary illnesses. The ailing monk, receiving permission to be bled, would don his night clothes, report to the house, and afterward spend several days convalescing. Rest, warmth, dietary indulgences, and recreation speeded his recovery. This therapy was so popular it had to be scheduled to avoid major holy days. Superstitious beliefs about moon, tide, and seasons somewhat restricted the practice, but abuse of bleeding eventually caused its suppression.

15

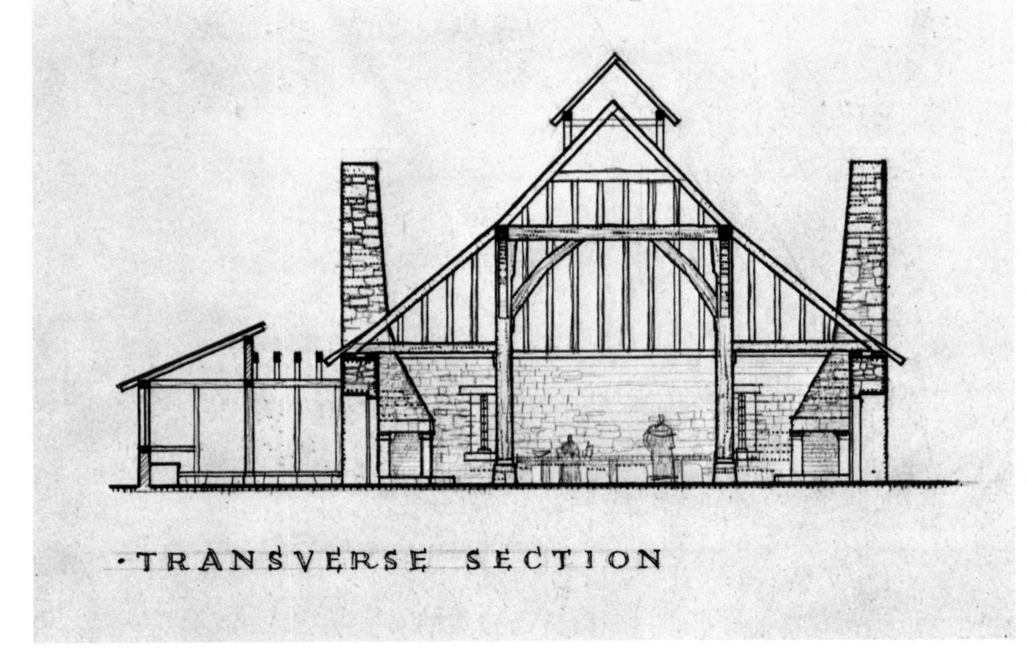

The vulnerable condition in which patients found themselves through the process of bleeding required that the House for Bloodletting be well heated. This was accomplished by installation of four corner fireplaces, in addition to the traditional open fireplace in the center of the building. Safety from fire hazards would require that the walls of the House for Bloodletting be built in masonry.

TRANSVERSE SECTION LOOKING EASTWARD

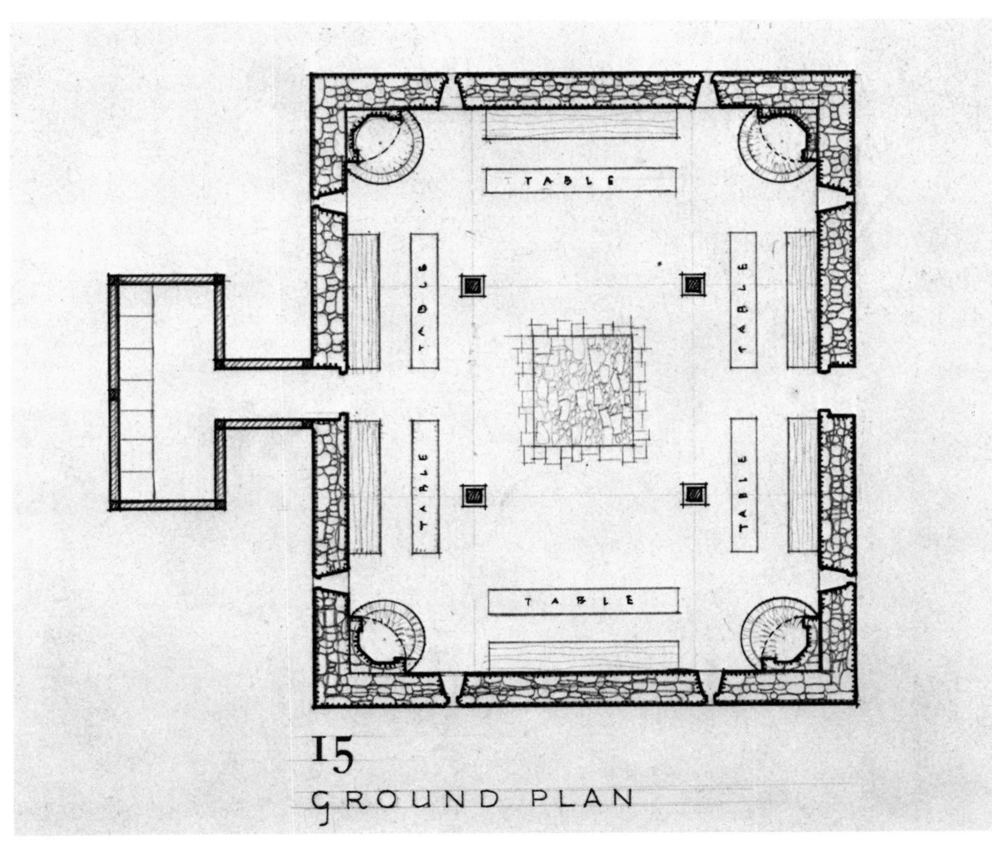

Without doubt Carolingian builders could have covered a house 35 feet wide with a single span (the nave of the Church after all had a span of 40 feet) but in most medieval buildings such a span would have had additional support in two rows of free-standing inner posts, if more than 25 feet wide. For this reason in our reconstruction we have introduced four additional inner posts carrying roof plates, which in the longitudinal direction of the building are slightly cantilevered to support the rafters of the hips of the roof.

PLAN AT GROUND LEVEL

SCALE: 1 INCH = 16 FEET [1:192]

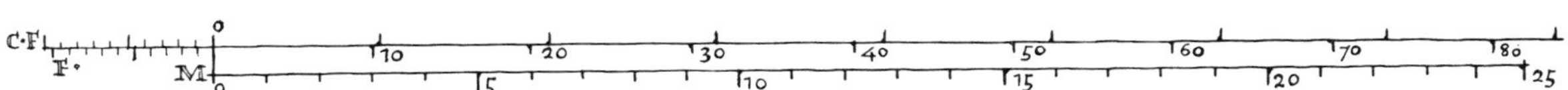

PLAN OF ST. GALL. HOUSE FOR BLOODLETTING

AUTHORS' INTERPRETATION

16

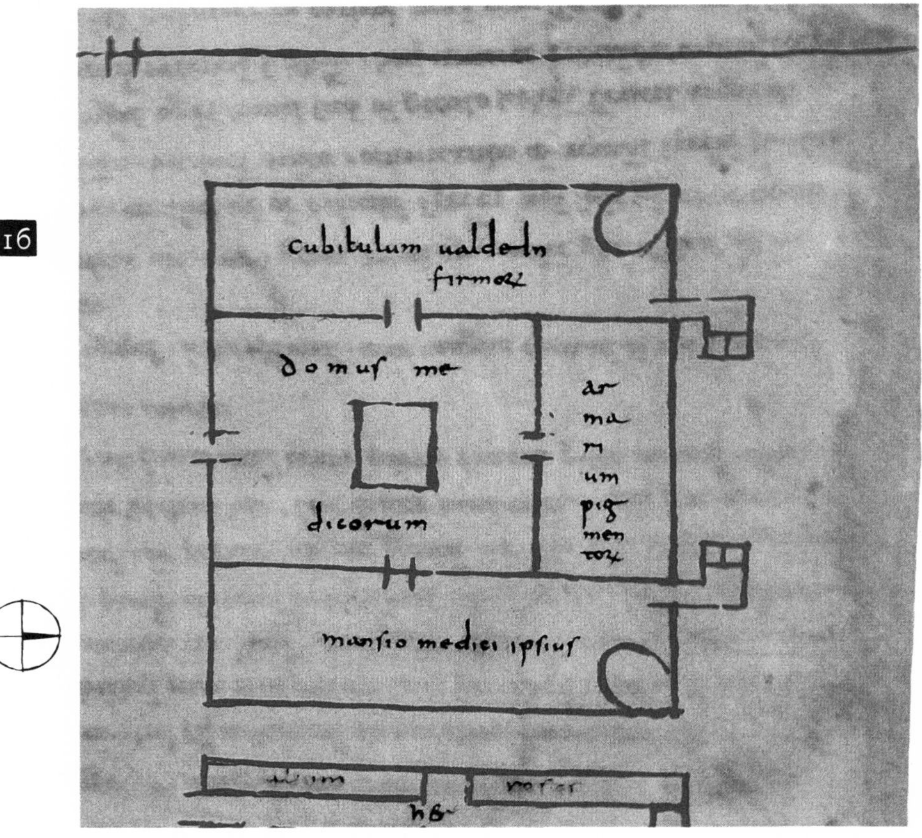

The Physicians' House shares a site with the Medicinal Herb Garden in the northeast corner of the monastery tract. The house belongs to a sub-group of the guest and service buildings of the Plan, of which the communal hall is surrounded on only three sides by peripheral rooms. Other variants of this smaller format are the House of the Gardener, the House for Cows and Cowherds, and the House for Foaling Mares and their Keepers.

The proximity of the physicians to their garden reflects the contemporary state of pharmacy, which lay largely in the realm of botanicals, as the authorities of Dioscurides, Isidore, and many others attest. The physicians' duties included compounding and dispensing medicines; their house is provided with a secure room especially designated for storage of medication.

PLAN OF ST. GALL. HOUSE OF THE PHYSICIANS

SHOWN FULL SIZE; 1:192

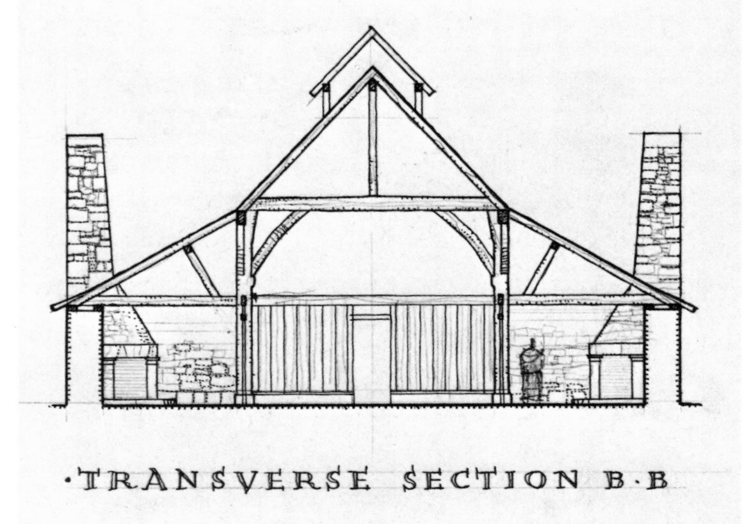

SCALE: 1/16 INCH EQUALS ONE FOOT [1:192]

GRAPHIC SCALE ON NEXT PAGE

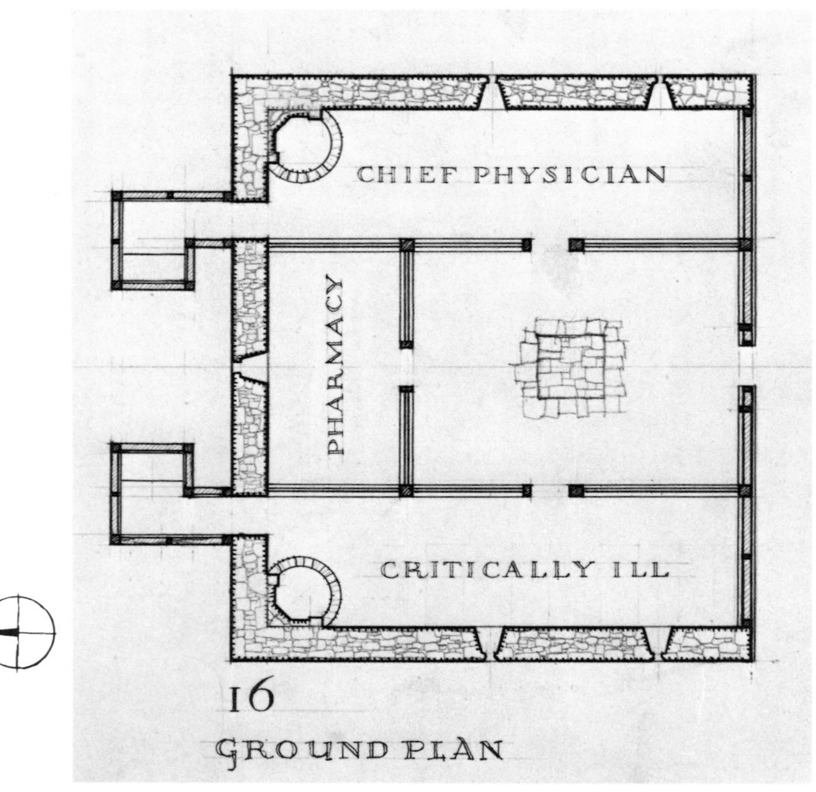

PLAN OF ST. GALL. HOUSE OF THE PHYSICIANS. AUTHORS' INTERPRETATION

GROUND PLAN AND TRANSVERSE SECTION

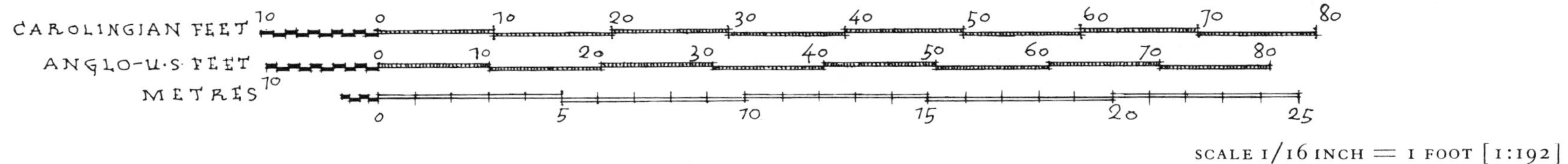

SCALE 1/16 INCH = 1 FOOT [1:192]

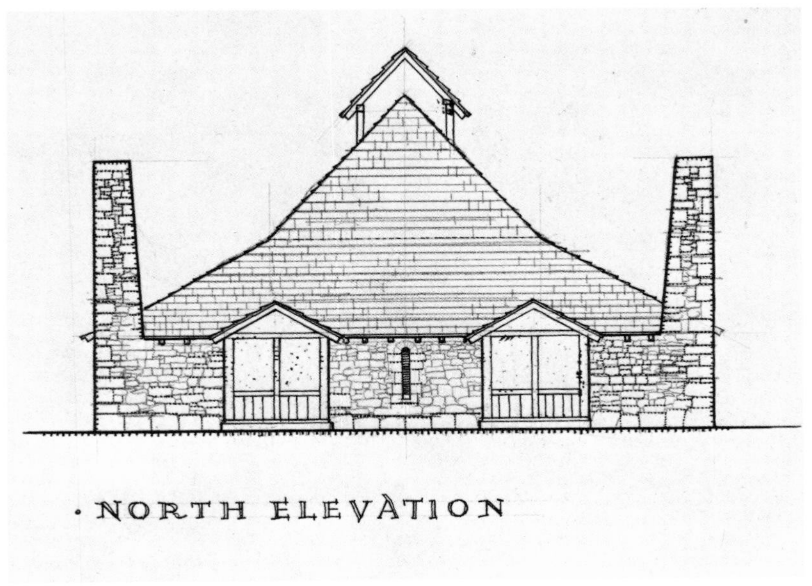

In the center: a window admitting light to the room where the pharmaceutical drugs are stored. To either side: the privies of the physicians and the critically ill.

WEST ELEVATION

Locating the fireplaces in the outer corners of the aisles keeps the chimney stacks at a safe distance from the inflammable roof.

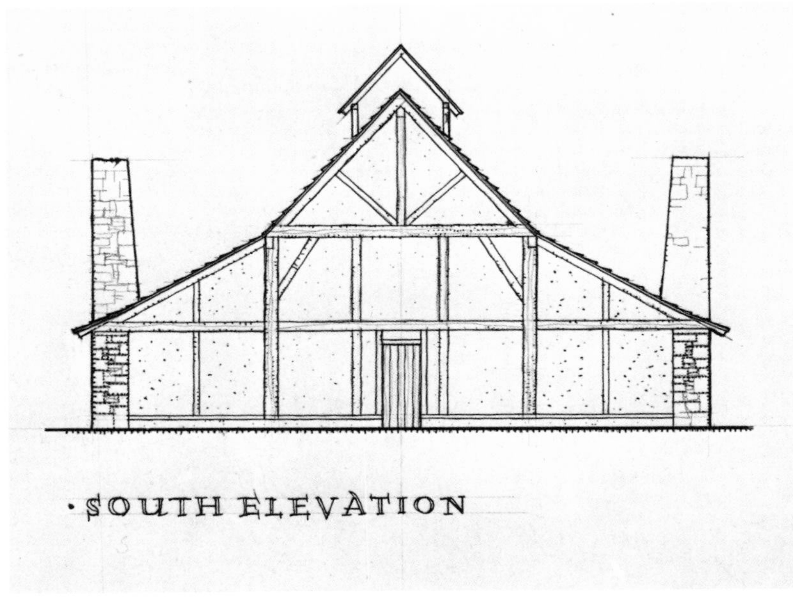

Our assumption that the gable walls were half-timbered is purely conjectural. They could of course as well have been built in masonry.

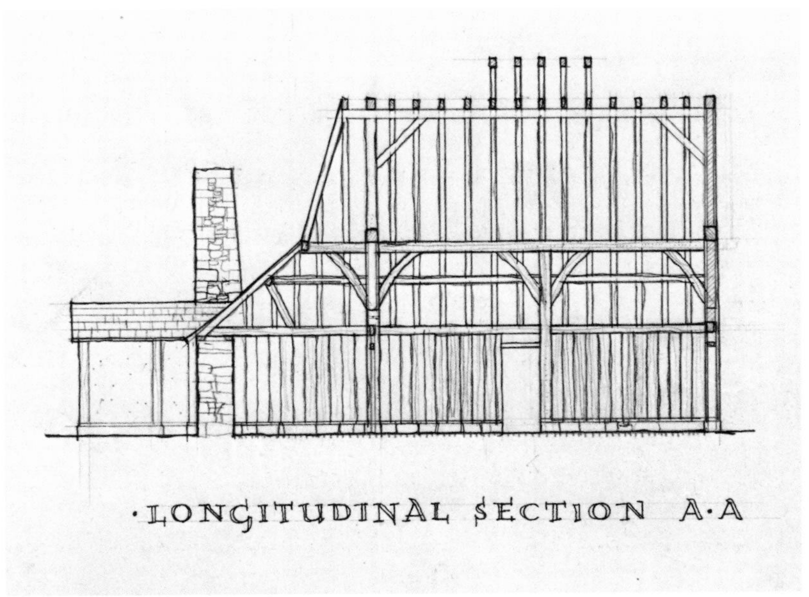

Two trusses, in addition to the gable walls, would have been entirely sufficient to carry the roof of this relatively small building.

PLAN OF ST. GALL. HOUSE OF THE PHYSICIANS. AUTHORS' INTERPRETATION

NORTH, SOUTH AND WEST ELEVATIONS AND LONGITUDINAL SECTION

ABBOT'S HOUSE

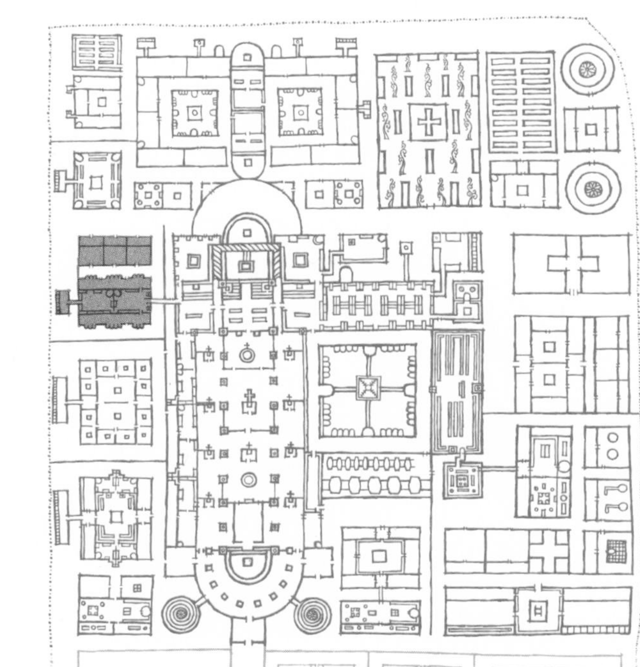

THE ABBOT'S AUTHORITY WAS ABSOLUTE within his community. He was, however, obligated in all major issues to take counsel with each monk. The office, supposedly elective, in practice was often awarded by the emperor for service, as was the case with Alcuin of York, a layman, who ended his days as abbot of St Martin of Tours. Prudence, justice, reason, moderation, were prime attributes in an abbot, accountable to God for the welfare of his community and responsible for the manorial estates upon whose sound management the welfare of the monastery depended.

In administration the abbot was assisted by a hierarchy of monastic officials (page 93). He was linked to two worlds as emissary and diplomat, roles exemplified in the strategic location of his house. It had direct access to the church; on the east it overlooked the monastic infirmary and novitiate; on the west, the outer school where secular clergy and the sons of nobles were trained, and the house for distinguished guests where emperor and courtiers were received when traveling or attending religious celebrations. St Benedict granted the abbot the right to live in his own house. Periodically this right was challenged or modified, as the privilege seemed out of keeping with other monastic practices. The Plan of St Gall affirms the abbot's separate quarters, but provides eight beds so that he might, in accord with the Rule, sleep with other monks. At ground level the house has bedroom, parlor, and two open porches. Above are a storeroom, and a solarium*—a distinctive feature of Roman architecture, usually of aristocratic dwellings. An annex contains a bathhouse, cellar, kitchen, and three rooms for servants. These facilities permitted the abbot to provide his numerous guests with food and drink appropriate to their status, while maintaining the desirable separation of monastic from worldly pursuits. Lacking guests, the abbot was charged to invite brothers to his table, being mindful, as one abbot cautioned, to call upon those who were weak and might benefit from his company.

* Location of access stair not shown on Plan. Similar conditions exist elsewhere. See note, page 24.

size of original drawing in carbon pencil 25 x 31 cm

PLAN OF ST. GALL. ABBOT'S HOUSE

AUTHORS' INTERPRETATION

BASED ON THE RECONSTRUCTION MODEL DISPLAYED AT THE EXHIBITION *KARL DER GROSSE*, AACHEN, 1965

As the lord of a vast web of manorial estates, the Abbot was the connecting link between the monastery and the secular world. The location of his house in a narrow plot of land to the north of the Church is an expression of this fact. It is an area outside of the claustral compound of the monks, and in addition accommodates the Outer School where the secular clergy and the sons of noblemen were trained, as well as the House for Distinguished Guests where the emperor and members of his court were received while on travel or in attendance of great religious festivities such as Christmas, Easter or Pentecost.

We have assumed that the roof covering the upper level of the Abbot's House did not extend over the entire width of the building. The arched openings of the two porches ranging along the east and west side of the Abbot's House suggest that it was a masonry structure. Privy and free standing annex containing the Abbot's Kitchen, Cellar, and Bath may well have been built in timber.

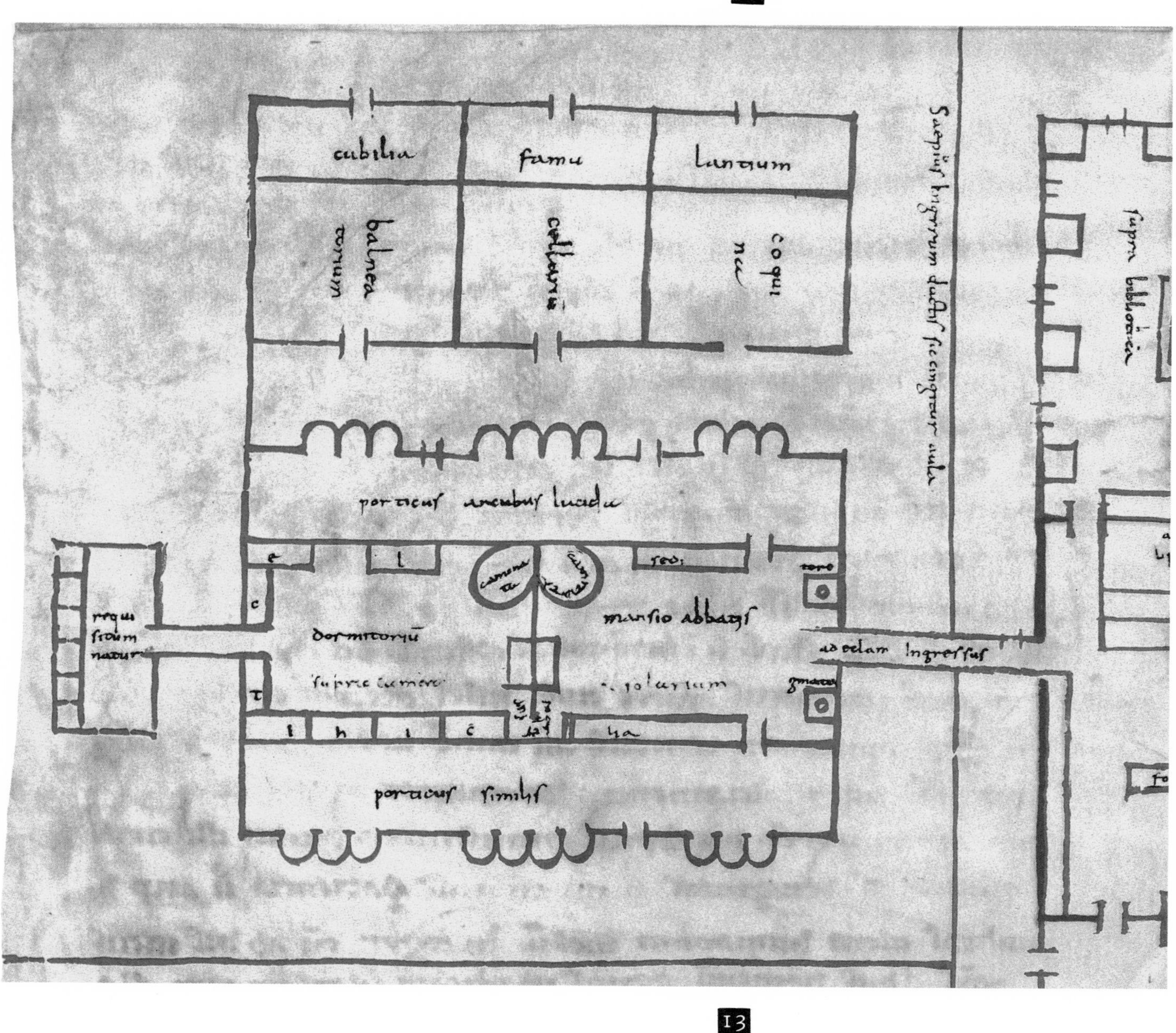

PLAN OF ST. GALL. ABBOT'S HOUSE

The House of the Abbot lies in axial prolongation of the northern transept arm of the Church, in a position corresponding to that of the Monk's Dormitory on the opposite side of the Church. In contrast to the Guest and Service Buildings which have peripheral suites of outer spaces ranged symmetrically around an inner hall with a central hearth that emits smoke through a hole in the roof, it consists of two oblong spaces separated by a median partition wall, one serving as the abbot's living room (MANSIO ABBATIS)*, the other as dormitory* (DORMITORIU)*. Along each long side of the house is an arcaded porch opening on the surrounding yard. Like the corresponding arches in the Monks' Cloister and in the cloisters of the Novitiate and Infirmary these are shown in horizontal projection. The inscription* SUPRA CAMERA ET SOLARIUM *written in the pale brown ink of the correcting scribe leaves no doubt that the abbot's house had two levels. The upper story accommodated a supply or treasure room* (CAMERA) *and a sun room* (SOLARIUM)*. This arrangement precludes the use of an open central hearth, and necessitates installation of chimney-surmounted corner fireplaces in the abbot's living and bedroom.*

ABBOT'S HOUSE

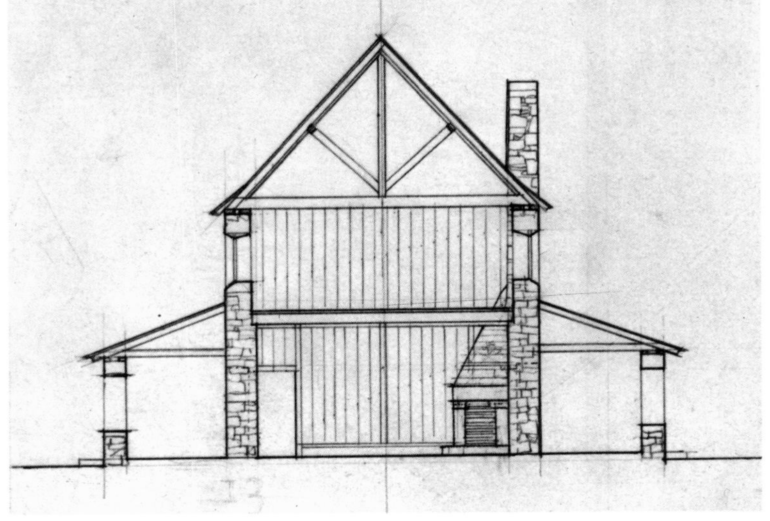

The reconstruction of the various elevations of the Abbot's House shown here is purely conjectural, but based on the assumption of comfortable minimum heights for each of its component spaces.

TRANSVERSE SECTION

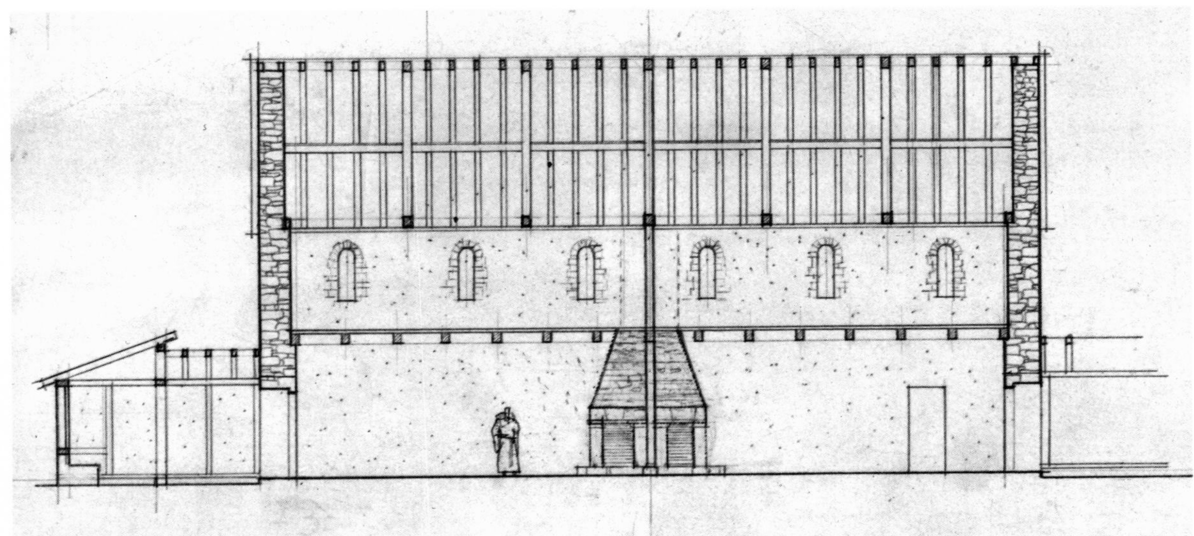

Since the drafter of the Plan does not tell us how the ground floor was connected with the upper level, we have not included such a feature in our reconstruction.

LONGITUDINAL SECTION

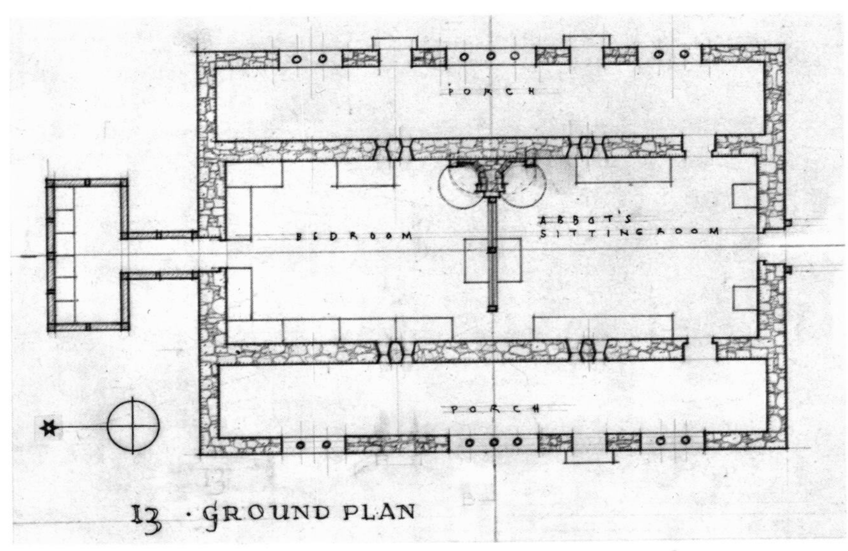

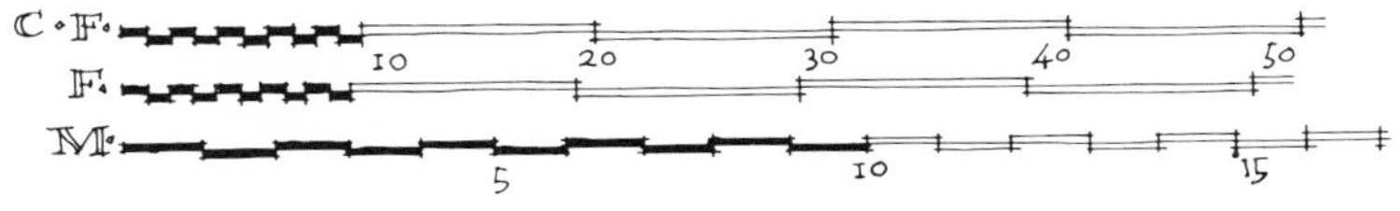

SCALE: SECTION & ELEVATION, 1:192

PLAN

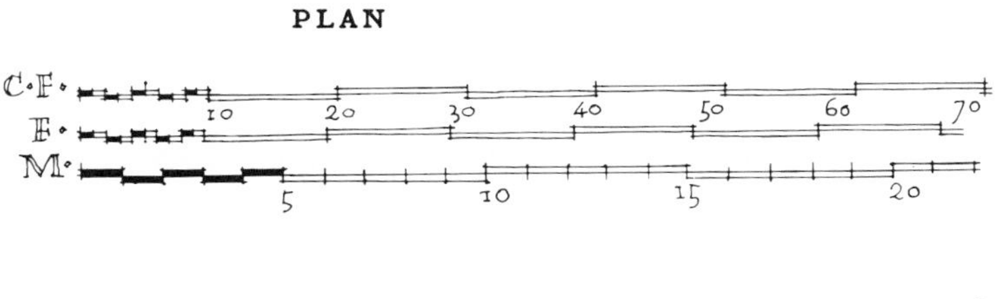

SCALE, PLAN: 1:256

13

The orientation of this building which places the Abbot's living room on the south side, his dormitory and privy to the north, and its two open porches east and west, enables the abbot and the brothers who share his quarters, to enjoy the benefits of the morning and afternoon sun, both on the ground floor and on the level of the solarium. Since the house has two stories it cannot draw its heat from open fireplaces on the lower level. To put two corner fireplaces which service living room and dormitory back to back simplifies the task of smoke emission, which can be accomplished by a common smoke stack.

HOUSE FOR DISTINGUISHED GUESTS
&
ITS KITCHEN, BAKE & BREWHOUSE

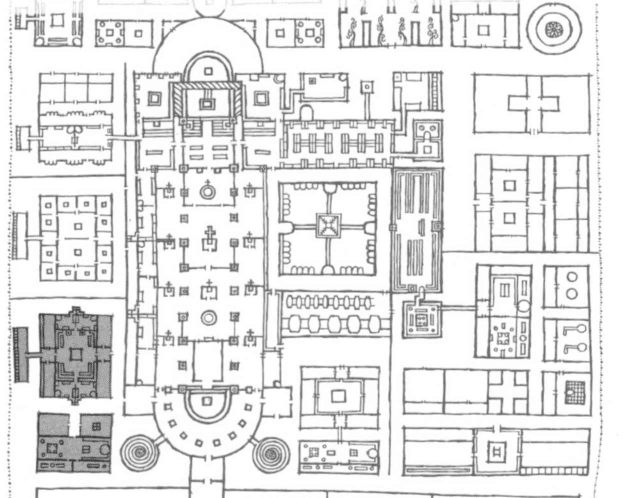

LET ALL WHO COME BE RECEIVED LIKE CHRIST FOR HE WOULD SAY, 'I was a stranger and ye took me in'. St Benedict's instructions on monastic hospitality came to be extended to the exalted and the lowly: emperor, servant, monk, knight, pilgrim and pauper are all received in five separate guesthouses of the Plan of St Gall. The monastery porter, greeting guests, bowed to the great, nodded to the humble, sent them to proper quarters, issued appropriate rations and drink, ordered used clothing and alms for the poor. He distributed these charities using one tenth of the abbey's produce and income, for which he was required to account. By the early 9th century visitors came in such throngs that the witty Bishop Theodulf of Orléans remarked in desperation, "If St Benedict had known how many would come he would have barred the door before them."

The right of kings and bishops to draw on monastic hospitality was old custom in transalpine Europe. Interdependence of the Frankish church and state encouraged this royal prerogative. Throughout his reign Charlemagne traveled extensively—along with wives, children, courtiers, servants, mounts, and baggage. This building, largest of the Plan's guesthouses, provided high-ranking visitors 4 bedrooms, each with corner fireplace and privy. Benches, tables, cupboards, and a hearth occupied an inner hall. Outer rooms held a host of attendants and the party's horses.

The roof-supporting timber frame of this structure partitioned the space into a center hall and peripheral rooms. The guest house is reconstructed in the historical tradition of the Germanic all-purpose house (page 76f), as is its kitchen, bake, and brewhouse.

ST. GALL

HOUSE FOR DISTINGUISHED GUESTS

PLAN OF ST. GALL. HOUSE FOR DISTINGUISHED GUESTS

AUTHORS' RECONSTRUCTION

This perspective shows the large center nave of the house, the communal living and dining area, and bedrooms of servants to the left, with stables to the right. Tables and benches ranged around the walls of the center space presumably could be rearranged to meet particular needs of a group of guests, or moved back altogether when not in use.

In each building of the Plan housing both animals and men, the layout is similar: servants' quarters flank (or guard) the entrance while animals pass through the common room to the rear. This disposition may reflect a defensive posture of ancient antecedents. In the House for Distinguished Guests it had the further convenience of proximity to the privy where, as an amenity afforded guests of high rank, refuse and manure from the stables might be readily disposed of.

Carpentry details shown here derive from later medieval examples; but the concept of a timber-framed roof dividing the house into nave, aisles, and bays, is clearly in the historical tradition of the Germanic all-purpose house. ▶

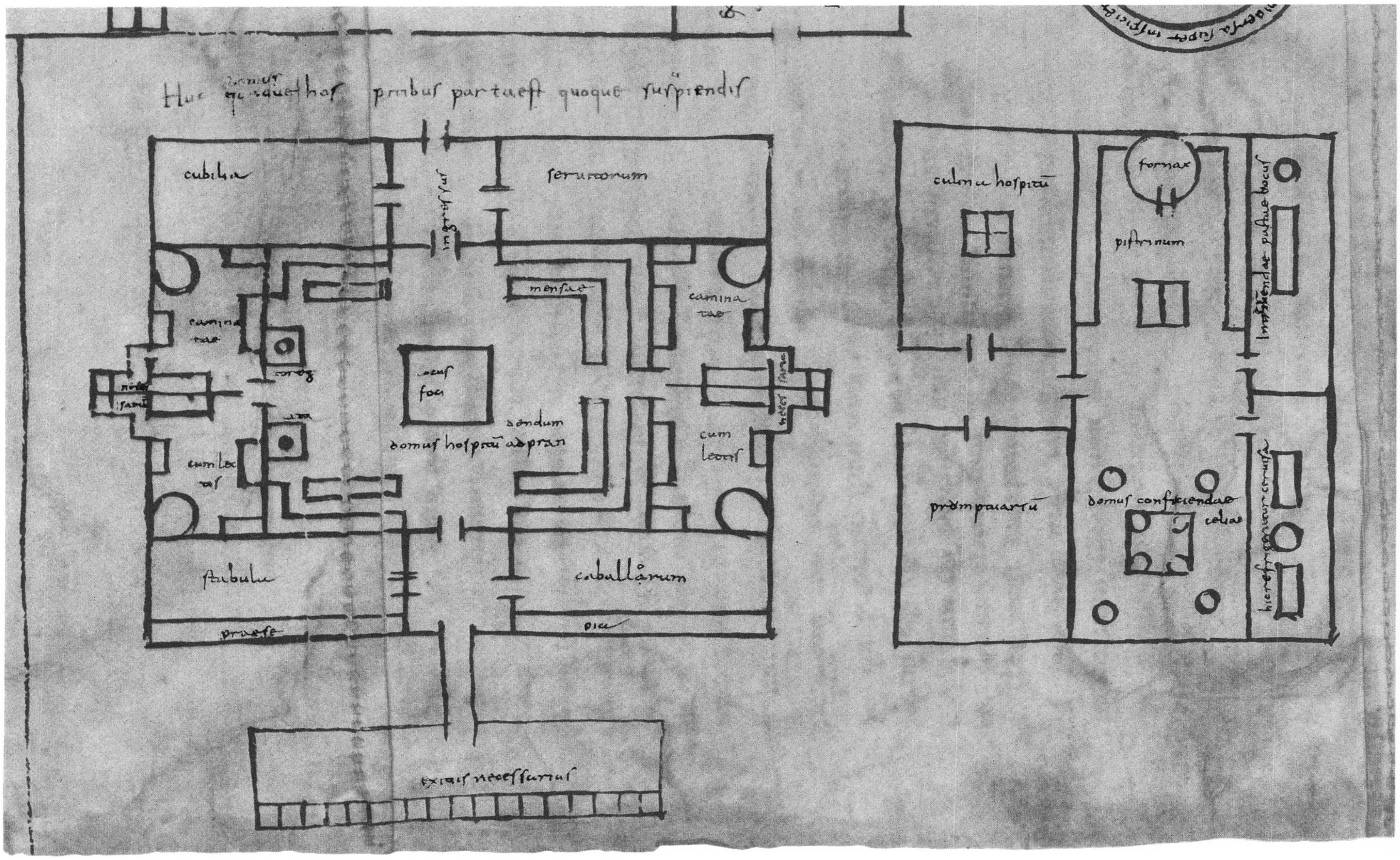

SEE SITE PLAN PAGE 42

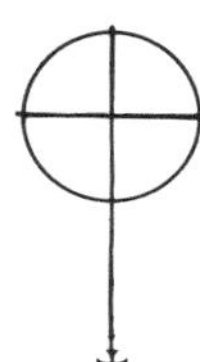

PLAN OF ST. GALL

HOUSE FOR DISTINGUISHED GUESTS, WITH ANNEX CONTAINING KITCHEN, BAKE & BREWING FACILITIES

The layout of this structure is in its basic dispositions the same as the Hospice for Pilgrims and Paupers. It also consists of a main house with an annex to accommodate services involving fire hazards. Likewise the main house here consists of a central hall for dining and a subsidiary suite of outer rooms used for sleeping, the accommodation of servants, and when appropriate, even horses. But the layout of the House for Distinguished Guests is more explicit than its humbler counterpart. Here with great precision is portrayed placement of tables and benches in the center hall, as well as the furnishings in bedrooms of the Distinguished Guests. These rooms are provided with corner fireplaces, making their comfort independent of the open fireplace in the middle of the center hall, and thus affording their occupants the luxury of privacy. The presence of these corner fireplaces induced us to assume that the outer walls of this house were intended to be of masonry.

The use of masonry and timber in a royal Carolingian hall is well attested through an important literary source, the BREVIUM EXEMPLA.

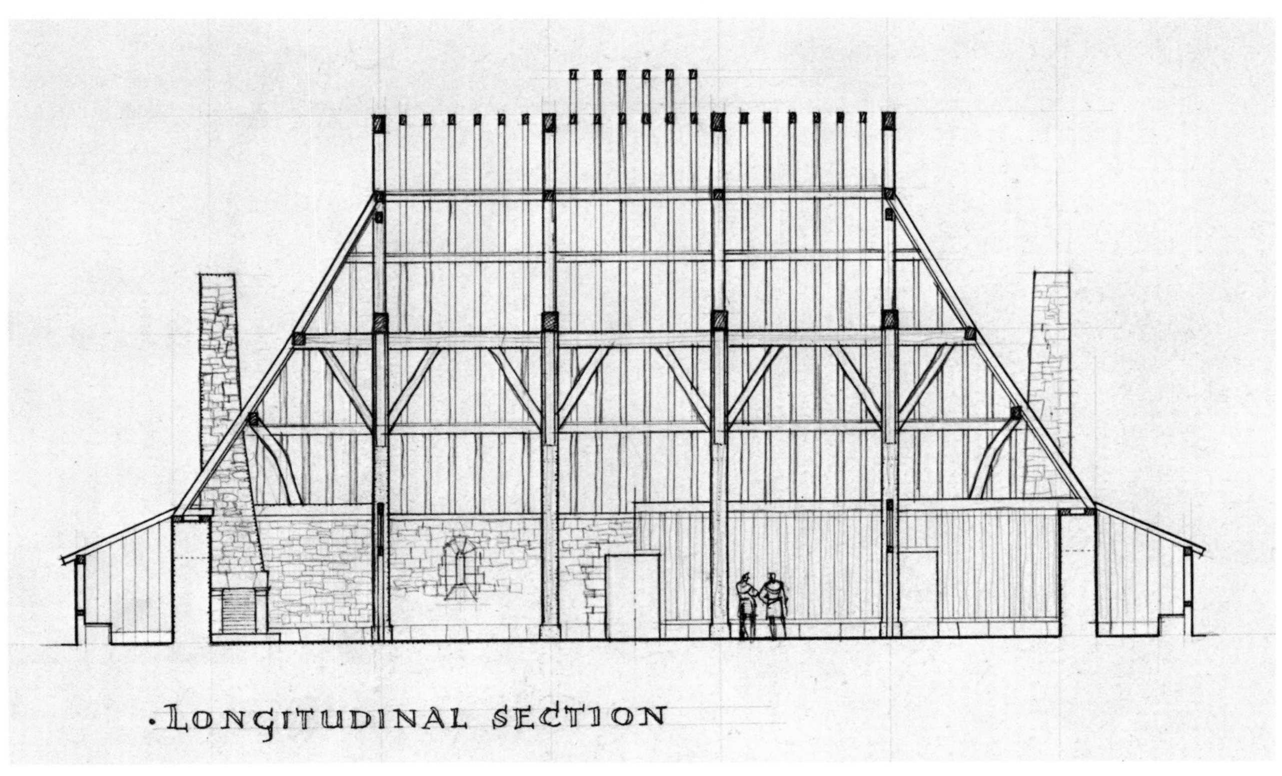

LONGITUDINAL SECTION

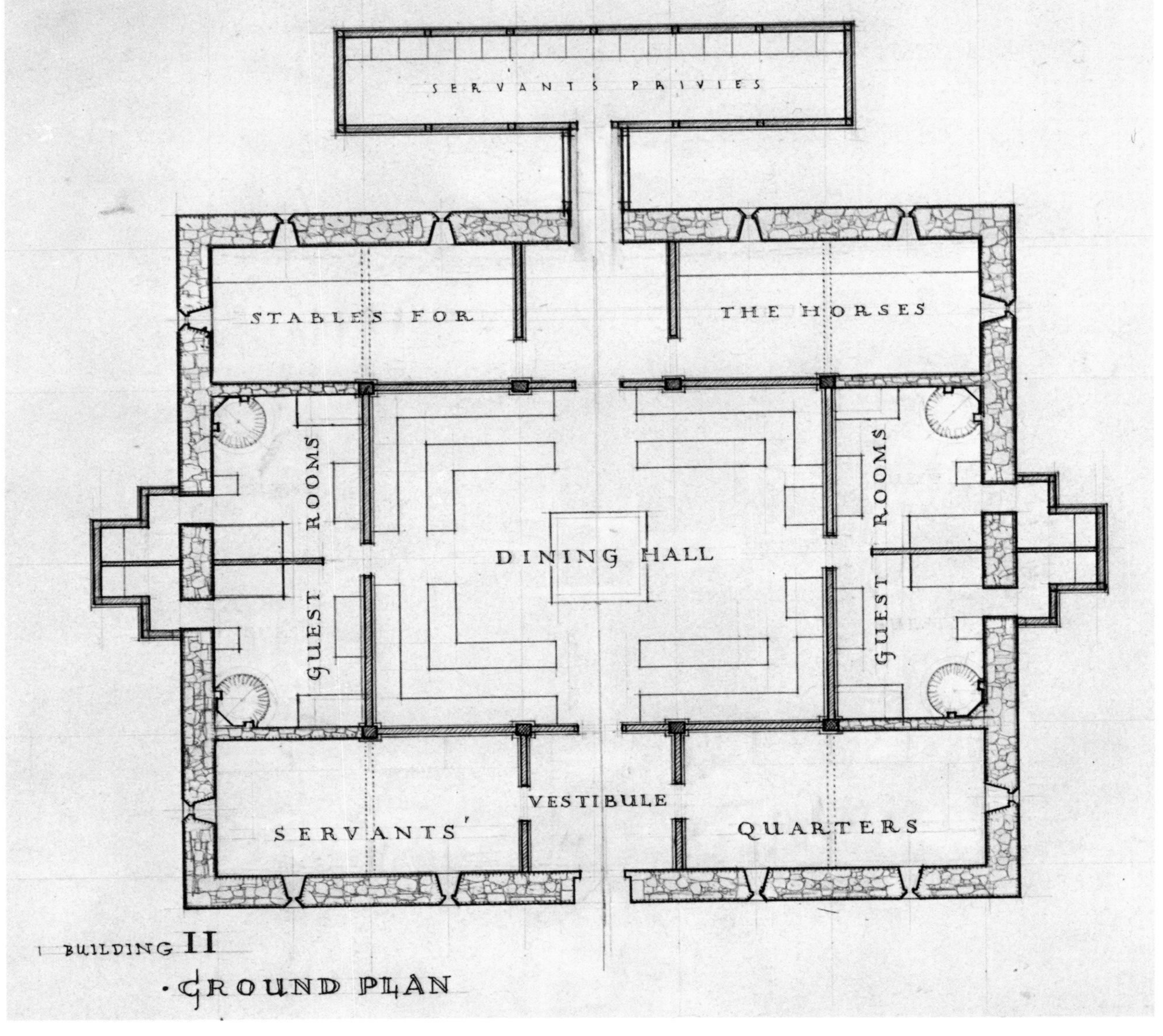

PLAN

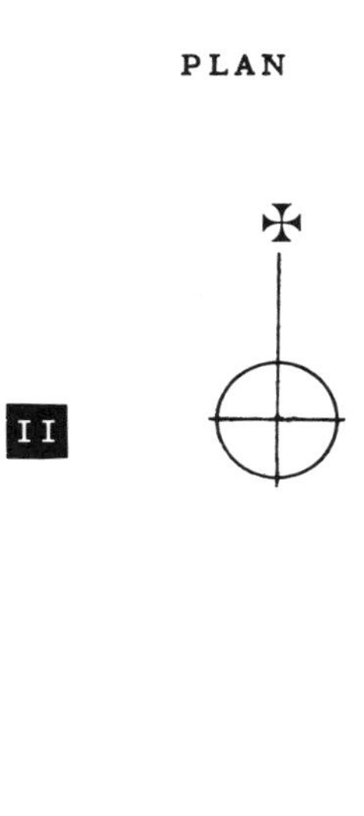

PLAN OF ST. GALL

HOUSE FOR DISTINGUISHED GUESTS. AUTHORS' INTERPRETATION

SCALE: 1/16 INCH = ONE FOOT [1:192]

KITCHEN, BAKE & BREWHOUSE FOR

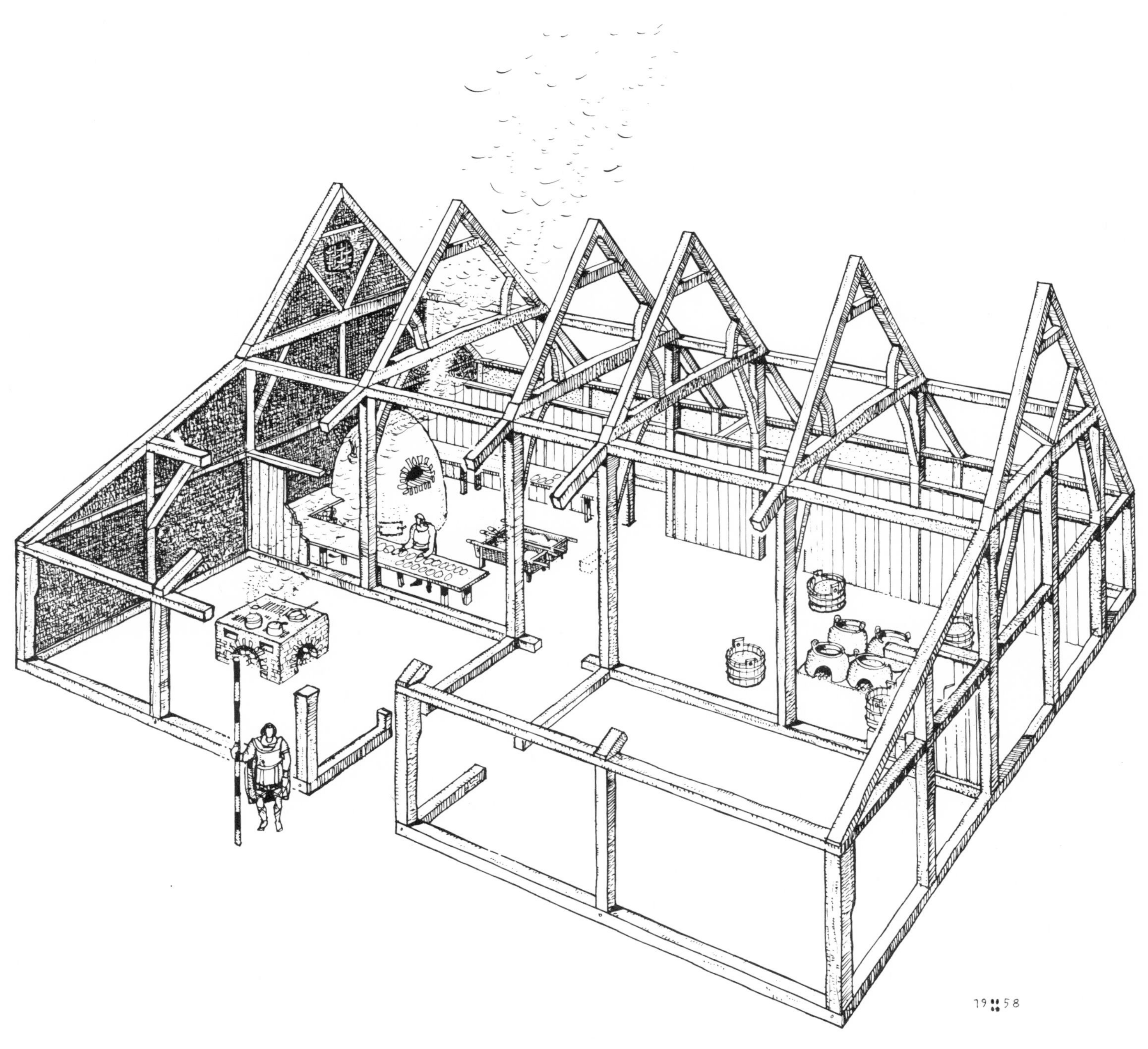

ST. GALL

KITCHEN, BAKE, AND BREW HOUSE FOR DISTINGUISHED GUESTS

PLAN OF ST. GALL

KITCHEN, BAKE AND BREWHOUSE FOR DISTINGUISHED GUESTS. AUTHORS' RECONSTRUCTION OF ROOF FRAMING, WITH SOME TIMBERS REMOVED

A widened aisle forms an extended lean-to accommodating kitchen and larder on either side of the entrance. The wall plate for the main space of the house provides footing for rafters over this enlarged lean-to. In the nave space are the oven, kneading troughs, and tables for shaping loaves. At right are the brewing range and four tubs or cauldrons for steeping brew. The narrow aisle beyond and to the rear (its interior not visible here) is of conventional width in relation to the main space, and houses at one end containers for cooling beer and at the other, troughs for leavening dough.

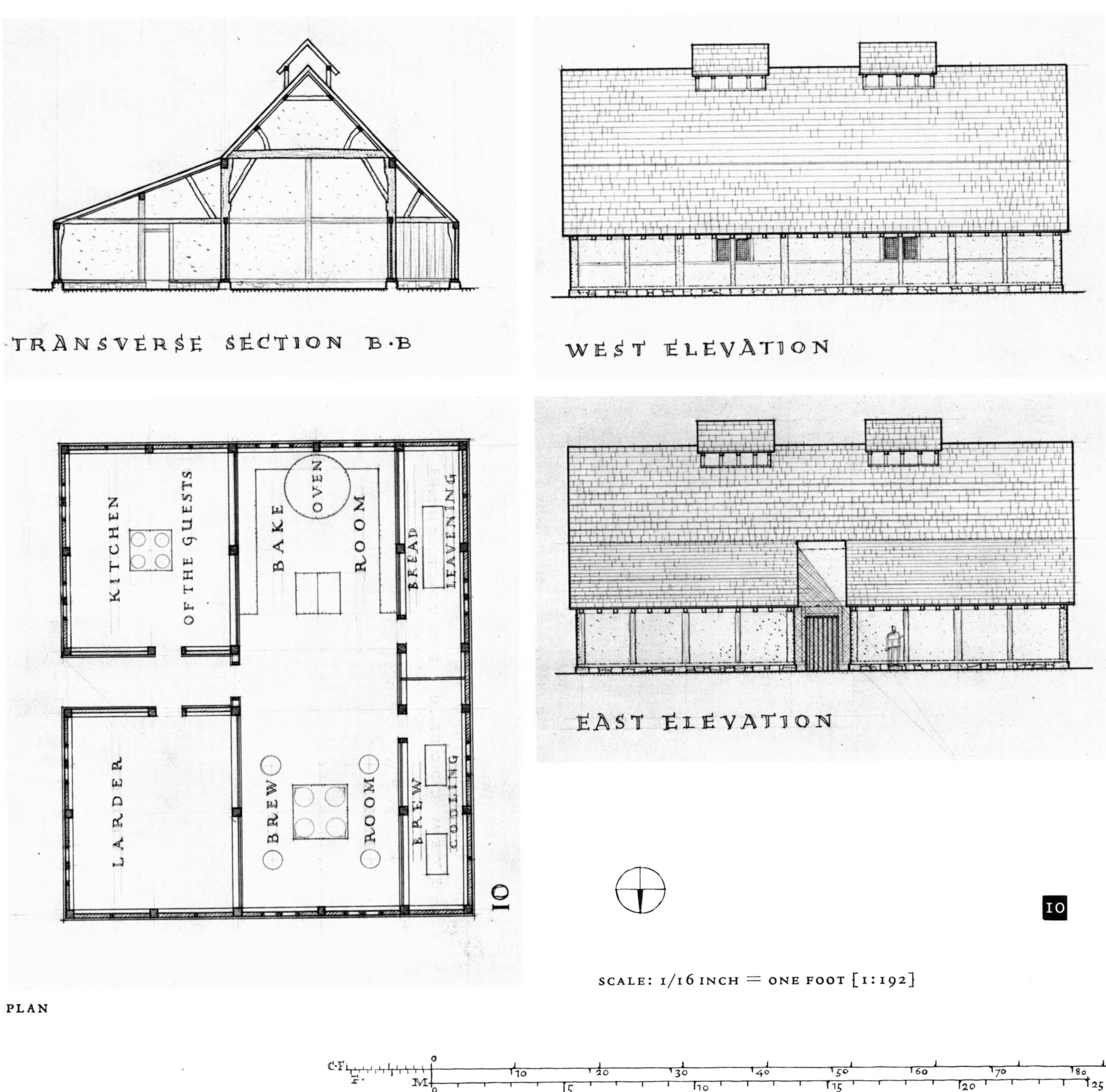

PLAN

PLAN OF ST. GALL

KITCHEN, BAKE AND BREW HOUSE FOR DISTINGUISHED GUESTS. AUTHORS' INTERPRETATION

The layout of this structure is a striking example of the extraordinary functional flexibility of the building type to which it historically belongs. The drafters of the Plan found themselves faced with having to enlarge facilities for baking and brewing, installed in the nave of this building, with a large kitchen and larder. They accomplished this by increasing the width of one of the two aisles of the structure (usually about half that of the nave) to a ground area equalling the nave, and by accommodating larder and kitchen in this enlarged aisle to either side of an entrance corridor directly into it. The aisle at the back of the house, used for leavening dough and cooling beer, retained its traditional width.

HOSPICE FOR PILGRIMS & PAUPERS & ITS KITCHEN, BAKE & BREWHOUSE

LXVI. *DE HOSTIARIIS MONASTERII*

1 *Ad portam monasterii ponatur sense sapiens, qui sciat accipere responsum et reddere et cuius maturitas eum non sinat uacari.*

2 *Qui poratrius cellam debebit habere iuxta portam, ut uenientes semper praesentem inueniant, a quo responsum accipiant.*

66 THE PORTERS OF THE MONASTERY

At the gate of the monastery let there be placed a wise old man, who understands how to give and receive a message, and whose years will keep him from leaving his post. This porter should have a room near the gate, so that those who come may always find someone to answer them.

Benedicti regula, ed. McCann, 1952, 152-53.

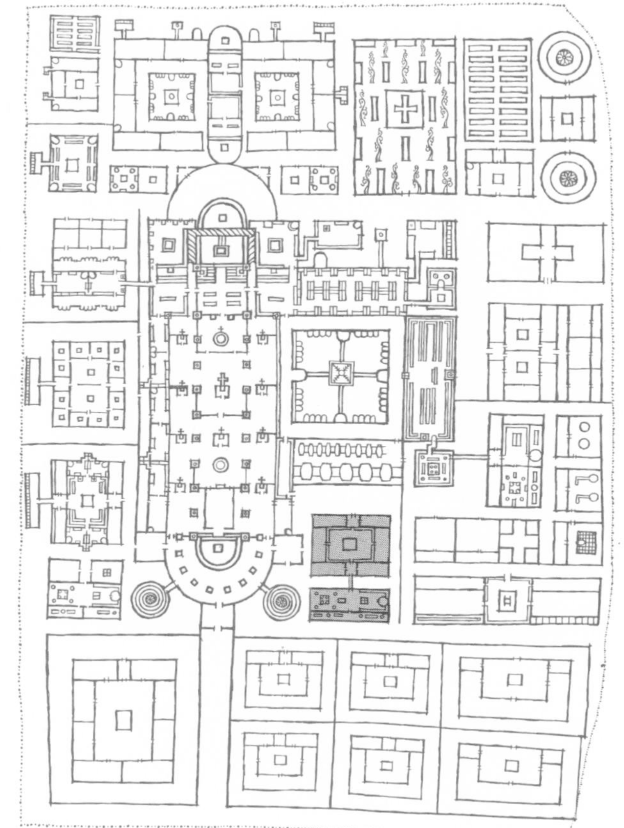

THE MASTER OF THE HOSPICE SERVED UNDER THE ABBEY PORTER and supervised arriving pilgrims and paupers. Although almost as large as that for noble visitors, this hospice lacks refinements of furnishing and sanitation afforded guests of higher status. Sixteen pilgrims could be housed here, more at need. Their kitchen, bake, and brewhouse provided food and drink different from that for noble guests. Adalhard, abbot of Corbie and Gozbert's contemporary, instructed his hosteler on the care of Corbie's pilgrims. Each was to receive a 3½ pound loaf of bread daily, as well as a ration of two tankards of beer or, at the prior's discretion, wine. They were also fed beans, lard, cheese, eel, and meat. The needy received alms, clothing, and shoes. Pilgrims continued on their way provided with a half loaf of wheat and rye bread.

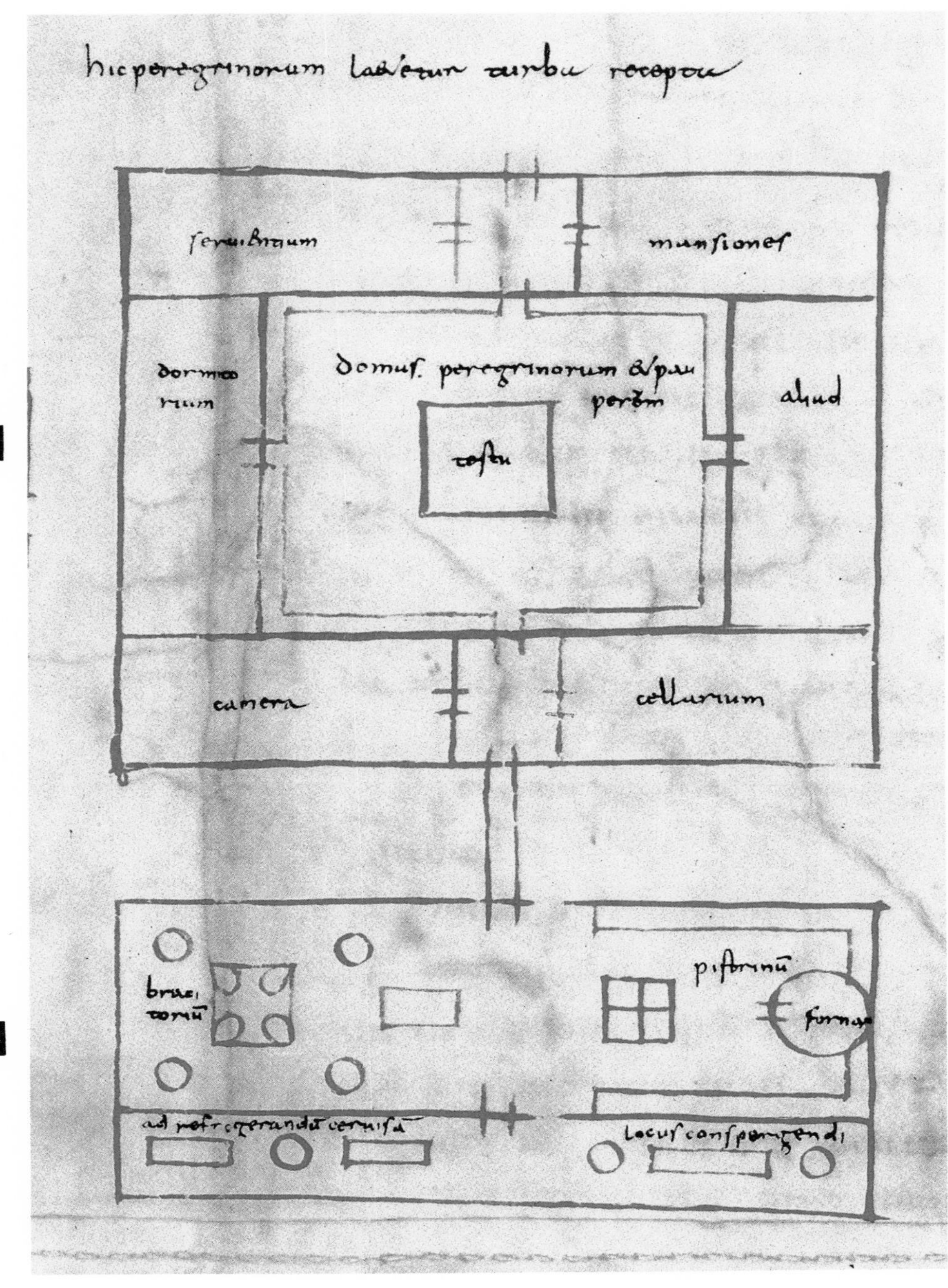

HOSPICE FOR PILGRIMS & PAUPERS (31) & ITS KITCHEN, BAKE, & BREWHOUSE (32)

(SEE SITE PLAN BELOW)

Of three baking and brewing houses on the Plan, that of the monks is largest, but it also includes two rooms for servants' sleeping quarters and a lean-to for flour storage. Servants attached to houses for pilgrims and distinguished guests lodged in their respective main buildings, not in the bakeries. The size of the bake and brewhouse for distinguished guests is augmented by its separate larder and kitchen. But when areas used solely for baking and brewing are compared, only minor differences in size occur among the three like facilities. This replication of facilities for baking and brewing, in function and layout of each, apparently marks traditional juxtapositions as well as recognition of the combined bakery-brewery plan to adapt to efficient service for a widely varying number of people—on the Plan from as few as twelve pilgrims to as many as 300 monks, if the monastery ever attained its full population.

Routes between grain supply (mills, mortars, brewer's granary) and breweries of pilgrims' and guests' facilities are highly circuitous and lie right through the western paradise of the church. But traffic of burdened servants in this most public area of the site would hardly have presented an interruption. The sacrifice in efficiency in this pattern was regained in maintaining the desired segregation between worldly and claustral activities.

▼

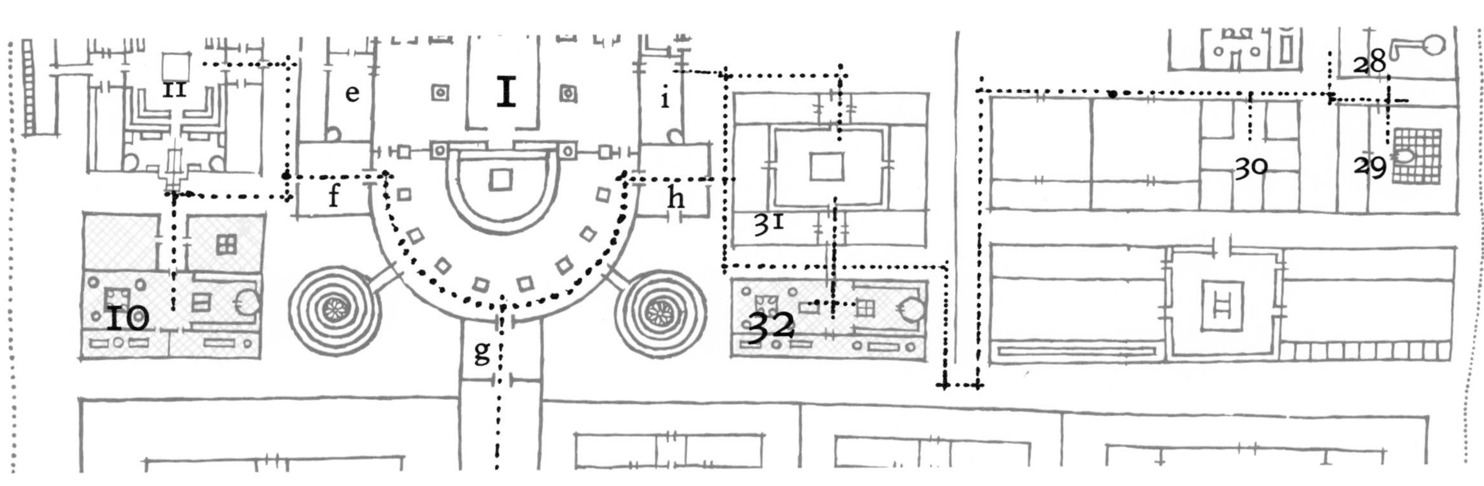

SITE PLAN

e. PORTER'S LODGING
f. PORCH ACCESS TO HOUSE FOR DISTINGUISHED GUESTS
i. LODGING, MASTER OF HOSPICE FOR PILGRIMS & PAUPERS
h. PORCH ACCESS TO HOSPICE FOR PILGRIMS & PAUPERS
9. MONKS' BAKE & BREWHOUSE
10. KITCHEN, BAKE & BREWHOUSE FOR DISTINGUISHED GUESTS
30. BREWERS' GRANARY, ETC.
31. HOSPICE FOR PILGRIMS & PAUPERS
32. KITCHEN, BAKE & BREWHOUSE FOR PILGRIMS & PAUPERS
28. MORTAR 29. DRYING KILN

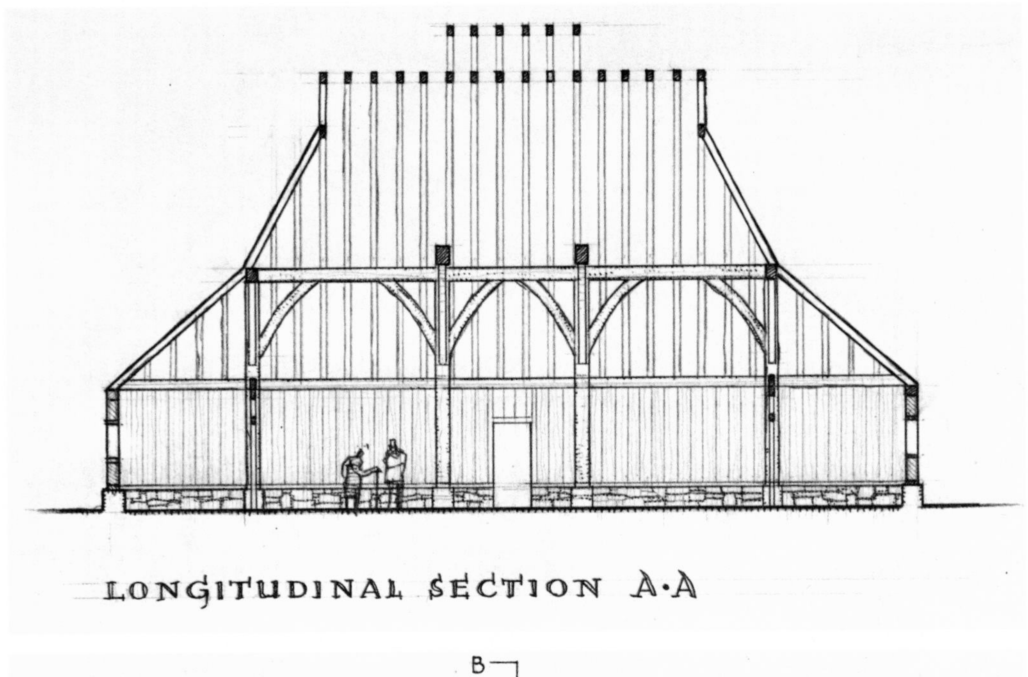

LONGITUDINAL SECTION

The presumption in these reconstructions is that the roof was supported by a frame of freestanding inner posts connected lengthwise by roof plates and crosswise by tie beams. The rafters rise in two tiers, the lower from wall plates to roof plate, the upper, at a slightly steeper angle, from the roof plates to the ridge.

32

31

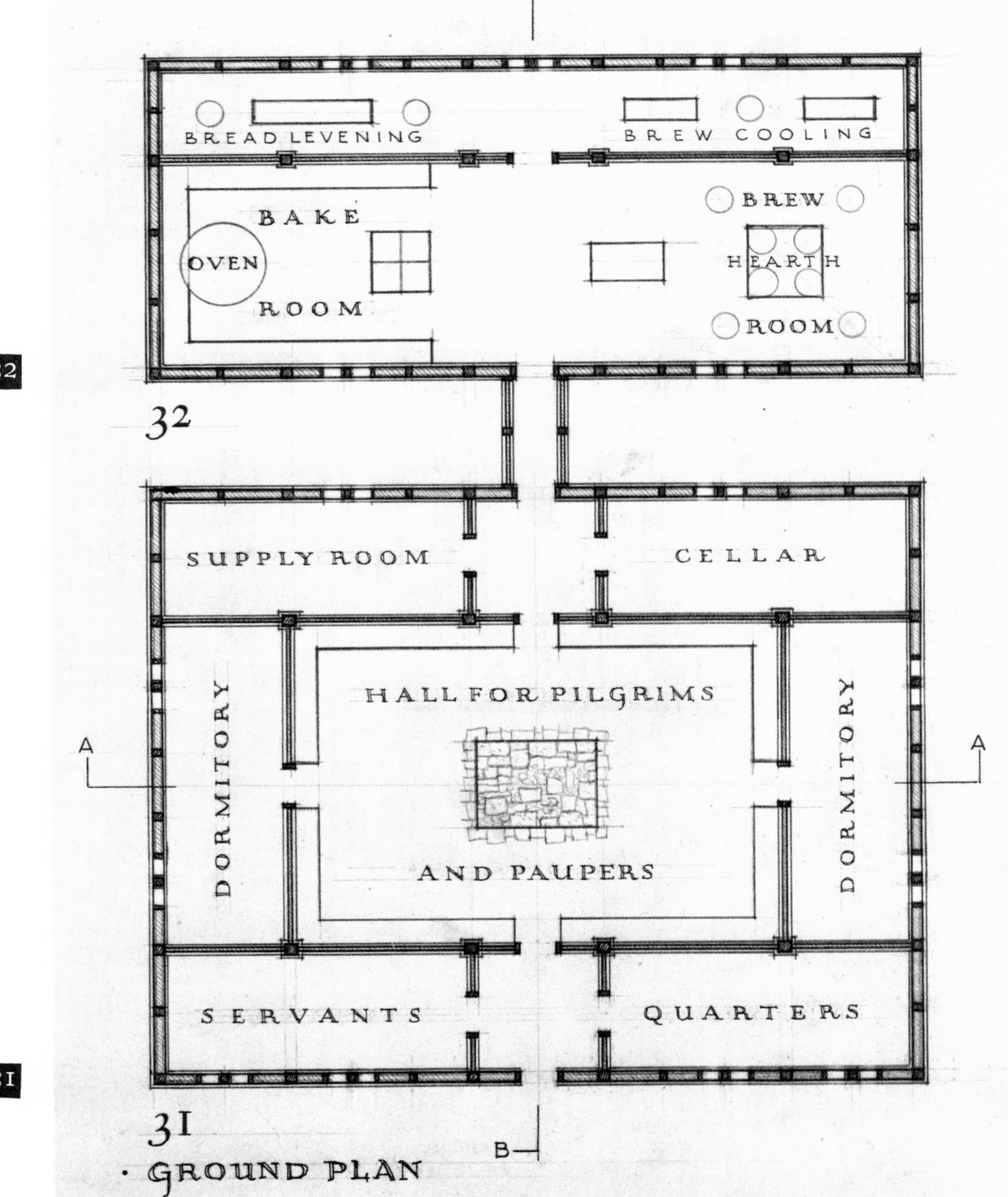

PLAN OF ST. GALL. HOSPICE FOR PILGRIMS AND PAUPERS

AUTHORS' INTERPRETATION

PLAN

For historical justification of the reconstructions shown in this series of illustrations we refer to pages 75–80 above, where it has been shown that the guest and service buildings of the Plan of St. Gall belong to a vernacular building tradition traceable in the Germanic territories of the Lowlands to the 14th century B.C. The traditional material for this building type was timber.

All the guest and service buildings of the Plan were freestanding; in reconstructing their plans and elevations, we have used the simple lines of the Plan as indicating their interior dimensions. The elevations shown here are purely conjectural but based on the assumption of comfortable minimum heights required by the functions of each component of the building. Carpentry details derive from later medieval buildings.

SCALE 1/16 INCH = ONE FOOT [1:192]

FOR GRAPHIC SCALE SEE PAGE 59

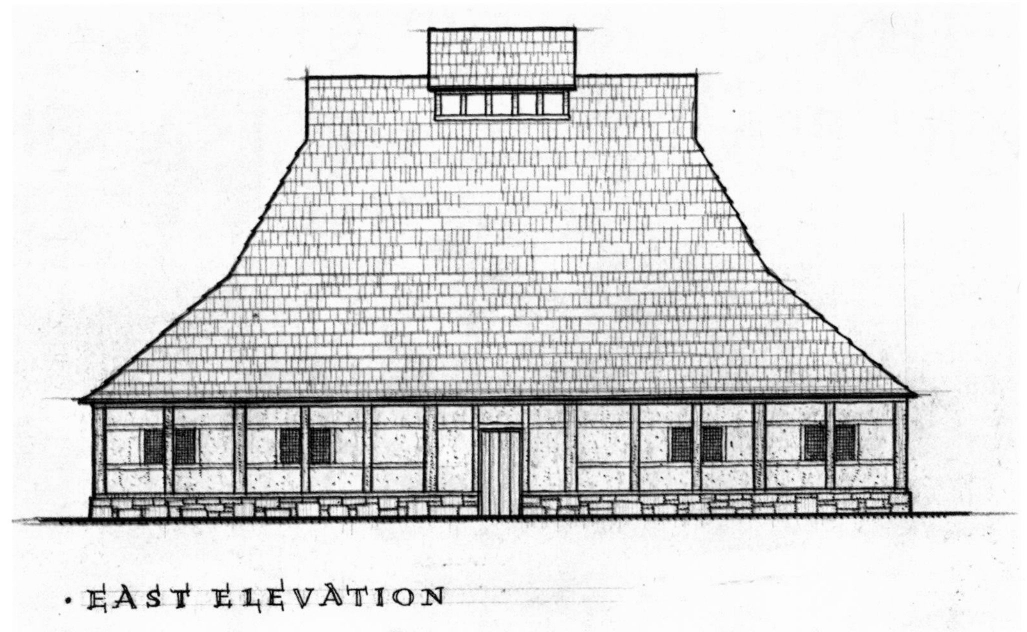

EAST ELEVATION

The roof lines might have been straight. We have chosen to show them broken, because they thus reflect more clearly in the exterior appearance of the building the composition and boundary lines of its inner spaces. To hip the roof over the narrow ends of the building is a sound constructional assumption, since it steadies the roof in the longitudinal orientation and is a feature archaeologically well attested as early as the Iron Age.

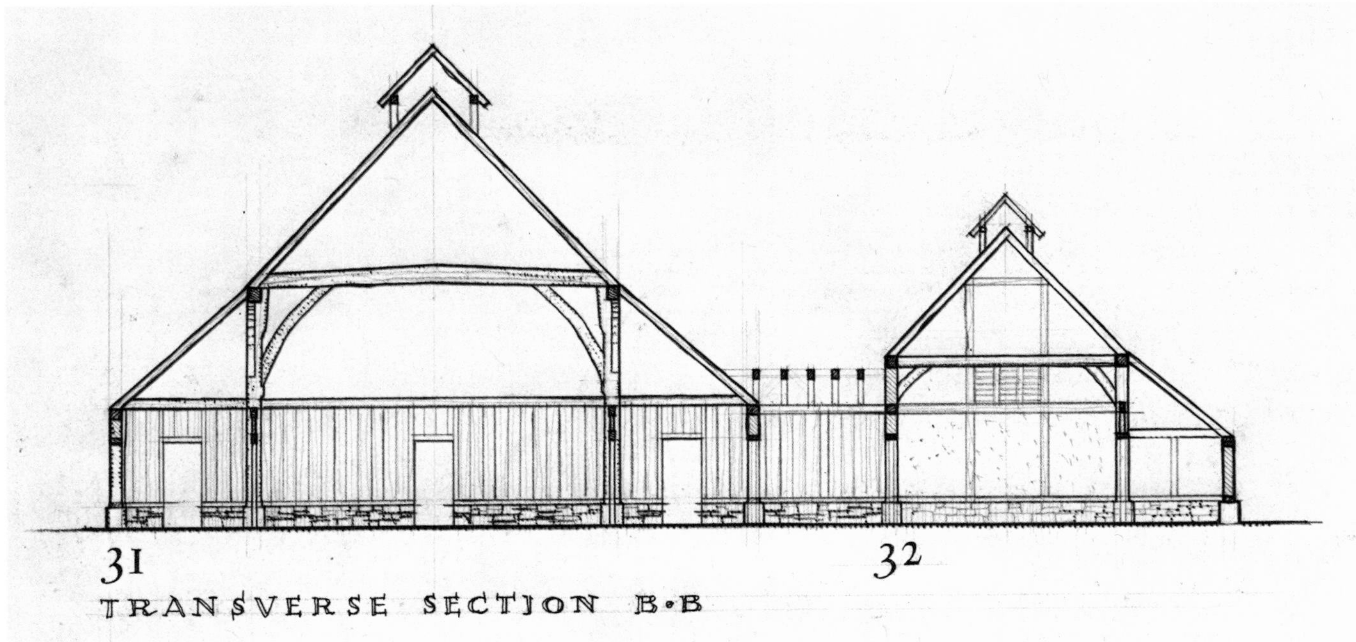

TRANSVERSE SECTION

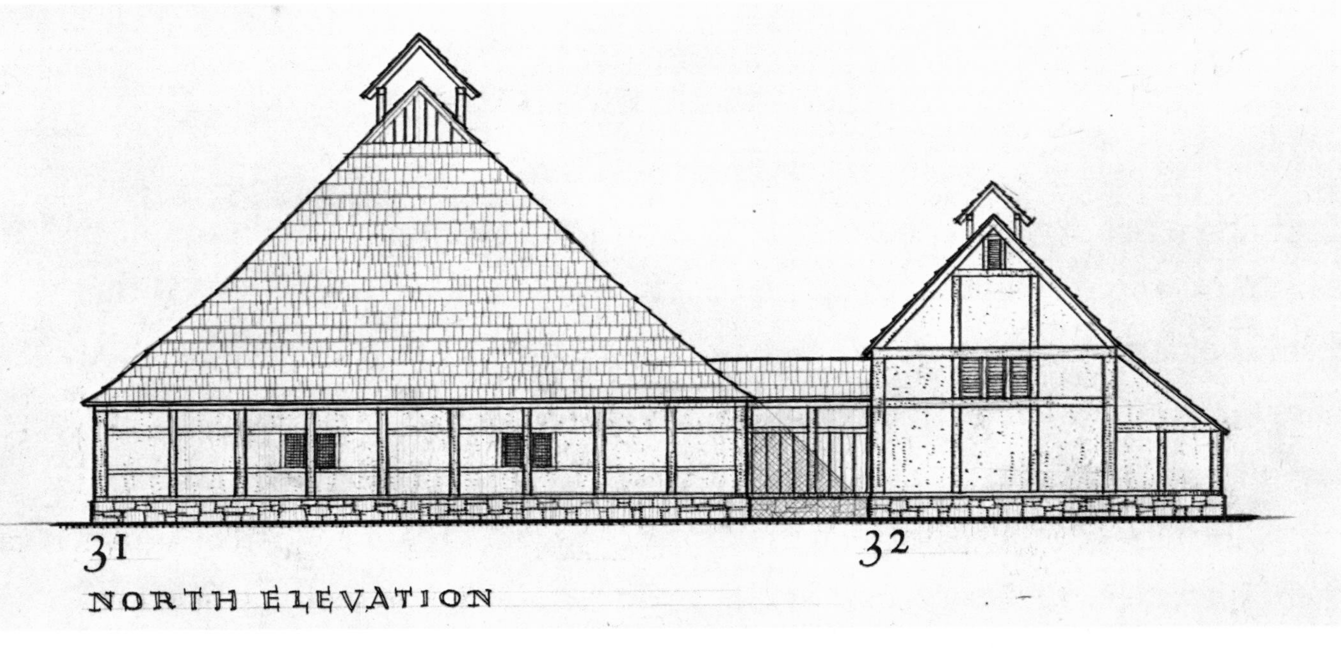

NORTH ELEVATION

PLAN OF ST. GALL. HOSPICE FOR PILGRIMS AND PAUPERS

AUTHORS' INTERPRETATION

WORKSHOPS & QUARTERS FOR ABBEY CRAFTSMEN & ARTISANS

LVII. *DE ARTIFICIBUS MONASTERII*

1 *Artifices si sunt in monasterio, cum omni humilitate faciant ipsa artes si permiserit abbas.*
2 *Quod si aliquis ex eis extollitur pro scientia artis suae, eo quod uideatur aliquid conferre monasterio,*
3 *hic talis erigatur ab ipsa arte et denuo per eam non transeat, nisi forte himiliato ei iterum abbas iubeat.*

52 THE CRAFTSMEN OF THE MONASTERY

If there be craftsmen in the monastery, let them practise their crafts with all humility, provided the abbot give permission. But if one of them be puffed up because of his skill in his craft, supposing that he is conferring a benefit on the monastery, let him be removed from his work and not return to it, unless he have humbled himself and the abbot entrust it to him again.

Benedicti regula, ed. McCann, 1952, 110-13.

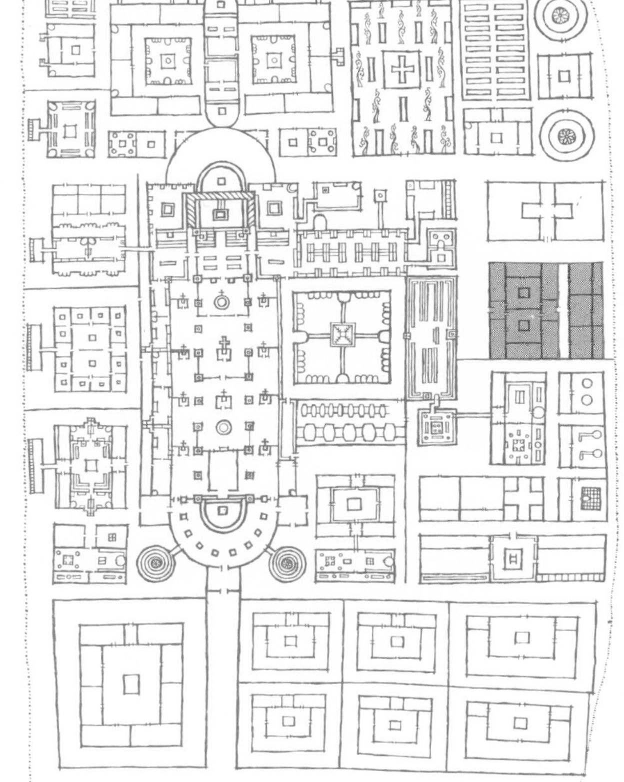

THE MAIN WORKSHOP of the Plan houses nearly all crafts needed to supply the community's material amenities. In systematic architectural integration it is as accomplished as the church-cloister and novitiate-infirmary complexes. The presence of workshops on the Plan seems to confirm the determination of the 816 Synod of Aachen that craftsmen should henceforward "practice within, rather than outside, the monastery walls."

The monastery chamberlain supervised craftsmen and assigned their tasks. Shoemakers, saddlers, curriers, and turners produced leather goods, parchment, smaller wooden objects; shieldmakers and sword grinders furbished military equipage. Fullers prepared and cleaned cloth, blacksmiths' anvils rang, goldsmiths pursued their art. These shops housed 28 to 40 workers; coopers and wheelwrights had quarters closer to need served.

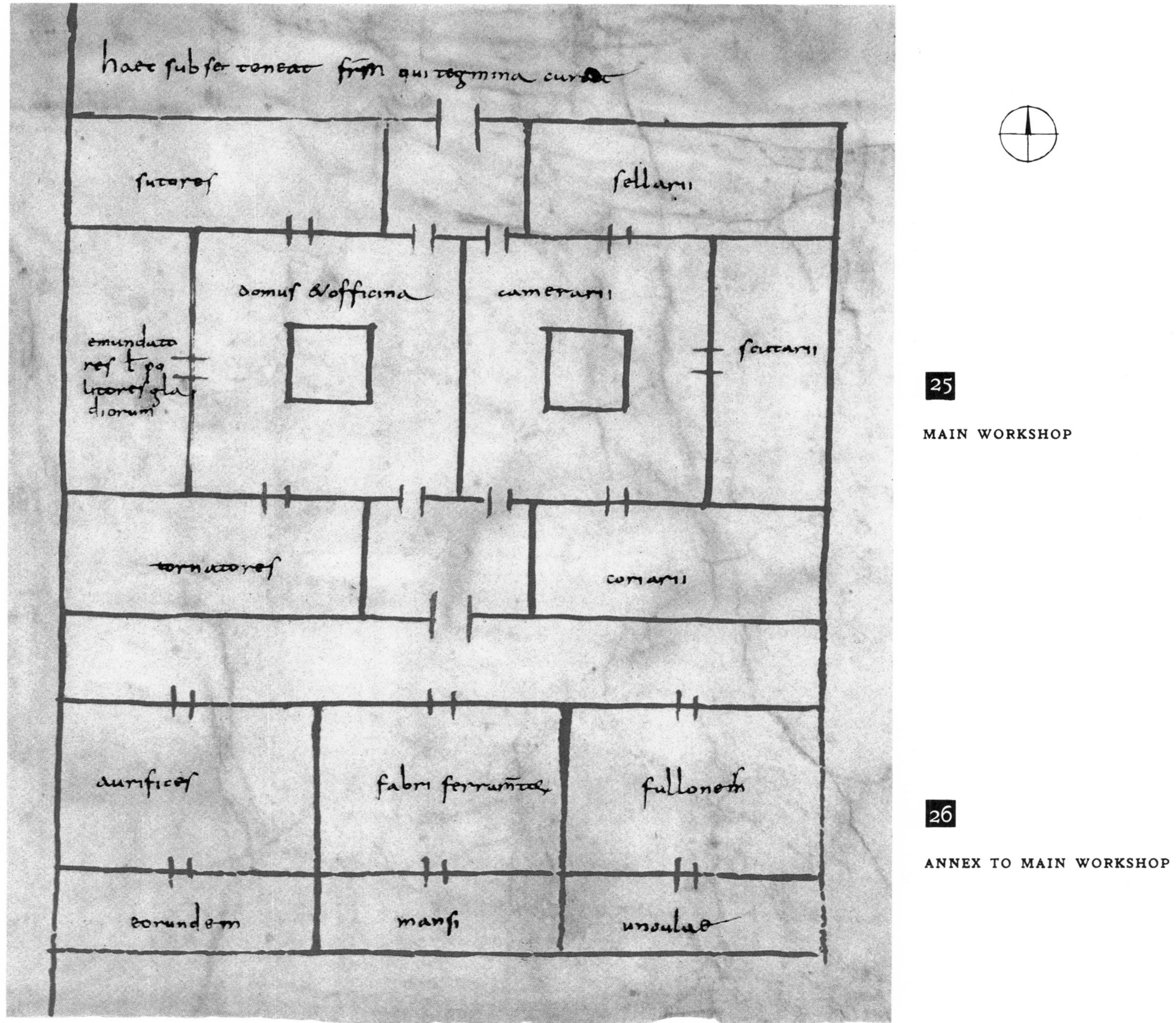

25 MAIN WORKSHOP

26 ANNEX TO MAIN WORKSHOP

PLAN OF ST. GALL. GREAT COLLECTIVE WORKSHOP

MAIN WORKSHOP AND ITS ANNEX

The layout of the main house here is identical with what we refer to as the "standard house" of the Plan: a large rectangular center space with open fireplace serving as living room, with peripheral outer rooms around it. The Workshop, as in the Outer School, is divided by a median wall partition into two center areas, each with its own fireplace. These rooms are designated the office and dwelling of the chamberlain, whose duty it was to oversee the craftsmen who used the shop.

Although housing a great variety of activities, the shop was neatly balanced in its division: flanking the north vestibule were leatherworkers (shoemakers, saddlers); in the center, flanking the chamberlain's quarters were metalworkers (grinders, sword polishers); on the south were those engaged in finish work: woodworkers who made tools and utensils, and curriers who prepared leather for various purposes. In the Annex were placed those activities involving fire hazards (goldsmithing, blacksmithing) and the fullers, who probably shared some craft facilities with the curriers, across the aisle to their north.

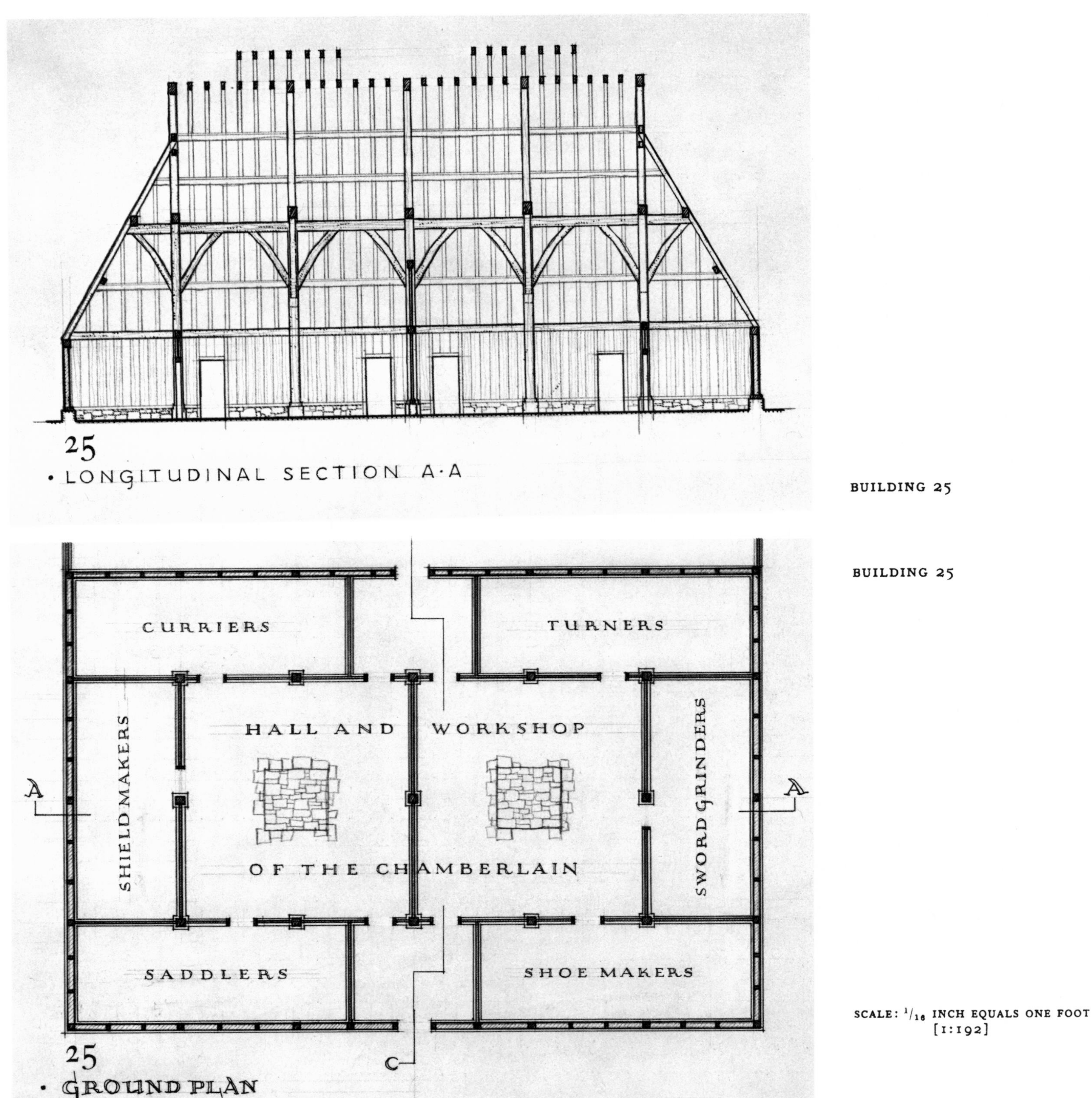

BUILDING 25

BUILDING 25

SCALE: 1/16 INCH EQUALS ONE FOOT [1:192]

PLAN OF ST. GALL. GREAT COLLECTIVE WORKSHOP. AUTHORS' INTERPRETATION

GROUND PLAN AND LONGITUDINAL SECTION

This Workshop affords a notable embodiment of the enterprising and innovative spirit of the men who developed the Plan. In marked contrast to the secular world, where craftsmen tended to be isolated and scattered over a wider geographic area, perhaps among several villages, the workmen of the Plan were assembled under one roof. Here they manufactured tools, utensils, harness and saddle gear and footwear, as well as weaponry; the farrier as well as the goldsmith were housed here. The aisled hall, with its constructionally conditioned bay division, lent itself with ease to such intensive and disparate use.

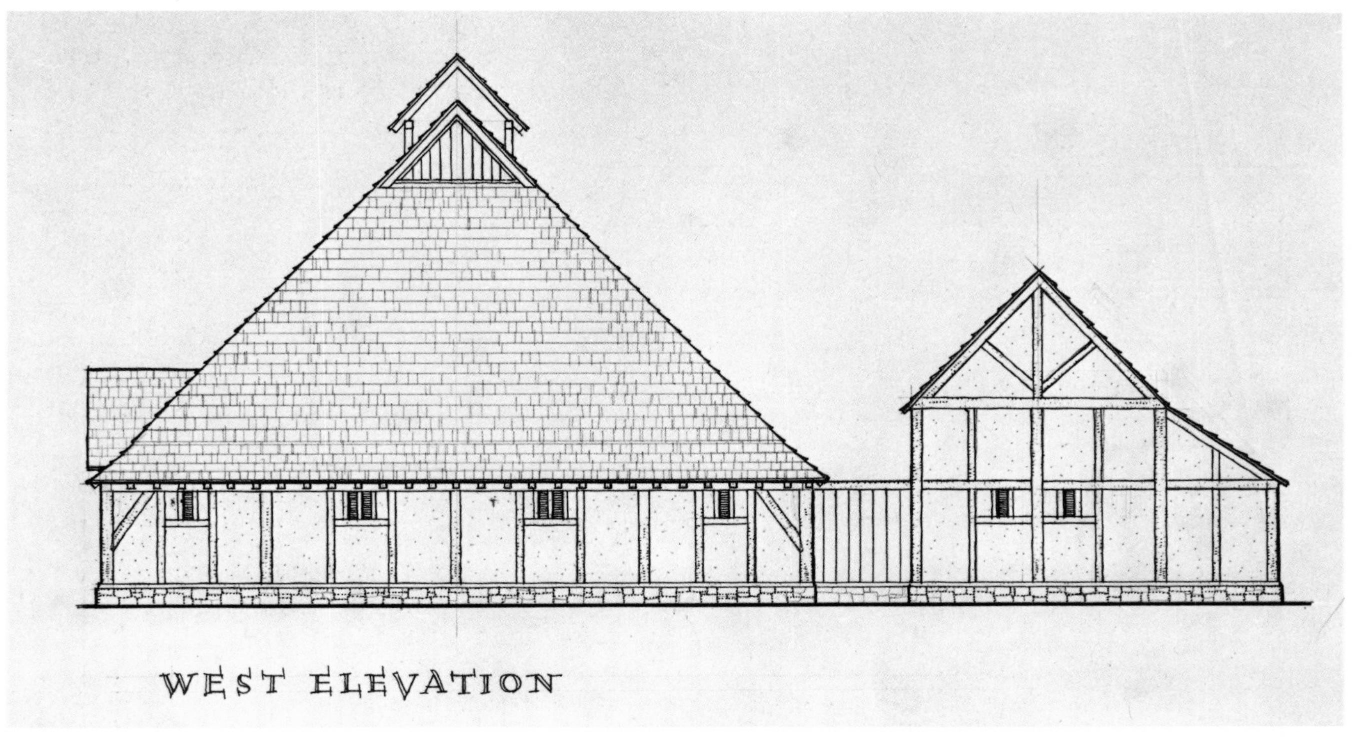

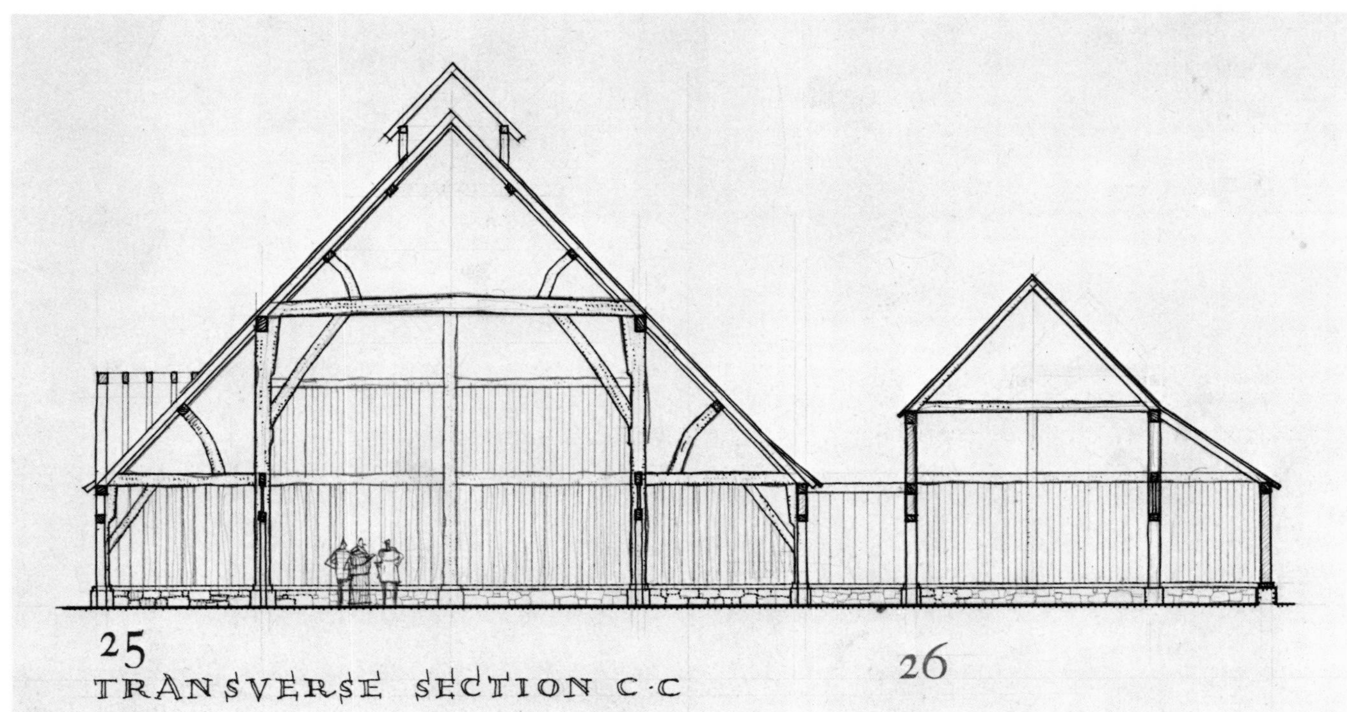

SCALE: 1/16 INCH = ONE FOOT [1:192]

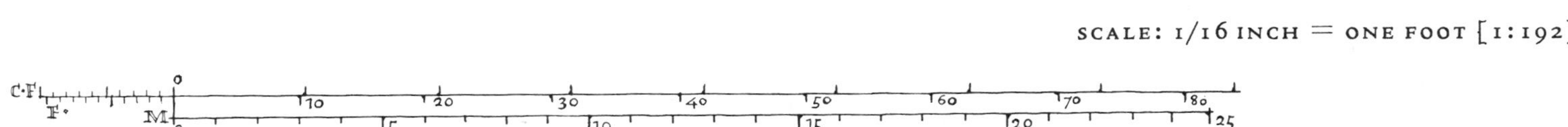

PLAN OF ST. GALL. GREAT COLLECTIVE WORKSHOP. AUTHORS' INTERPRETATION

WEST ELEVATION AND TRANSVERSE SECTION WITH ANNEX (AT RIGHT)

Our assumption that the house had windows to admit light to the outer rooms is purely conjectural. They may have been needed for functional reasons, since these rooms were probably to be used for both sleeping and working. Windows were not part of the pre- and protohistoric tradition of this building type, because they afforded the risk that a house could be entered through them by enemies, a primary consideration for people living in small groups and at considerable distance from one another, and dependent solely upon themselves for defense.

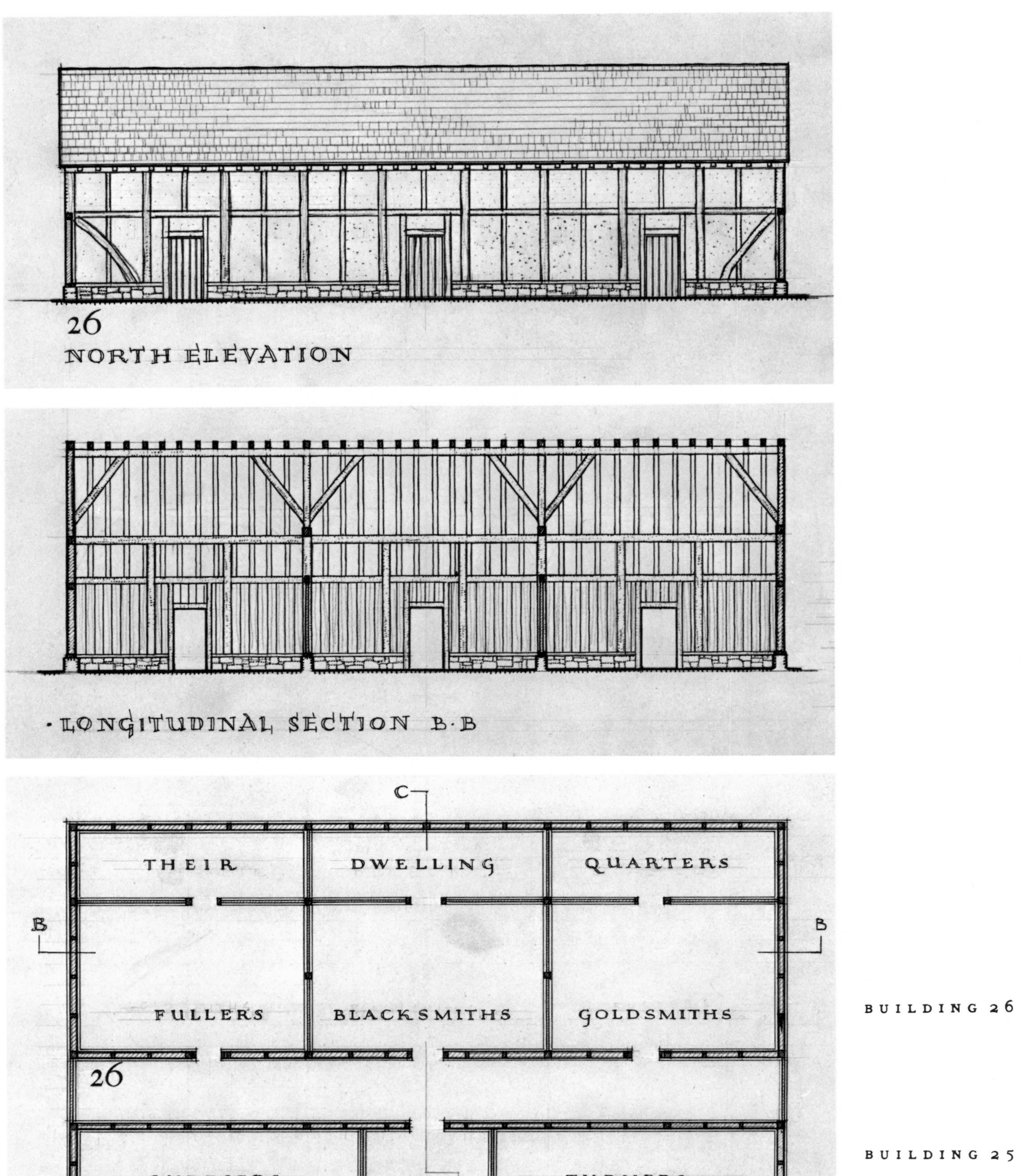

BUILDING 26

BUILDING 25

PLAN OF ST. GALL. GREAT COLLECTIVE WORKSHOP, ANNEX. AUTHORS' INTERPRETATION

PLAN, LONGITUDINAL SECTION, AND NORTH ELEVATION

The layout is identical with that of the Annex of the Abbot's House: a main space, internally divided into three areas for the performance of different tasks, plus a lean-to, also tripartite, serving as bedrooms for the Coopers and Wheelwrights. That the space between the main house and the annex should be interpreted as an open court may be inferred from its comparison with the Abbot's House and the Hospice for Pilgrims and Paupers where main house and annex are separated in a similar way.

THE MONKS' BAKE & BREWHOUSE

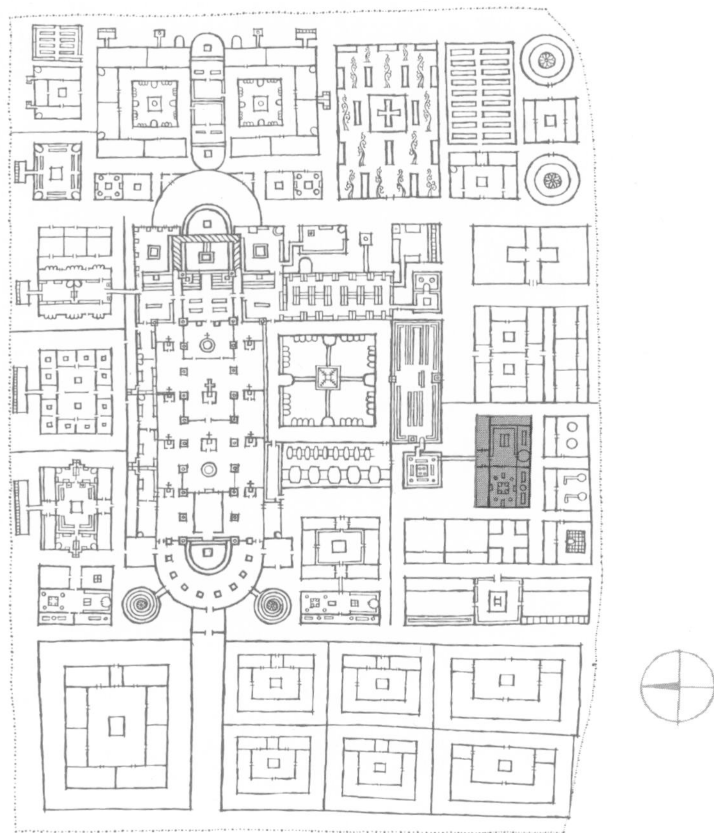

*Values [of western culture], and the motivations springing from them—even those underlying many activities that to us today seem purely secular—were often expressed during the Middle Ages in religious terms and shaped in some measure by religious presuppositions. Engineering was so creative in Europe partly because it came to be more closely integrated with the ideology and ethical patterns of Latin Christianity than was the case with the technology and the dominant faith of any other major culture.**

THE UNION OF EFFICIENT PLANNING WITH TECHNOLOGY emerges with exemplary clarity in the carefully planned proximity of the monks' bake and brewhouse with mortars, mills, drying kiln, and brewer's granary. Northern European monastic and secular diet focussed on cereal grains needed to produce both bread and beer. Efficient interaction was needed in the community of the Plan where, at full complement of residents, 260 pounds of bread and 350-400 liters of beer would be distributed daily. The Plan provides a large storage granary and a smaller one for the brewer's special needs.

In medieval times baking and brewing came to be associated under one roof. Besides processed grain they required warmth in common; the ambient furnished by the great bakery oven of the Plan could have caused bread to rise and beer to ferment. Alignment of mills and mortars on the Plan indicates that given a source and the correct land gradient, water power could

concluded on page 60 ▶

* Lynn White, Jr., *Medieval Religion and Technology. Collected Essays,* 1978, p. ix.

9

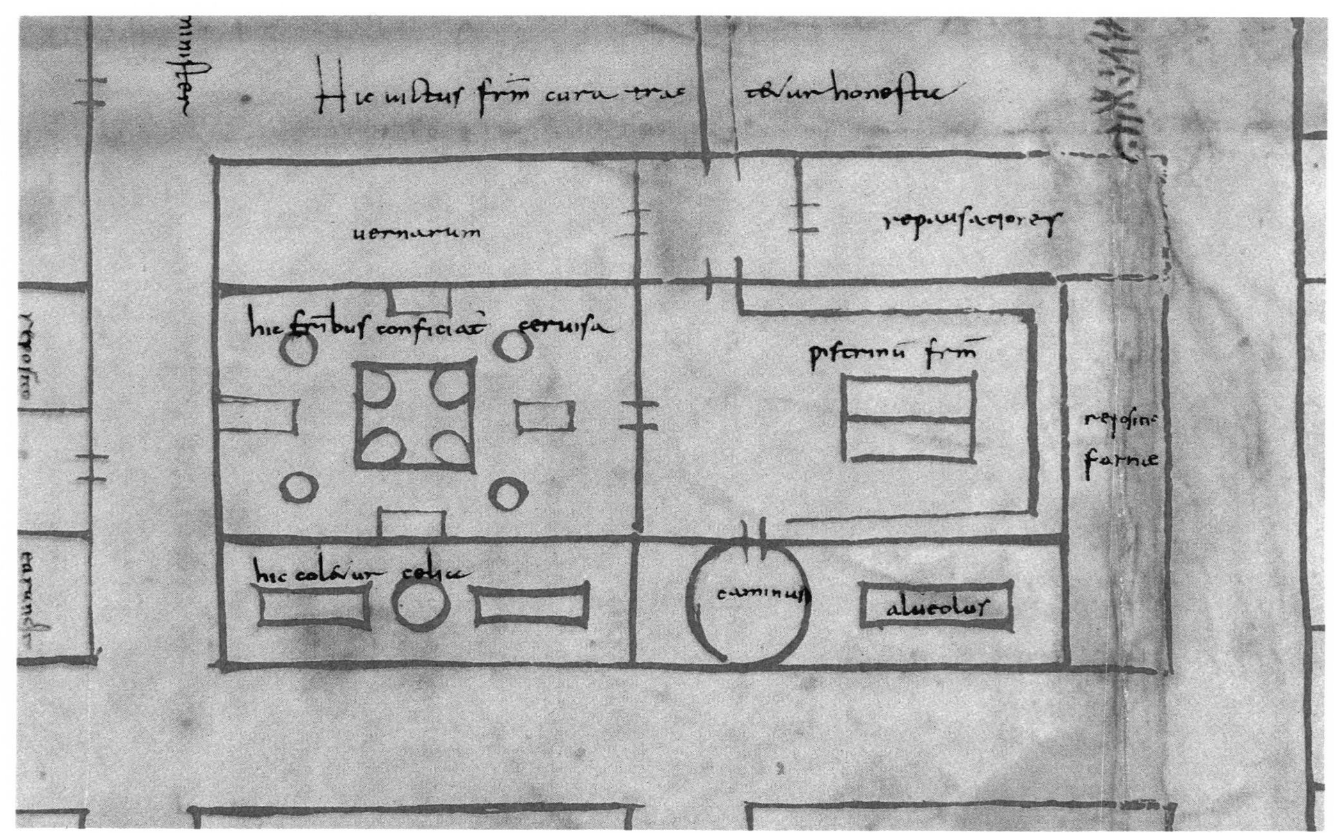

6. MONKS' REFECTORY
7. MONKS' CELLAR
8. MONKS' KITCHEN
9. MONKS' BAKE & BREWHOUSE
27. MILL
28. MORTAR
29. DRYING KILN
33. HORSES, OXEN & KEEPERS

THE SYMBIOTIC SCHEME IN PLANNING

The efficiency internal to the Plan of St. Gall is nowhere better demonstrated than in the relationships among the Brewers' Granary, Mortars, Mills, Drying Kiln, and Monks' Bake and Brewhouse. The traffic patterns demonstrate with what economy of movement raw material, grain—bulky and heavy even after threshing—could be moved from the Brewers' Granary to facilities where it was further refined, and finally into the Brewhouse where the end product, beer, was produced. Similar efficiency of movement existed between the Mill, the Bakehouse, and the Monks' Kitchen. However, planning for isolation of the monks' sanctum takes precedence over convenience where monastery met the world.

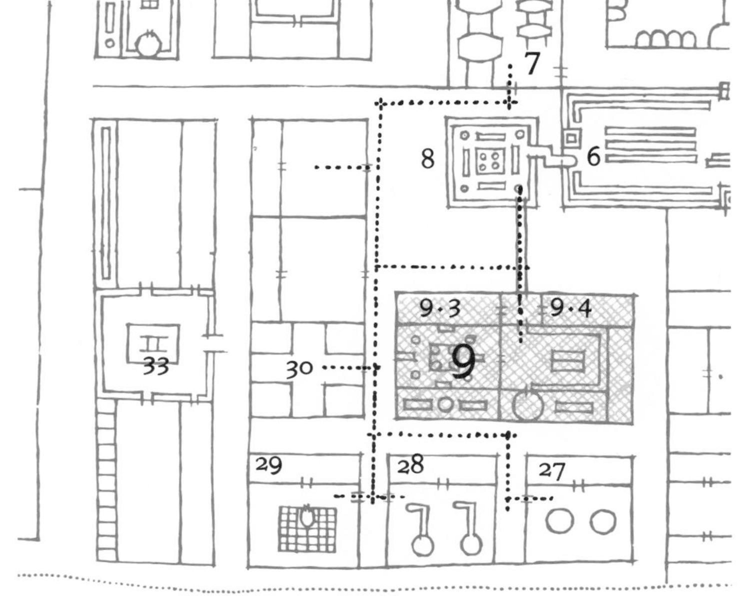

SITE PLAN

PLAN OF ST. GALL. MONKS' BAKE AND BREW HOUSE

The makers of the Plan devoted extraordinary attention to the visual detail and verbal instruction for this house, for it lay, in a most immediate sense, at the physical heart of the monastic complex, as the Church lay at its spiritual heart. The technology of this house is among the most highly elaborated and least abstract of all facilities of the Plan that existed to support daily life in the monastery.

The close proximity of facilities for processing raw material (grain), refining it (Drying Kiln, 29; Mortar; 28; Mill, 27), and using it in the Monks' Bake and Brewhouse assumes intense daily use—transporting sheaved grain, sacking threshed grain, carrying it after processing to bakery or brewery, carrying end products, new bread and new beer, to their destinations.

All the starting points and termini for these processes are found in a very small area relative to the size of the whole site of the Plan. Each day some major part of the cycles and processes for brewing and baking would be set in motion by monks assigned to such chores. The traffic in numbers of men, to say nothing of their burdens—grain, buckets, barrows, sacks, baked bread—achieved a density of use and compaction nowhere else found in the Plan. The planning of the associated facilities would therefore be highly specific, with little assumed and nothing left to improvisation that would affect efficiency adversely. In this small area of the overall site, the makers of the Plan demonstrated their thoroughness and ingenuity as administrators and architects.

THE MONKS' BAKE & BREWHOUSE

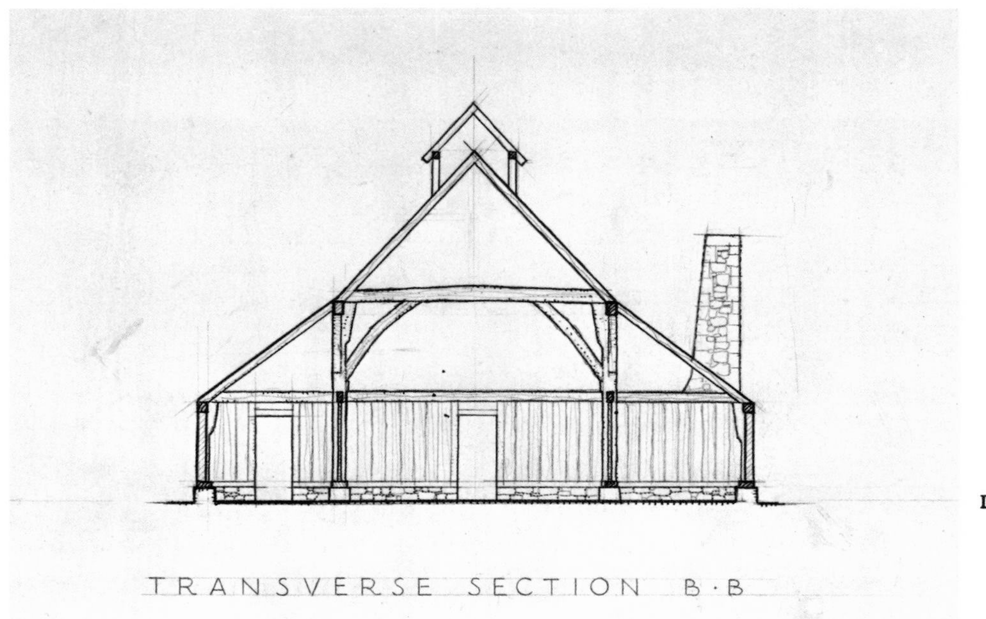

LONGITUDINAL SECTION

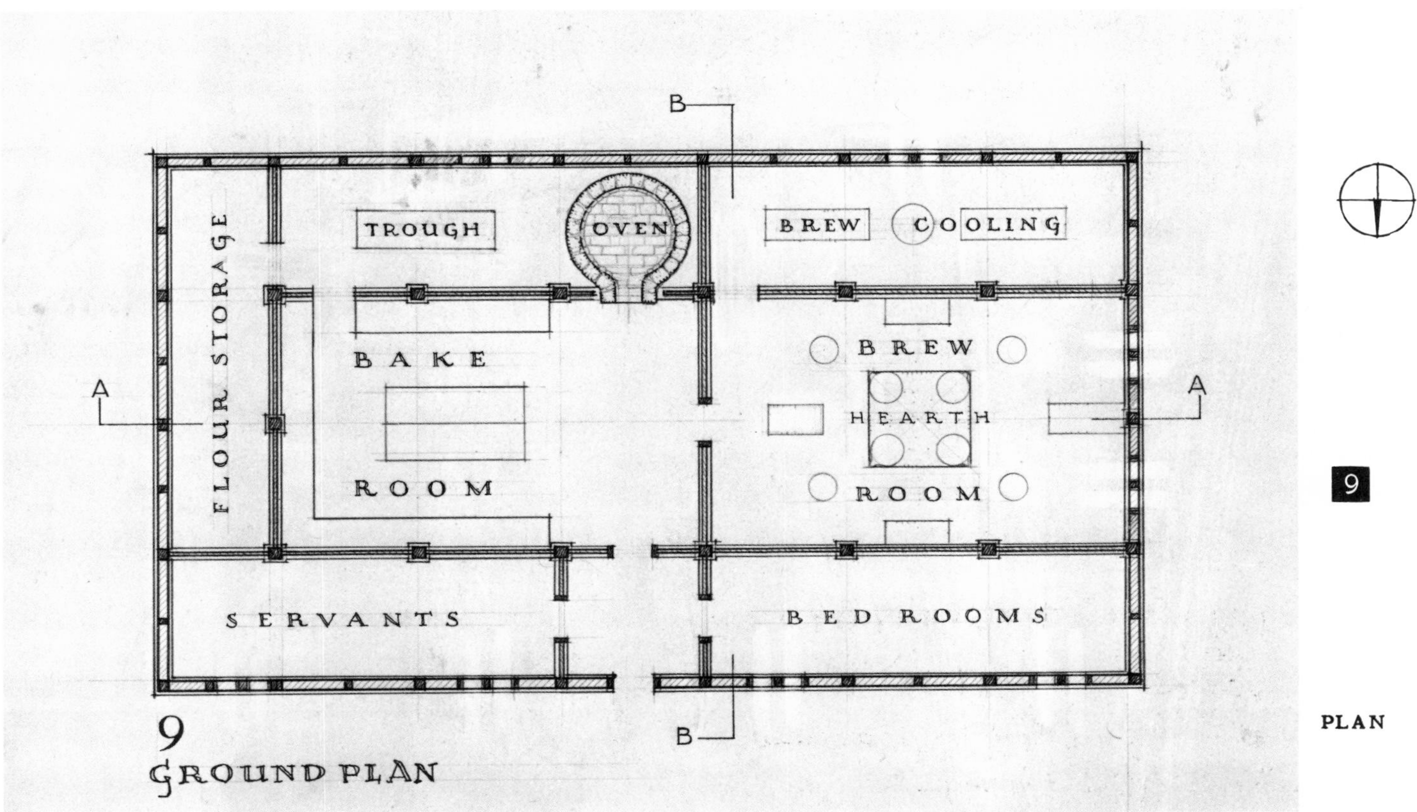

9

PLAN

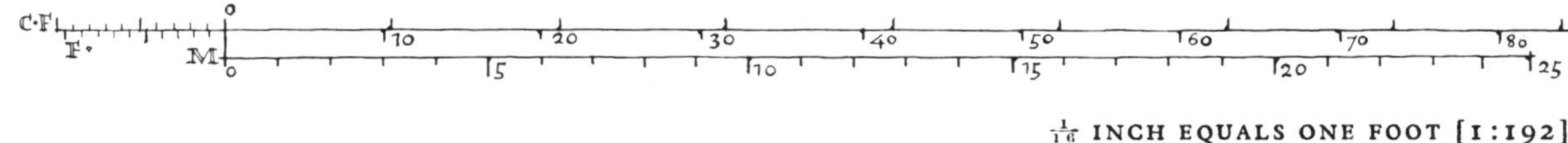

$\frac{1}{16}$ INCH EQUALS ONE FOOT [1:192]

PLAN OF ST. GALL. MONKS' BAKE AND BREW HOUSE. AUTHORS' INTERPRETATION

This facility belongs to the third variant of the building type from which the guest and service buildings of the Plan descend: a central hall with peripheral spaces on three sides. The partition wall in the central hall, dividing Bakery from Brewery, was not structural; in the Bake and Brewhouses for Pilgrims, and for Distinguished Guests, such a divider does not appear. In the Monks' Bake and Brewhouse the dividing wall allots more floor space to the Bakery, but in fact the work areas for each space were virtually identical. The location of the partition wall here in effect clears between entryway and oven; the task of loading or unloading loaves could go on without encumbering the bakers' working space. Certain doors connecting work and storage areas, not shown on the Plan itself, are provided here.

GRAIN STORAGE, GRINDING & CRUSHING

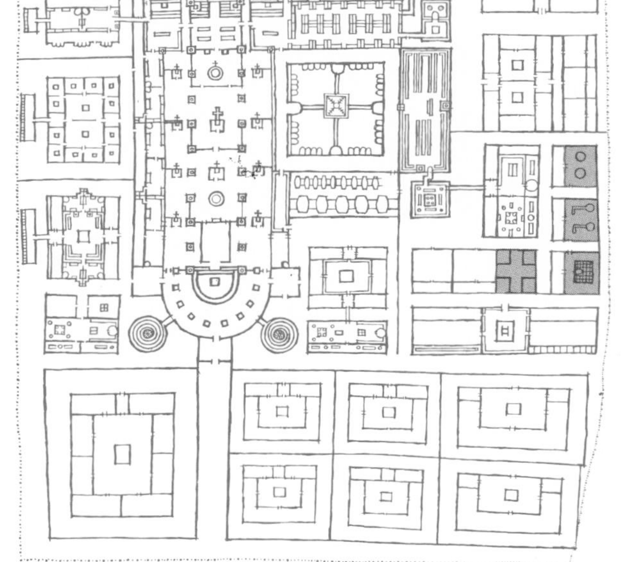

33

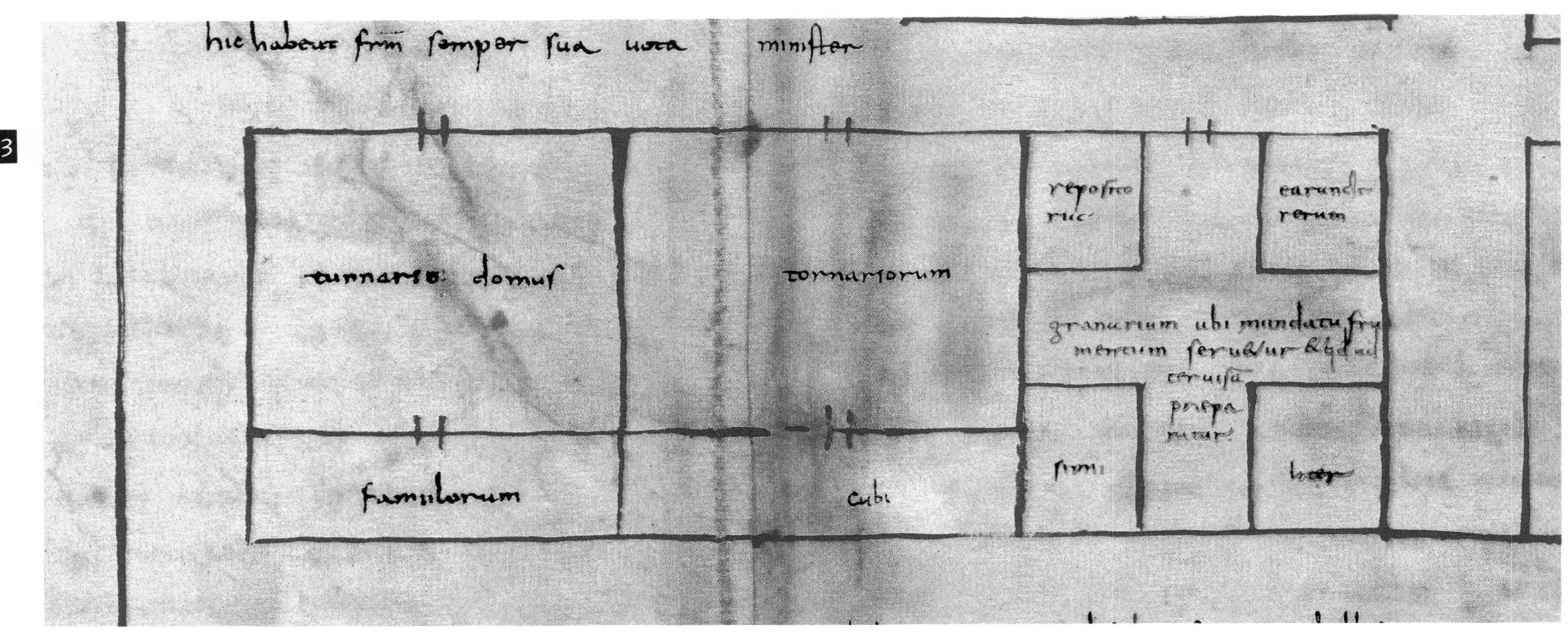

PLAN OF ST. GALL. HOUSE FOR COOPERS & WHEELWRIGHTS & BREWERS' GRANARY

concluded from page 57

have driven both. Although the Romans knew its use, their mills were largely hand- or animal-driven before the 4th century A.D.; in the 5th through 8th, water-powered mills were recorded in Frankish monastic communities. The impetus to apply water power may have spread in the West with Benedictine monastic life. Compelled for continuing existence to manage effectively large estates and complex economic interactions, the monastic community became a source of innovative and systematic technology. Unlike their secular counterparts, such communities possessed intellectual cohesion, physical integration, and the motivation to explore all means of lightening the burden of manual labor to better fulfill their ordained tasks.

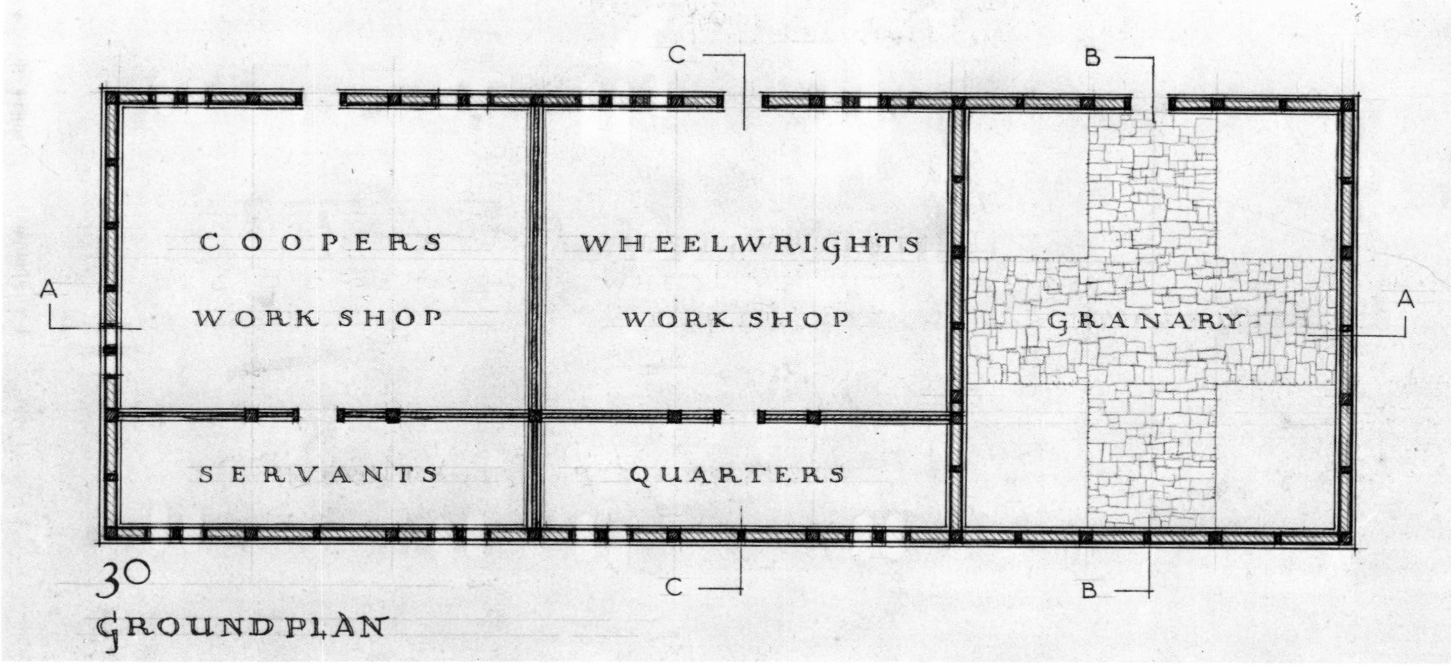

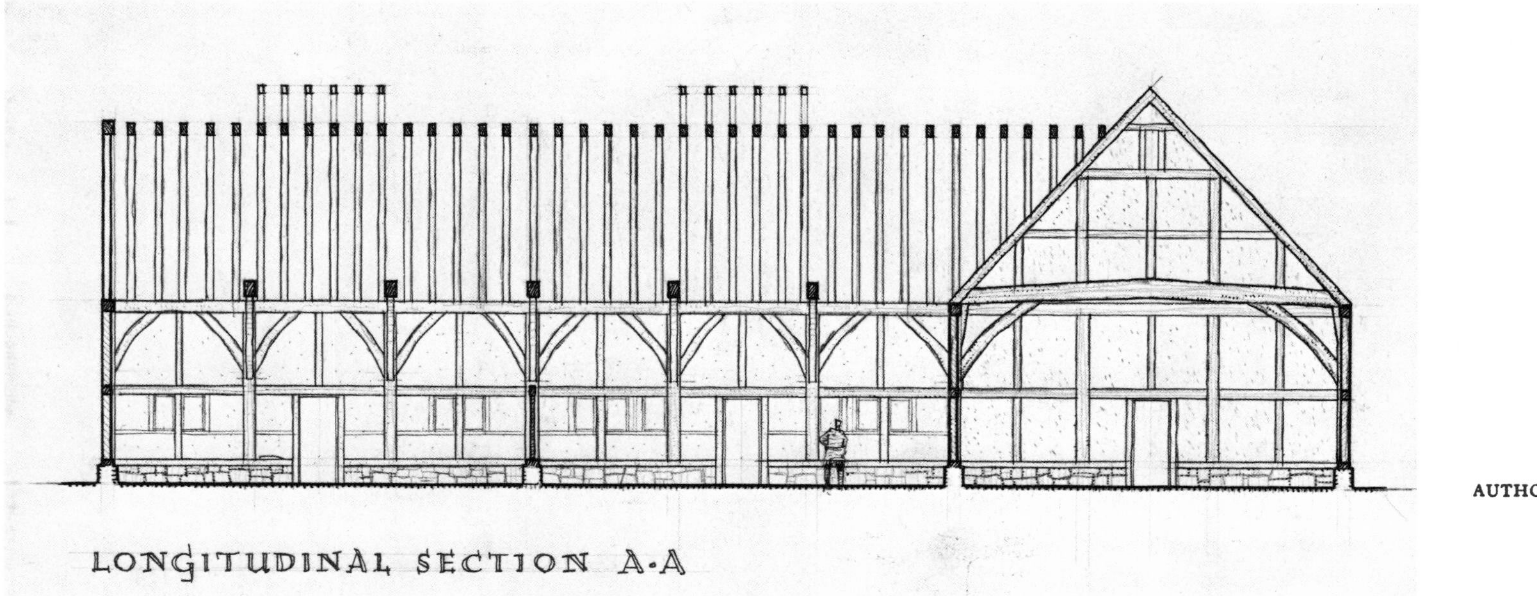

AUTHORS' INTERPRETATION

SCALE: 1/16 INCH = 1 FOOT [1:192]

PLAN OF ST. GALL. HOUSE FOR COOPERS & WHEELWRIGHTS & BREWERS' GRANARY

The association of two workshops with a granary is seemingly in recognition of the space required for all three activities: no less than a barn-size structure would provide sufficient floor space for making large barrels and utility carts and fittings, and a threshing floor. Temporary storage of unfinished and damaged carts and barrels was probably one consideration in determining the size of this building. We have reconstructed this house according to the same criteria that guided that of the Annex of the Great Collective Workshop and the Abbot's House.

Each workshop in this house is 30 feet long (12 standard modules) and 25 wide in the work areas (10 standard modules), suggesting that the part of the structure housing coopers and wheelwrights was divided lengthwise into six bays, each 10 feet deep. Such a division would be reflected externally and internally in the location of the roof-supporting uprights, as well as their connecting beams.

Reconstruction of the Brewer's Granary as a cross wing is conjectural, based on internal symmetry established by the great cross of the threshing floor. It appeared to call for a space based on the concept of a square.

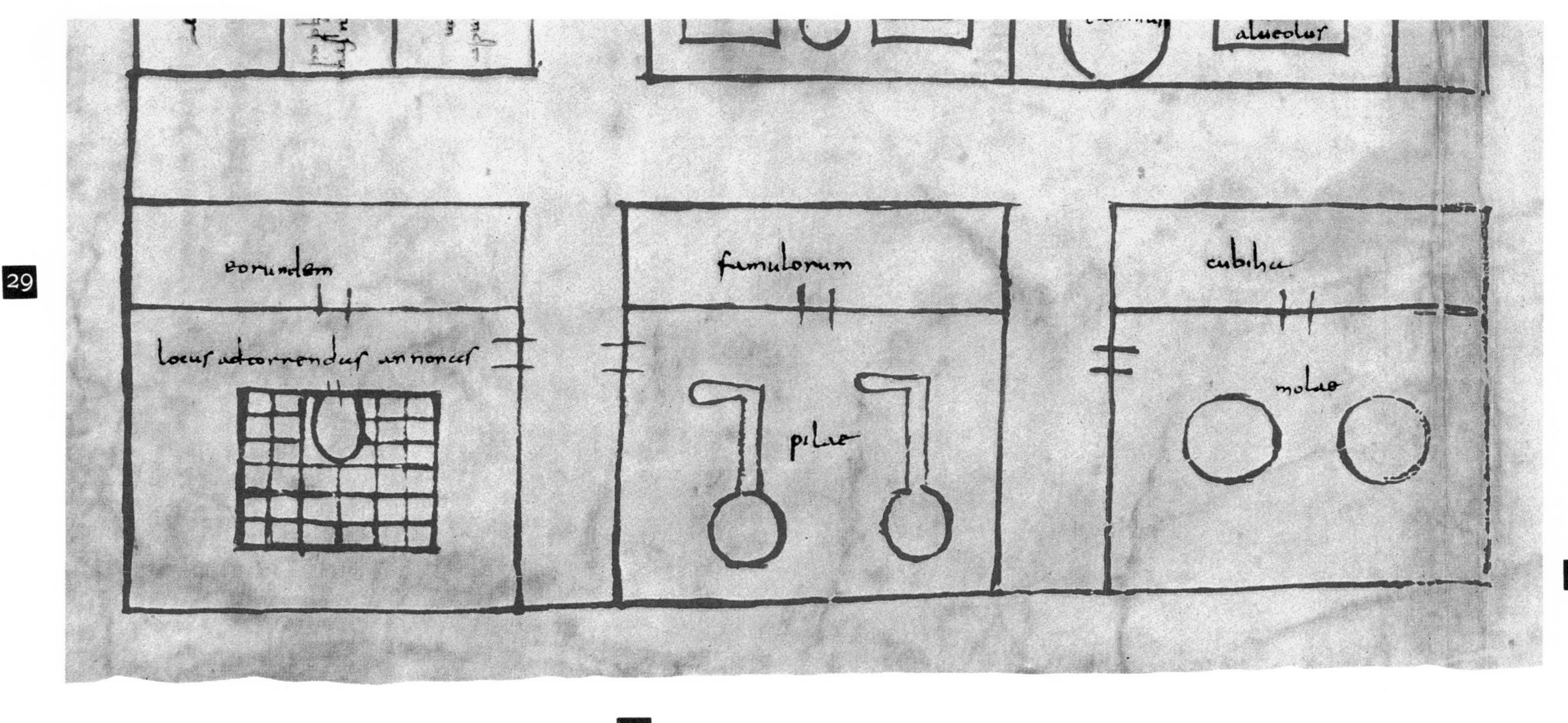

6. MONKS' REFECTORY
7. MONKS' CELLAR
8. MONKS' KITCHEN
9. MONKS' BAKE & BREWHOUSE
25. GREAT COLLECTIVE WORKSHOP
26. ANNEX OF GREAT COLLECTIVE WORKSHOP
27. MILL
28. MORTAR
29. DRYING KILN
30. HOUSE OF COOPERS & WHEELWRIGHTS AND BREWERS' GRANARY
33. HOUSE FOR HORSES AND OXEN AND THEIR KEEPERS
31. HOSPICE FOR PILGRIMS AND PAUPERS
32. KITCHEN, BAKE AND BREWHOUSE FOR PILGRIMS AND PAUPERS
A. FENCE OR WALL SEPARATING "OUTSIDERS" FROM "INNER" ACTIVITIES
B. FENCE OR WALL EXTENDING TO EXTERNAL BOUNDARY

Note: Proximity of Coopers to Monks' Cellar*

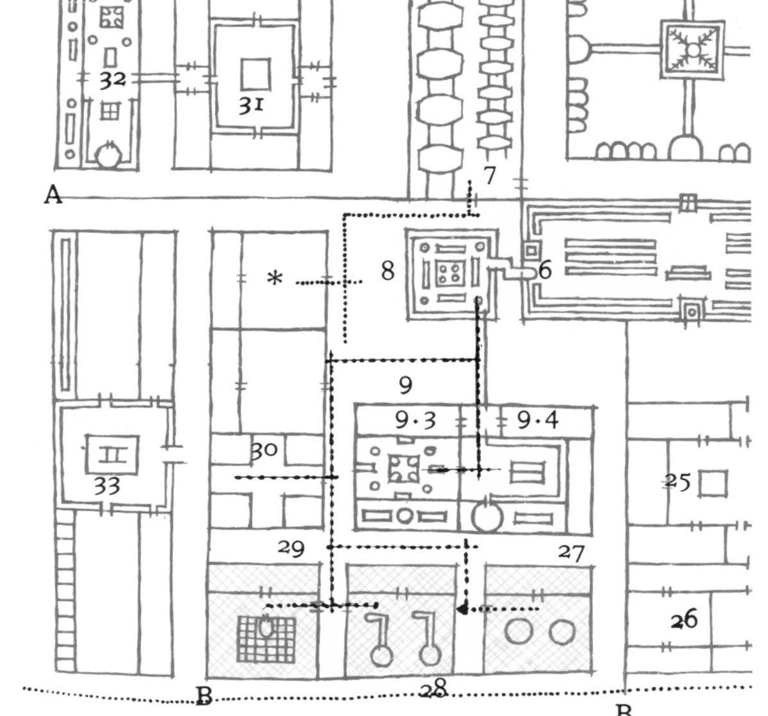

SITE PLAN

PLAN OF ST. GALL. DRYING KILN, MORTAR, AND MILL

The alignment of installations for grinding, crushing, and parching grain (27, 28, 29) at the southern edge of the monastry complex appears to have been purposeful. If the topography of the site were ideal, with stream and land gradient permitting the development of water power, these facilities on the Plan could all have been water driven.

The Drying Kiln, Mortar, and Mill are sited next to the Monks' Bake and Brewhouse (9) and the Monks' Kitchen (8), and near the Bake and Brewhouse of the Pilgrims and Paupers (32). Traffic patterns and usage demonstrated that the location of mills and mortars was carefully planned. The Monks' Bakery and Kitchen required flour from the Mill; the Mortar produced crushed grain for brewing and for many other dishes basic to the monks' diet. The Drying Kiln was used not only for parching grain but for drying fruit.

The noise of the mortars and mill would also have made it desirable to locate them at a distance from the center of monastic activities.

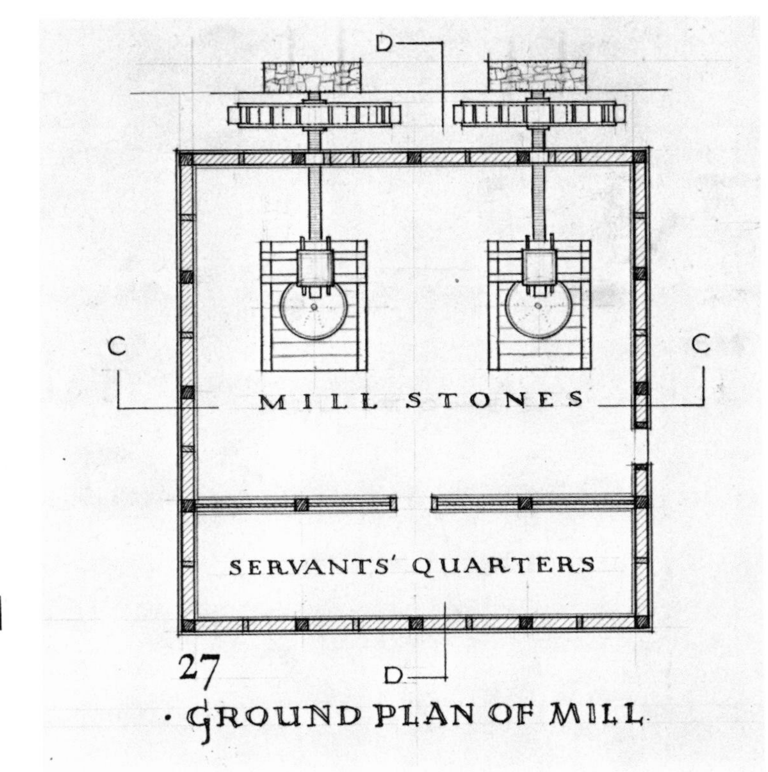

27

SCALE 1/16 INCH = ONE FOOT [1:192]

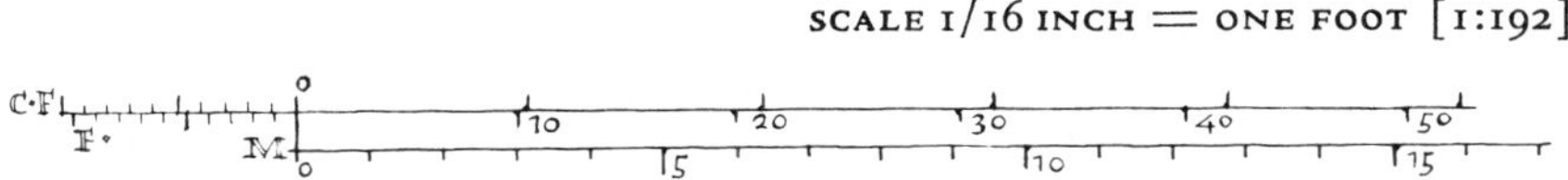

PLAN OF ST. GALL. MILL

AUTHORS' INTERPRETATION. GROUND PLAN

Waterpower for the Mill and Mortar of the Plan of St. Gall is a viable proposal; we have therefore reconstructed the mechanisms as water driven, for these reasons: As regards the millstones, their size, at a literal diameter of $7\frac{1}{2}$ feet, would tend to eliminate the possibility of hand operation. Their depiction on the Plan lacks any indication of drive systems, but that lack is consistent with other such omissions where practicalities, to be left to a master craftsman to execute, have been eliminated in favor of clarity of scale and function.

The alignment of mills and mortar on the southern edge of the Plan site would facilitate use of water power assuming that a stream existed on the site and could be channeled down a gradient sufficient to provide it. Abundant documentary evidence shows that from the end of the 5th century onward and with increasing frequency in succeeding centuries, monastic mills of transalpine Europe were water powered; finally, references to animal-driven mills in these same sources are almost entirely lacking.

We have already discussed the question of why the Romans, although they had it, made scant use of the water mill; whereas the young barbarian nations of the north adopted and diffused it with enthusiasm. To reasons already set forth we suggest here, as a factor so far overlooked, that the strongest impetus for the phenomenal spread of waterpower in the early Middle Ages came not from the secular world but from the ascendancy of Benedictine monasticism.

The records of many abbots show that extensive monastic estates included mills located far outside the immediate vicinity of the monastery; Gozbert himself doubtless would have controlled several beyond the two proposed by the Plan for the monastery. Adalhard records that Corbie's bakeries had to produce 450 one-pound loaves each day, for which the monastery drew on an annual volume of 5,475 modii of grain from 15 mills, each of six millstones, all of which had to be maintained in good working order. And the abbey of St.-Germain-des-Prés had several times again that number of mills.

Building and operating such facilities required impressive capital investment dependent on ownership of great acreage and an unparalleled degree of managerial competence. The monastic school-trained leaders of the period brought to the vast monastic holdings the ingenuity and spirit of radical innovation that necessity alone would have made welcome. In addition, the monastries and their high officials had the pressing moral committment to free the monks from long hours of arduous physical labor, in order to further the Opus Dei. By contrast the secular world, lacking intellectual advantages, integrated physical resources, administrative unity, and religious incentives, lagged behind the great monastaries in technical innovation; as in most labor-intensive societies, medieval secular institutions tended toward conservatism.

Gregory of Tours leaves as an anecdote about Abbot Ursus that constitutes the first documentary evidence of a monastic mill. After relating that "on account of this [water mill] the work that formerly had to be done by many monks could now be accomplished by a single brother," Gregory repeats a dialogue between Ursus and Sichlerius, a Visigoth and nobleman whose land bordered the abbey's, and who had seen first hand the installation of the new mill and its sluices:

"Covetous to acquire the mill, he told the abbot, 'Give me this mill, to become my property, and I shall give you, in return, whatever you ask for.' Replied the Abbot: 'It was only with the greatest of pain, on account of our poverty, that we were able to install this mill; and now we cannot give it to you lest our brethren die of hunger.' Sichlerius retorted: 'If you wish to give it to me by your own free will, I shall be grateful. Otherwise I will take it by force, or build another mill, for which I shall divert the water from your sluice; and in this way it will no longer be able to turn your wheel.' The abbot replied, 'You will not do what God shall not permit you to do, you will not take it at all!' Sichlerius, in ire, did what he had threatened to do, but because of divine intervention, the water failed to turn the wheels of his mill." Thus the intransigent noble was defeated.

The story, embodying all the social dichotomies between secular and religious spheres, is symptomatic and may have remained so for the most of the Middle Ages. Ingenuity and initiative, in addition to divine justice, were clearly on the side of the abbot.

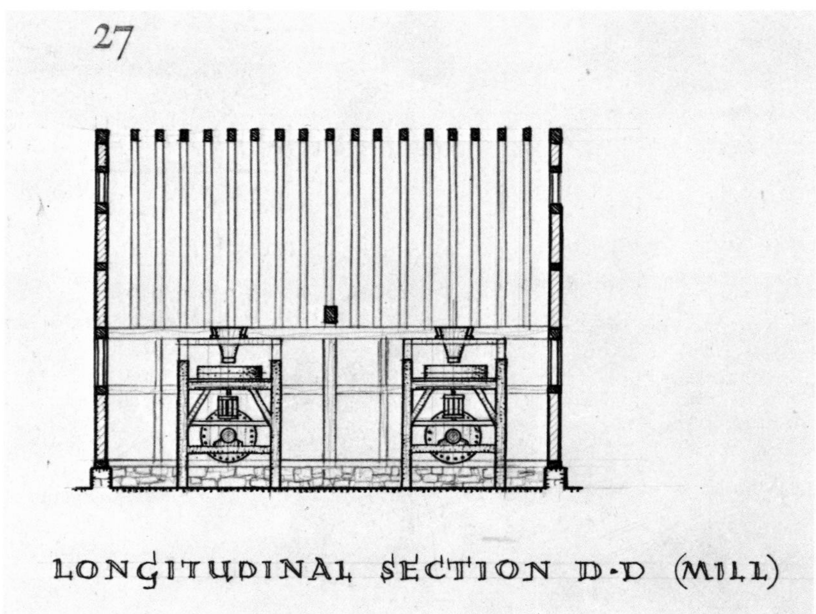

LONGITUDINAL SECTION

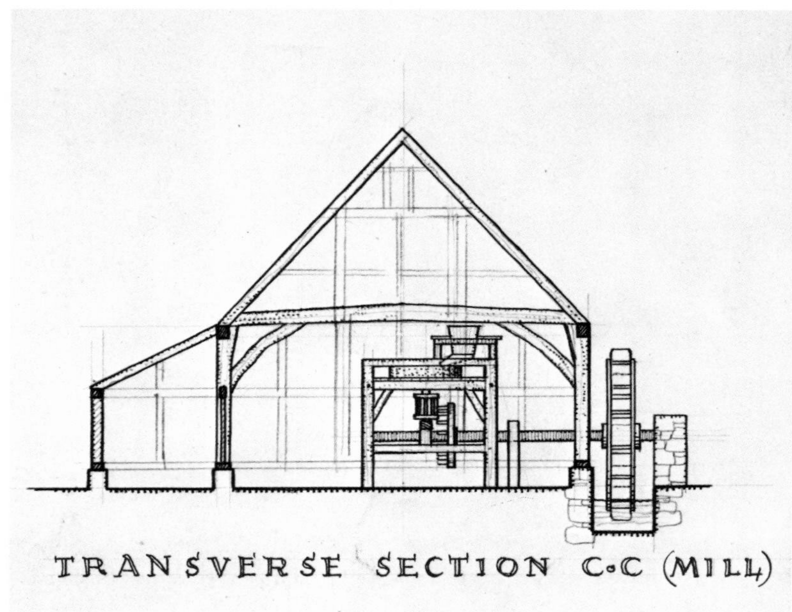

TRANSVERSE SECTION

PLAN OF ST. GALL. MILL AUTHORS' RECONSTRUCTION

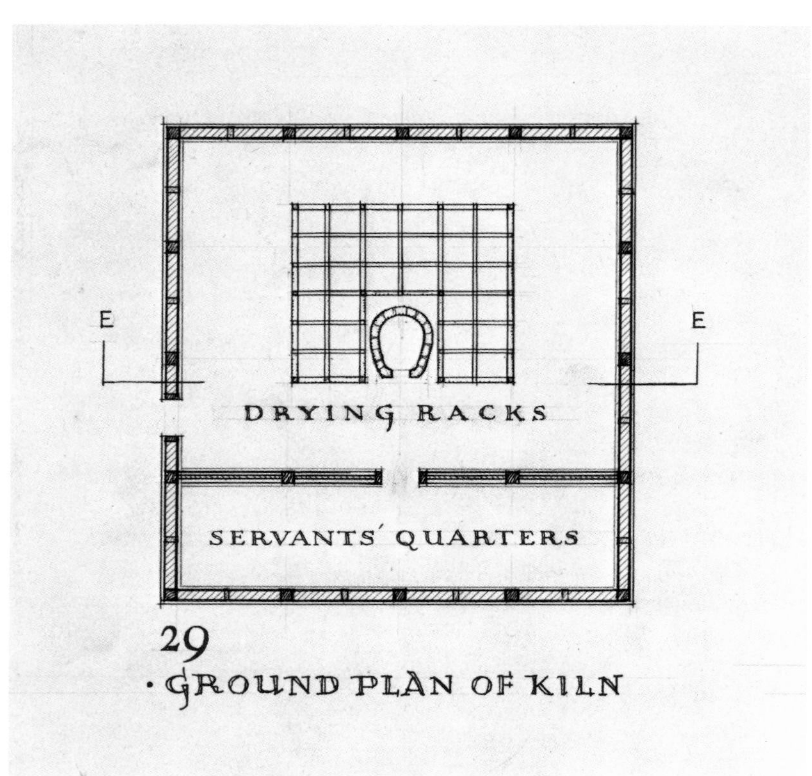

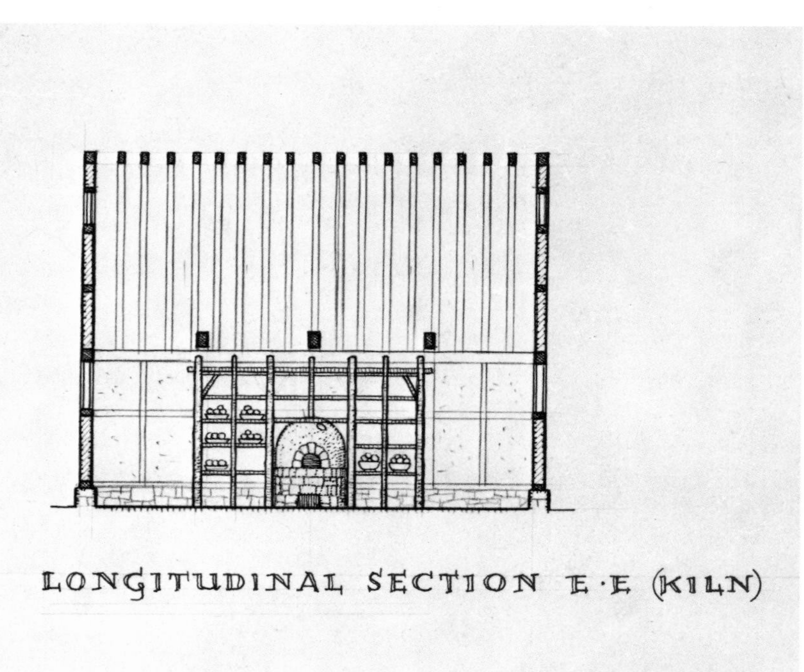

PLAN OF ST. GALL. DRYING KILN.

The shelter for the Drying Kiln is identical with those for the Mills and Mortars of the Plan. This house could have been the simplest kind of structure, perhaps even open-sided. Although the Drying Kiln would not develop temperatures so high as those needed for baking, some fire hazard would have existed in a closed building; the Plan does not show either smoke exit or stack port for this facility. We reiterate that these service structures of the Plan are highly abstract; their purpose and siting were of foremost importance to the Plan's makers; their constructional details, secondary.

POMPEII. CARBONIZED LOAF OF BREAD

The division of the loaf into equal-sized segments for easy distribution may have had some relevance for Benedict's later instruction that the monks' ration of bread be carefully and fairly weighed.

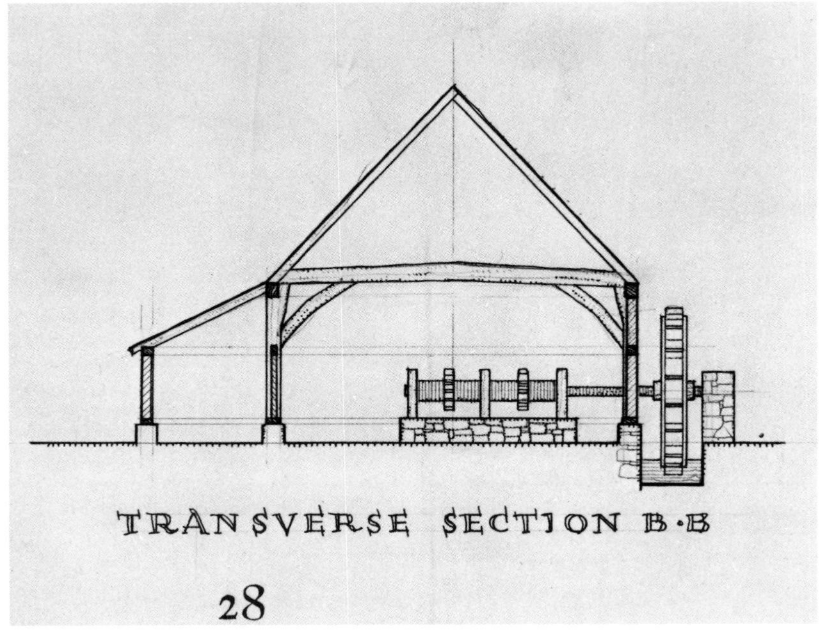

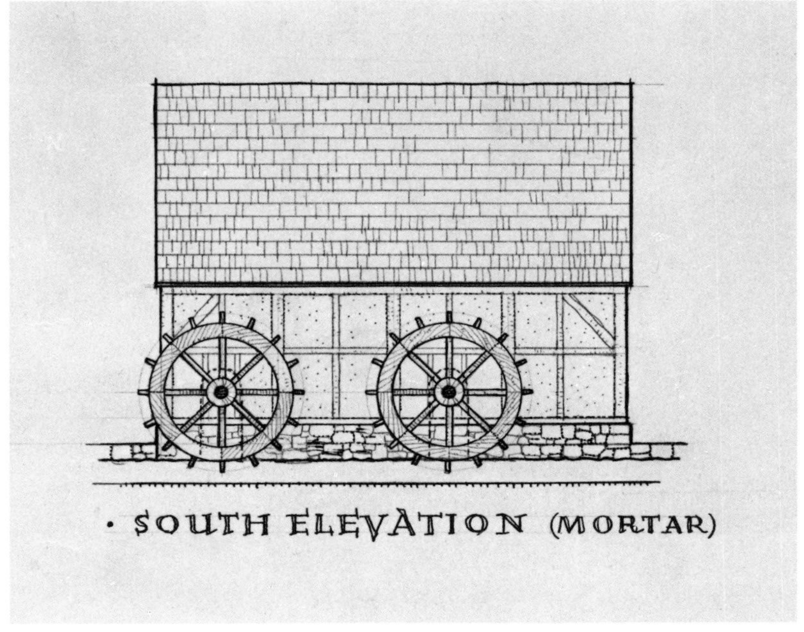

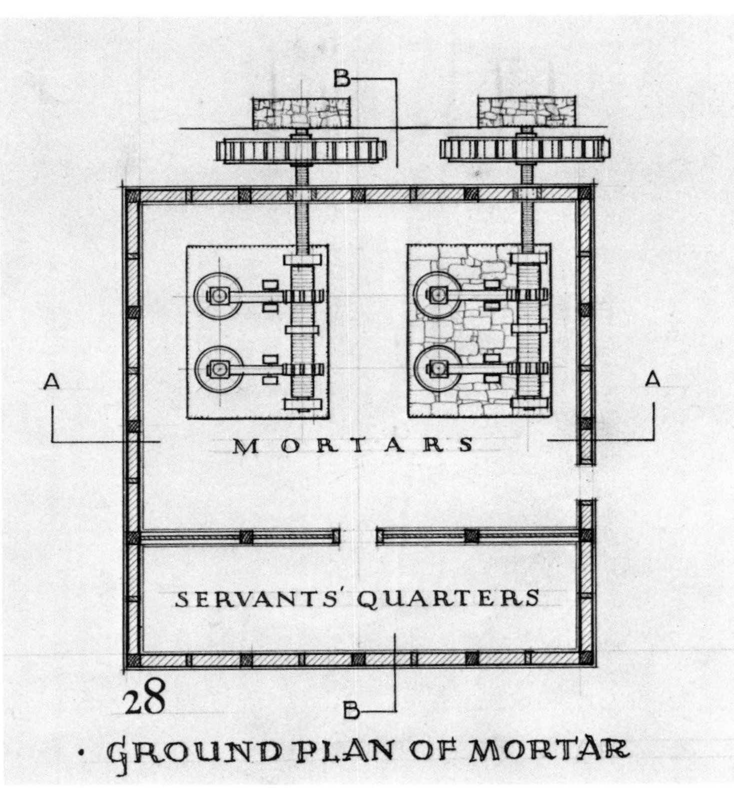

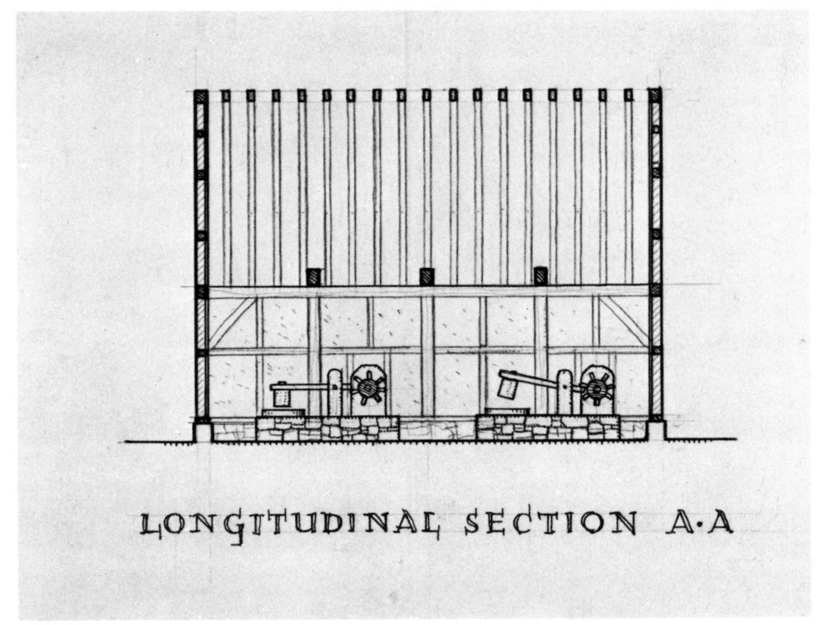

PLAN OF ST. GALL. MORTAR HOUSE. AUTHORS' INTERPRETATION

PLAN. TRANSVERSE SECTION, LONGITUDINAL SECTION; SOUTH ELEVATION

The Mortars of the Plan are here reconstructed as water-driven mechanisms, with their axle-trees oriented east and west and the presumptive waterwheels to which these were geared oriented in the same direction, as are the waterwheels of the reconstructed Mill.

THE MONKS' ORCHARD & GARDEN & GARDENER'S HOUSE

Inde noti conquitur flabris solisque calore
Areola et lignis, ne diffluat, obsita quadris
Altius a plano modicum resupina levatur.
Tota minutatim rastris contunditur uncis,
Et pinguis fermenta fimi super insinuantur.
Seminibus quaedam tentamus holuscula, quaedam
Stirpibus antiquis priscae revocare iuventae.
Denique vernali interdum conspergitur imbre
Parva seges, tenuesque fovet praeblanda vicissim
Luna comas. . . .

Then my small patch was warmed by winds from the south,
and the sun's heat. That it should not be washed away,
We faced it with planks and raised it in oblong beds
A little above the level ground. With a rake
I broke the soil up bit by bit, and then
Worked in from on top the leaven of rich manure.
Some plants we grow from seed, some from old stocks
We try to bring back to the youth they knew before.
Then come the showers of Spring, from time to time
Watering our tiny crop, and in its turn
The gentle moon caresses the delicate leaves.*

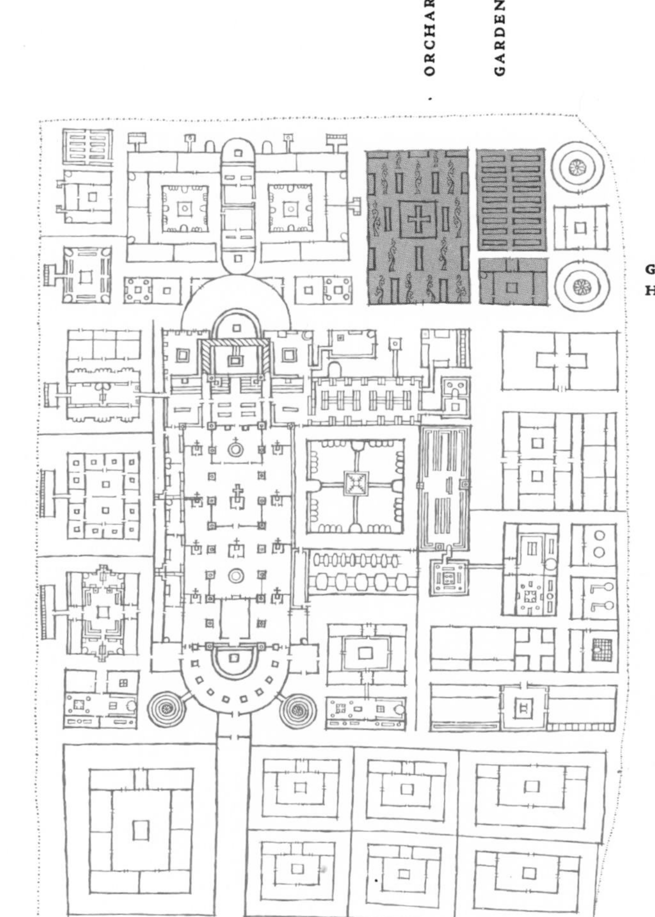

THE AWARENESS OF FUNCTIONAL INTERRELATIONSHIPS that distinguishes the architectural program of the Plan of St Gall emerges strikingly in the placement of the monks' vegetable garden between their orchard and the poultry runs. The birds' diet could be augmented by garden clippings; their manure provided fertilizer to renew the garden soil. The runs, also sited near the granary to the west, allowed the fowlkeepers easy access to grain supplies for feed.

While the monks did not regularly consume fowl, eggs were a major source of protein. The monks' garden produced mainly spicy or savory vegetables used for flavoring, mitigating the dullness of a largely vegetarian regime. Its 18 raised planting beds are laid out in 5-foot widths governed by the modular scheme and human scale of the Plan; wider beds would be difficult to hand-cultivate.

continue on page 71

* WALAHFRID STRABO, *HORTULUS*, verses 46-55. Payne and Blunt, eds., 1966, 28-29.

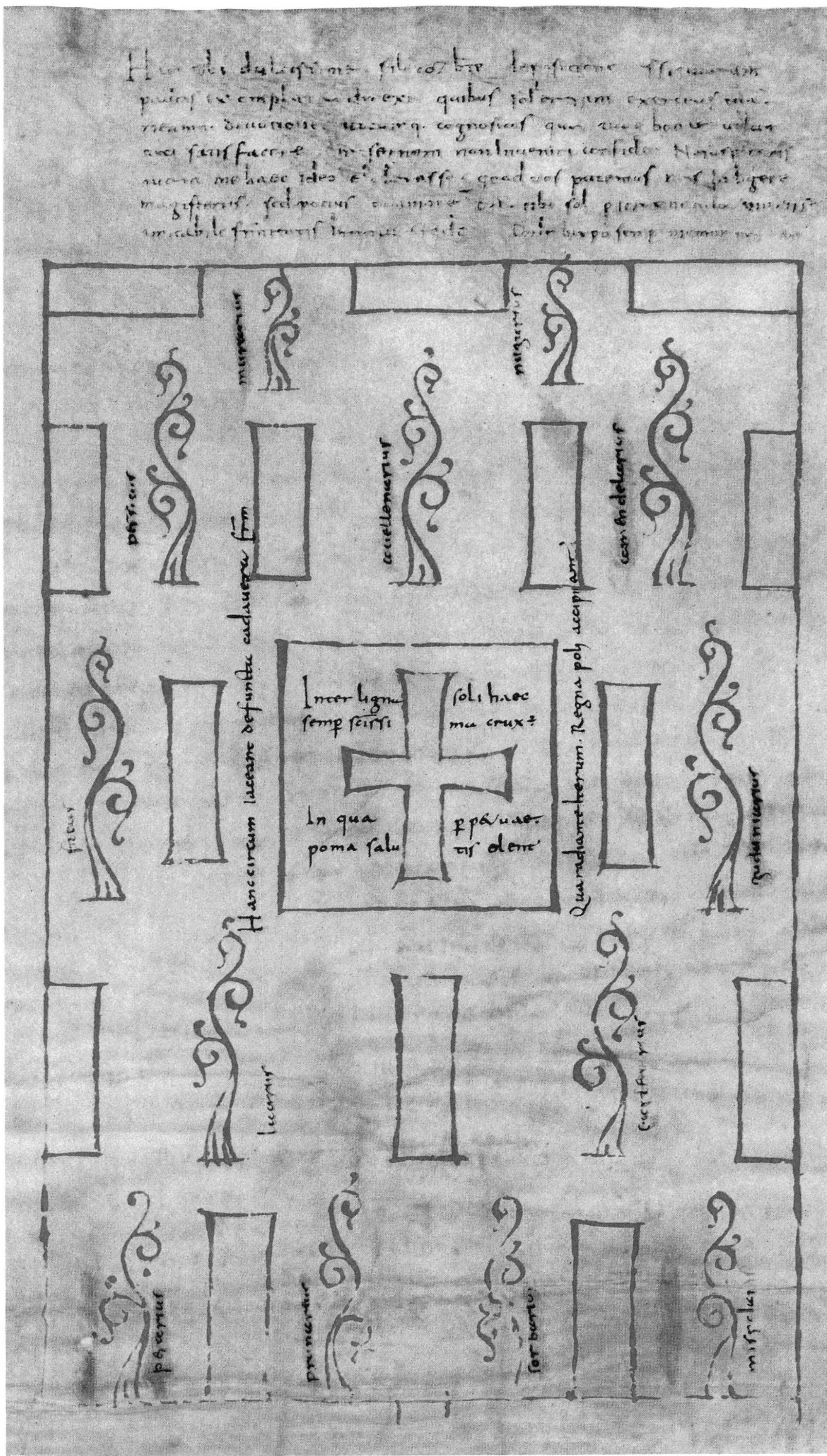

PLAN OF ST. GALL. MONKS' CEMETERY AND ORCHARD

◀ DEDICATORY LEGEND
See I.

Y

The cemetery contains thirteen planting areas for trees and fourteen (= twice seven) burial plots. Seven of them lie to the east of the great cross in the center, and seven of them at and below it. It is probably not an accidental arrangement but rather one of the countless examples of preoccupation of the drafters of the Plan with sacred numbers. Thirteen evokes the memory of Christ and the twelve Apostles and in particular their congregation at the supper that preceded His death. (The tendril-shaped symbol used to locate the trees of the orchard is a key to identifying the designer of the original Plan.

The number seven, Augustus writes, expressed "the wholeness and completeness of all created things". The modular scheme of the Plan applies to the burial plots: their width, $6\frac{1}{4}$ feet, is composed of two standard $2\frac{1}{2}$-foot modules plus one $1\frac{1}{4}$-foot submodule, while their length, at $17\frac{1}{2}$ feet, reflects once again the sacred number seven: $7 \times 2\frac{1}{2} = 17\frac{1}{2}$. Thus, in each plot the bodies of seven brothers could be accommodated, in keeping with the application of standard modules to achieve the human scale of the other facilities of the Plan. And as elsewhere, this compounding and multiplication of sevens can hardly be fortuitous, but on the contrary, quite purposeful in the planning of the Cemetery.

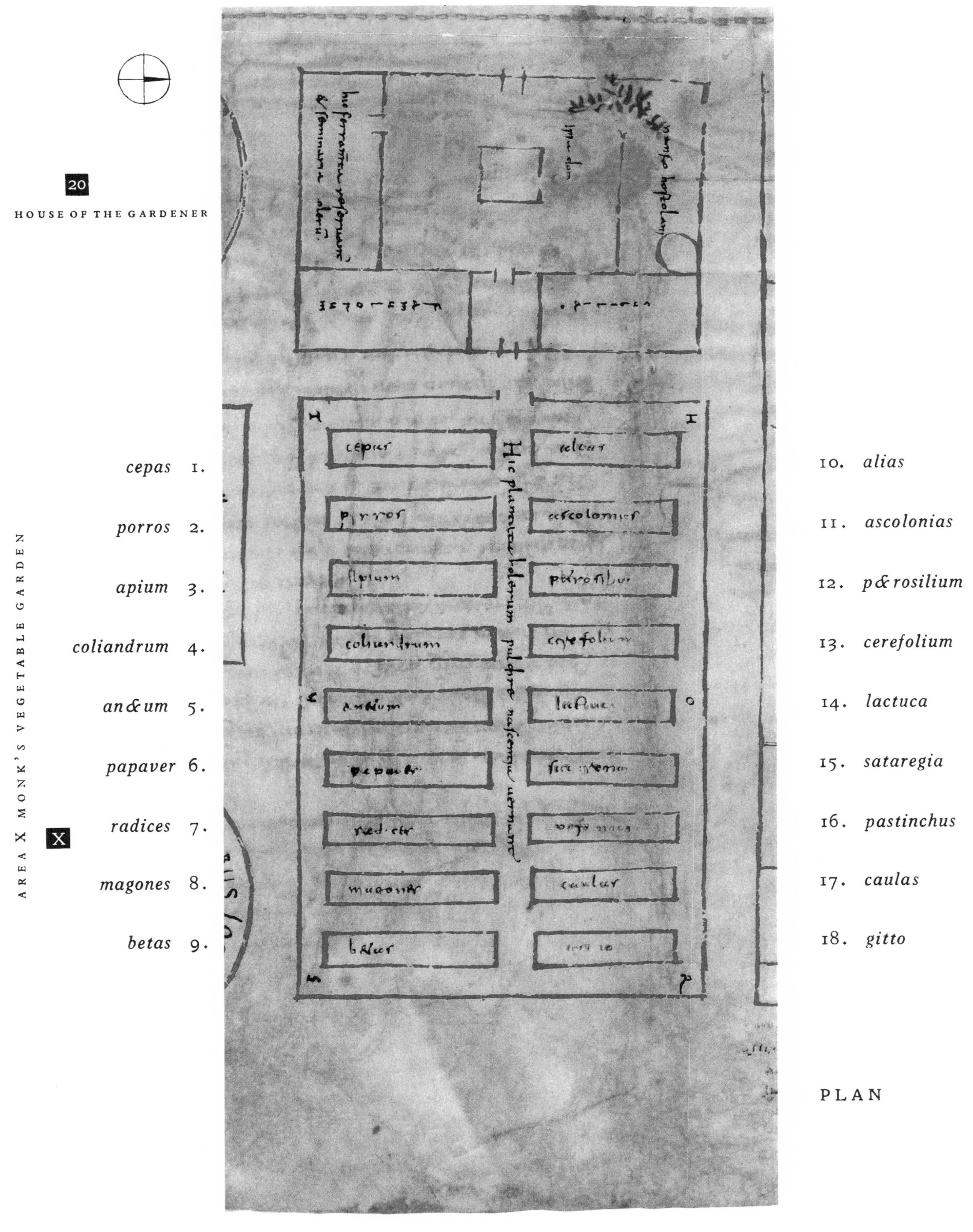
20
HOUSE OF THE GARDENER
AREA X MONK'S VEGETABLE GARDEN
X
cepas 1.
porros 2.
apium 3.
coliandrum 4.
an&um 5.
papaver 6.
radices 7.
magones 8.
betas 9.
10. alias
11. ascolonias
12. p&rosilium
13. cerefolium
14. lactuca
15. sataregia
16. pastinchus
17. caulas
18. gitto
PLAN

& GARDENER'S HOUSE

PLAN OF ST. GALL.
HOUSE OF THE GARDENER AND HIS CREW AND MONKS' VEGETABLE GARDEN

The position of the Monks' Vegetable Garden between the Orchard (y) and the poultry runs (21, 23) as well as its proximity to the Monks' Latrine (4) demonstrates the awareness for functional inter-relationships characterizing the intelligence of those who designed the Plan. Both Orchard and Garden come under the care of the Gardener. The Garden would have drawn the most effective fertilizer from the nitrogen-rich droppings of the nearby fowl yards; grain feed for chickens and geese (the Granary is in close proximity) could be augmented by trimmings from the vegetables. However, the most important source for fertilizer might have been the Monks' Privy, if the waste there was not swept away through water channels but (as seems more reasonable to assume) was gathered in settling tanks.

The garden plots were devoted largely to what we today consider to be seasonings or spices; with root crops in need of more space than that available within the monastic compound, and therefore grown on land outside the walls, the produce of the garden could be largely devoted to crops for enhancing the flavors of the monks' heavily vegetarian diet.

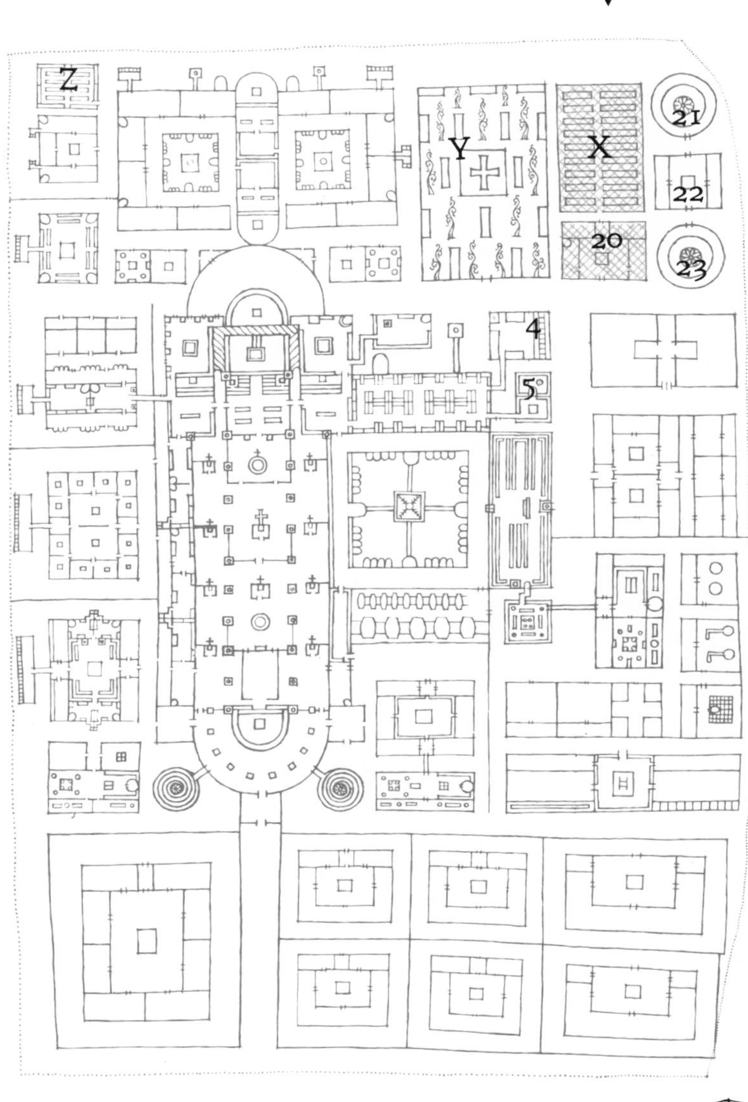

SITE PLAN

* X. MONKS' VEG. GARDEN
Y. ORCHARD & CEMETERY
* 20. GARDENER'S HOUSE
21. GOOSE HOUSE
22. HOUSE OF FOWLKEEPERS
23. HEN HOUSE
4. MONKS' PRIVY
5. MONKS' LAUNDRY & BATHHOUSE
Z. MEDICINAL GARDEN

Each bed of the Monks' Vegetable Garden is used for the cultivation of a specific type of plant, the name of which is entered by the hand of the second scribe in the pale ink that characterizes his writing. Read from top to bottom in the sequence in which they were written they are:

SOUTHERN ROW

1. *cepas* — onion (*allium cepas* L.)
2. *porros* — leek (*allium porrum* L.)
3. *apium* — celery (*apium graveolens* L.)
4. *coliandrum* — coriander (*coriandrum sativum* L.)
5. *an&um* — dill (*anetum graveolens* L.)
6. *papaver* — poppy (*papaver somniferum* L.)
7. *radices* — radish (*raphanus sativus* L.)
8. *magones* — poppy (*papaver . . .* L.)
9. *betas* — chard (*beta vulgaris or beta cicla* L.)

NORTHERN ROW

10. *alias* — garlic (*allium sativum* L.)
11. *ascolonias* — shallot (*allium ascolonicum* L.)
12. *p&rosilium* — parsley (*apium petrosilium* L.)
13. *cerefolium* — chervil (*anthriscus cerefolium* Hofmann)
14. *lactuca* — lettuce (*lactuca scariola* L.)
15. *sataregia* — pepperwort (*satureia hortensis* L.)
16. *pastinchus* — parsnip (*pastinaca sativa* L.)
17. *caulas* — cabbage (*brassica oleracea* L.)
18. *gitto* — fennel (*nigella satira* L.)

The modern Latin plant names listed in parentheses are taken from Wolfgang Sörrensen's article on the gardens and plants of the Plan. To Sörrensen we owe much other vital information on this subject; see Sörrensen in *Studien*, 1962.

The fact that poppy appears twice is bewildering. Sörrensen (*ibid.*, 210–11) feels certain that *magones* is poppy, but which variety of poppy remains uncertain.

GARDENER'S HOUSE

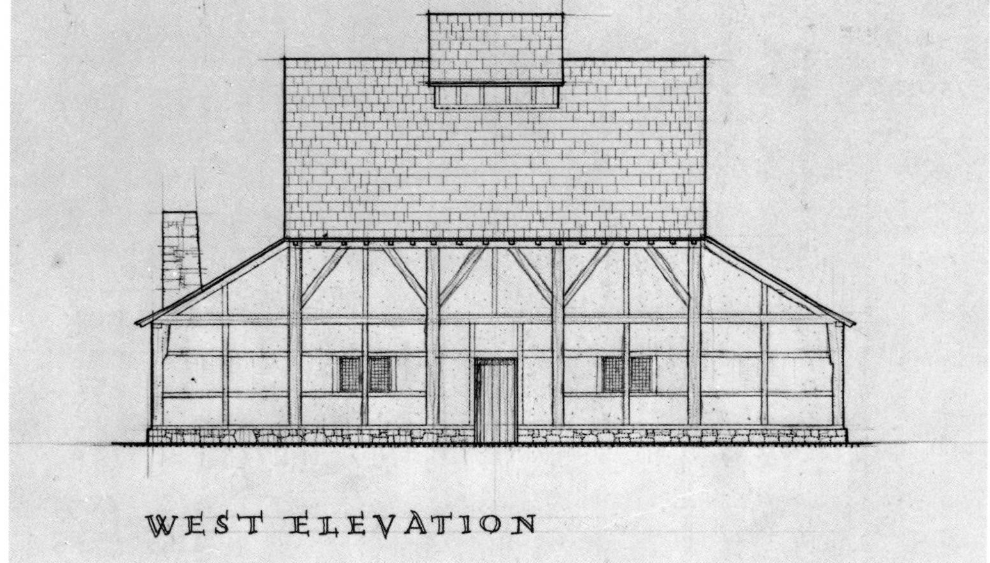

WEST ELEVATION

The entrance, located in the middle of the western long wall, leads directly into the common living room. The northern lean-to with corner fireplace serves as the Gardener's private dwelling.

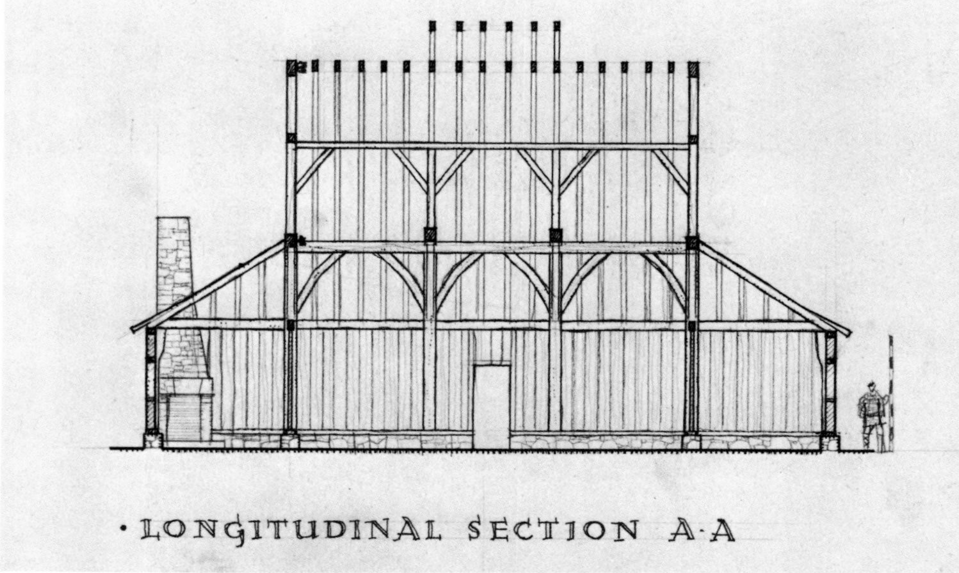

LONGITUDINAL SECTION

The door in the center leads from the common living room into a vestibule which gives access to the servants' quarters and has an exit to the Garden.

20

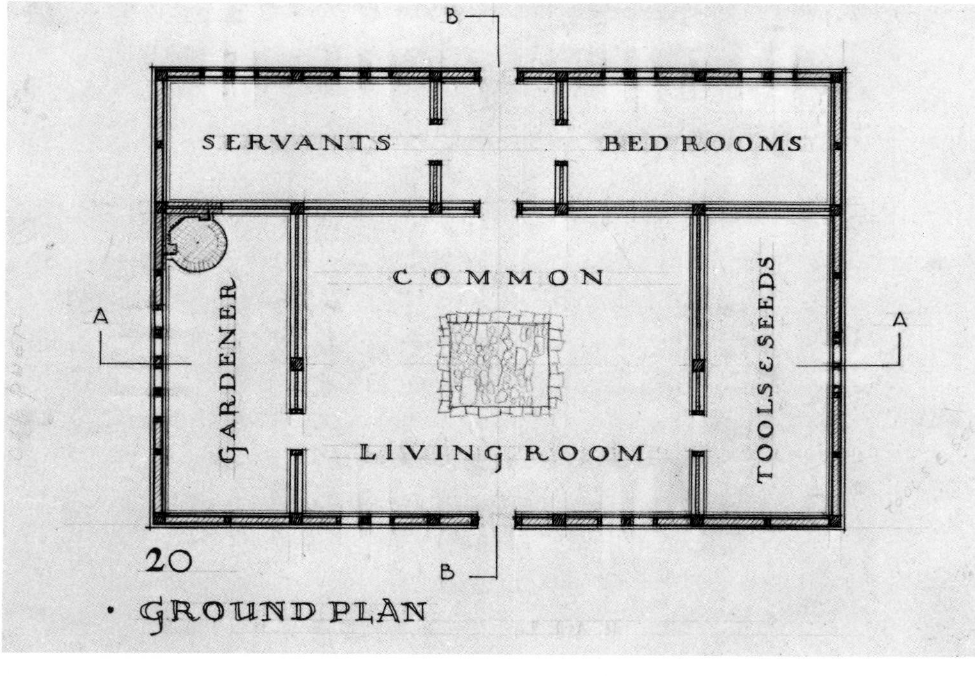

GROUND PLAN

Since the Gardener's private room had a corner fireplace, it was independent of the communal fireplace in the living room and could have been separated from the rest of the house by wall partitions as well as by a ceiling. If provided with a ceiling it would have needed windows in the outer wall for light and air.

SCALE $\frac{1}{16}$ INCH EQUALS ONE FOOT [1:192]

PLAN OF ST. GALL. HOUSE OF THE GARDENER AND HIS CREW

AUTHORS' INTERPRETATION

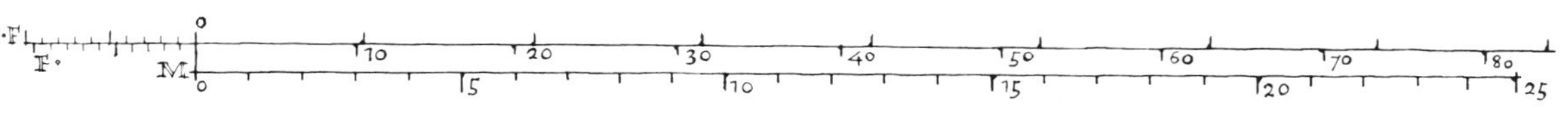

THE FOWLKEEPER'S HOUSE & HENHOUSE & GOOSEHOUSE

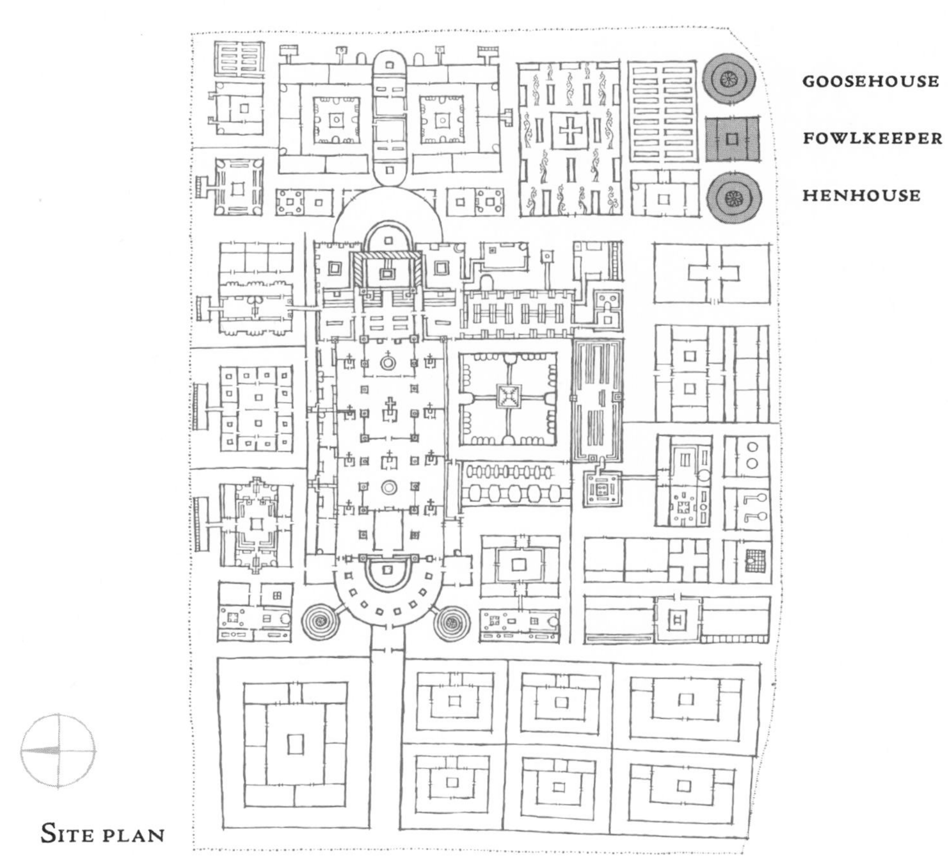

FOURTEEN FRUIT TREES in the orchard shaded the monastery's burial ground. Neither orchard nor garden yielded enough in season to feed the entire community; fruit and field crops were grown in quantity outside on monastic estates. But orchard and garden provided the monks with exercise and manual labor within the cloister. Some were skilled not only in plant propagation techniques, but became eloquent gardeners as well (page 66). The poultry runs lack clear architectural antecedents; they may be a traditional circular aviary form. The chief gardener, often a layman, had private quarters in a 3-aisled house with spaces for crew and supplies. The fowlkeepers lived in a simpler version of this building located conveniently between the fowl pens. Each house had a common living space, hearth, and roof lantern for smoke escape and light. They are variants of a basic building type that originates in Northern vernacular architecture (page 76f).

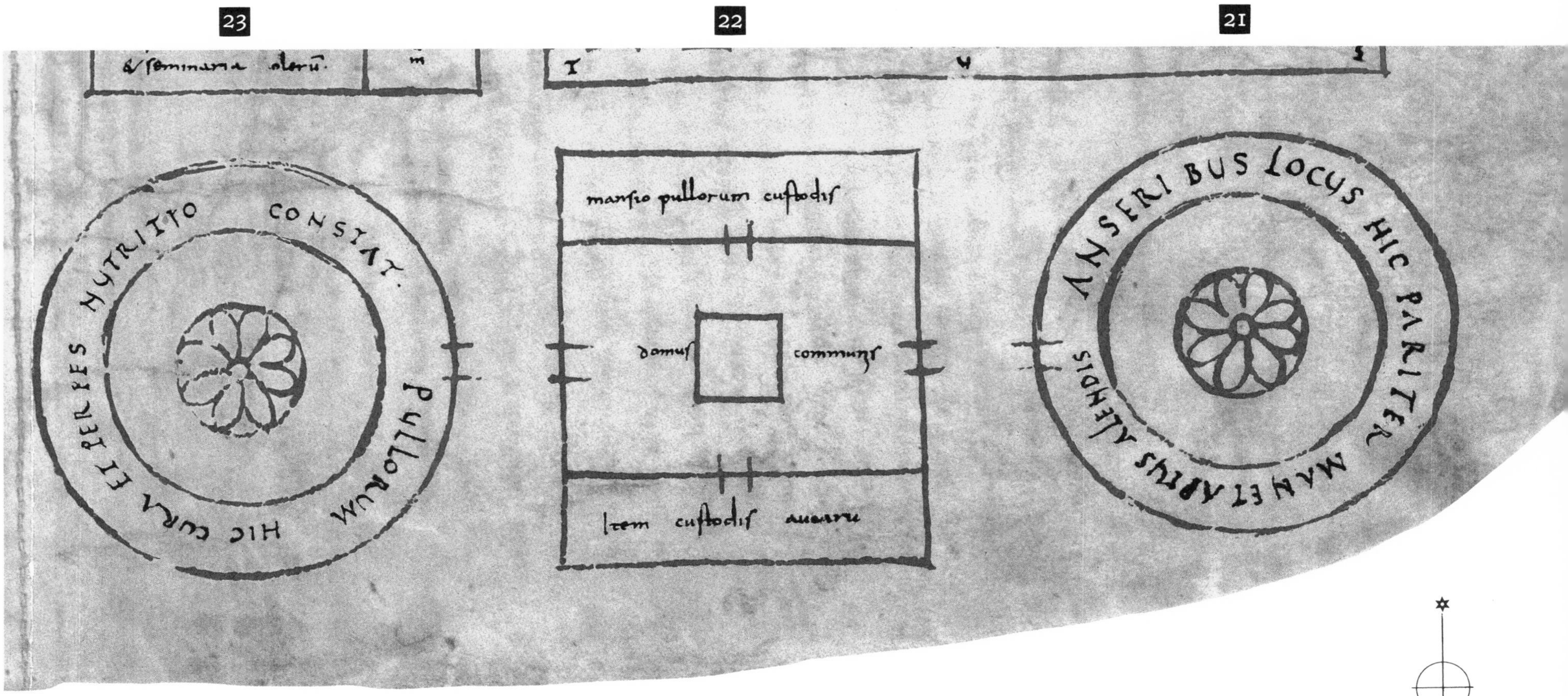

SITE PLAN

The proximity of the fowl runs to the Granary, Vegetable Garden, and Orchard shows with what degree of skill convenience and necessity were planned for by the makers of the Plan. Grain for feed could be gleaned or threshed at need in the Granary and carried to the fowl runs. Proximity to the gardens was a boon for both birds and their keepers—garden clippings might provide the chickens and geese with additional food, while in the beds and orchard manure from the pens could quickly be distributed, enhancing sanitation. In all facilities housing animals on the Plan of St. Gall, the herdsmen and keepers lived in close contact with beasts; while the fowlkeepers were spared the literal necessity of "going to bed with the chickens," their house is separated by only ten feet from the two poultry enclosures.

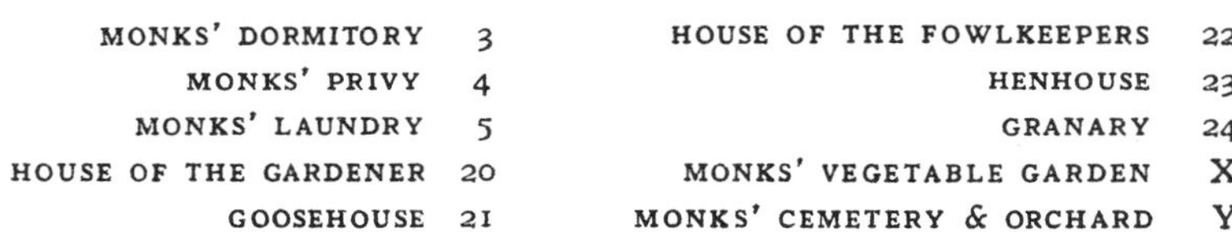

MONKS' DORMITORY	3	HOUSE OF THE FOWLKEEPERS	22
MONKS' PRIVY	4	HENHOUSE	23
MONKS' LAUNDRY	5	GRANARY	24
HOUSE OF THE GARDENER	20	MONKS' VEGETABLE GARDEN	X
GOOSEHOUSE	21	MONKS' CEMETERY & ORCHARD	Y

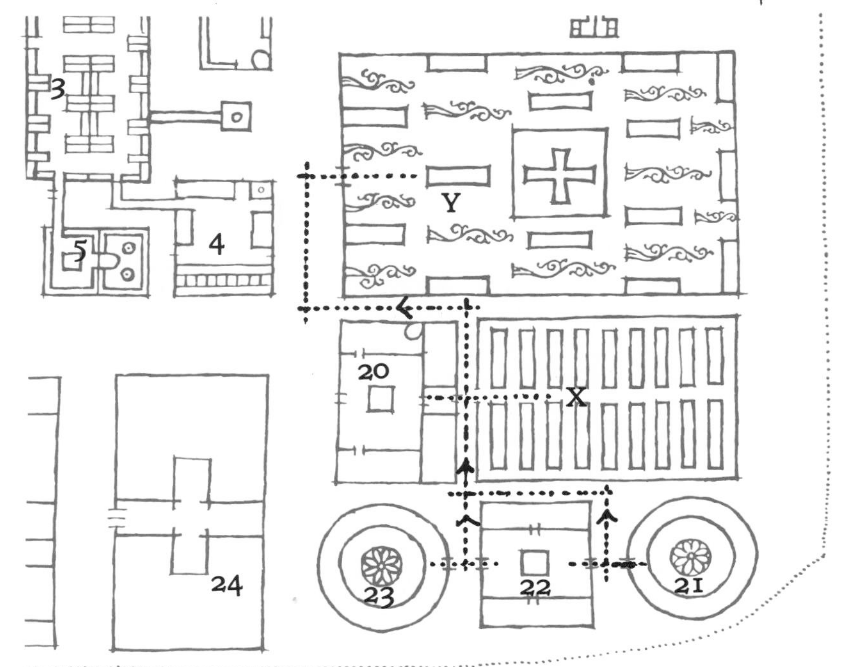

PLAN OF ST. GALL, HENHOUSE, HOUSE FOR FOWLKEEPERS, GOOSEHOUSE

The house for fowlkeepers is 35 feet in length (ridge axis E *to* W*) and 42½ feet wide. Its communal hall with fireplace measures 22½ × 35 feet, allowing two 10-foot aisles at either side for sleeping accommodation.*

The form that the pair of circular pens may have taken is discussed extensively on the following pages. Their sheer size, at a diameter of 42½ feet (across the outermost circle) is impressive evidence of the importance that poultry (perhaps including ducks) had in the monastic economy. A monastery population of the size postulated on the Plan of St. Gall would in itself have required many birds to augment diet; the guest facilities and lay dependents proposed for St. Gall made planning for fowl pens of this size a necessity. The poultry houses and that for their keepers are masterpieces of functional planning; they exhibit great charm in the symmetrical composition of circular with rectangular structures.

HENHOUSE & GOOSEHOUSE

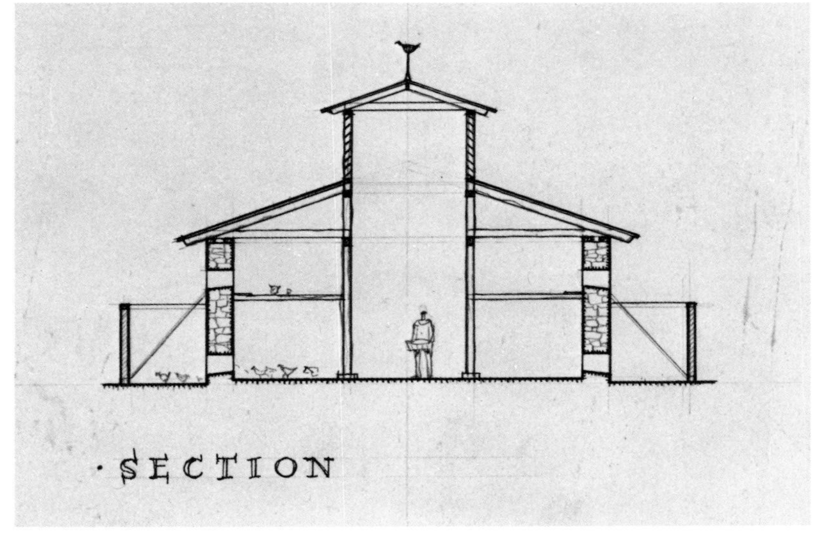

SECTION

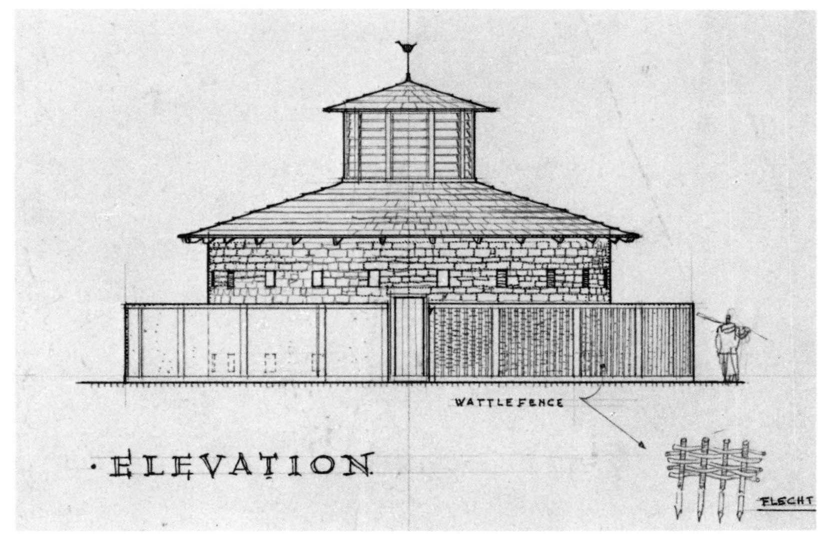

ELEVATION

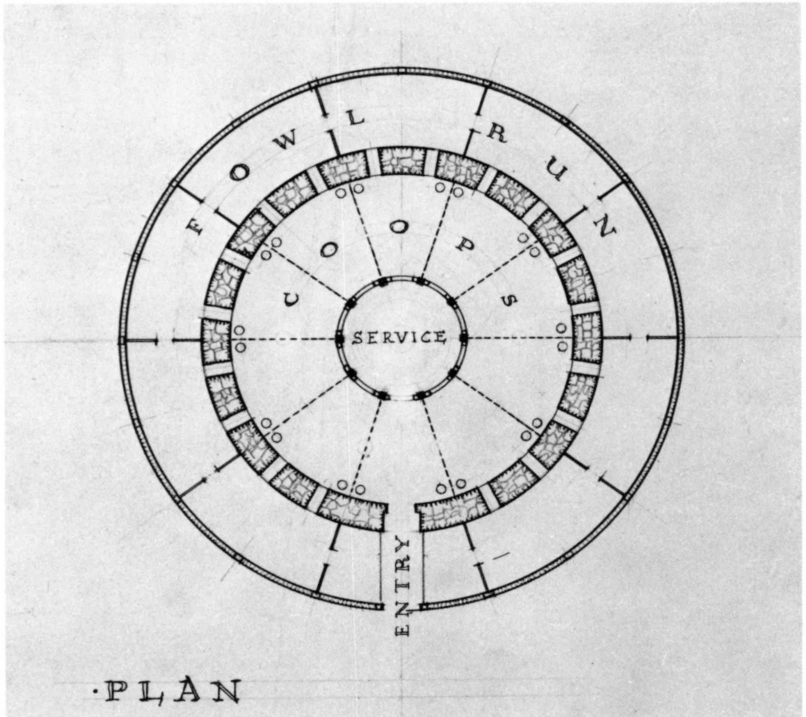

23

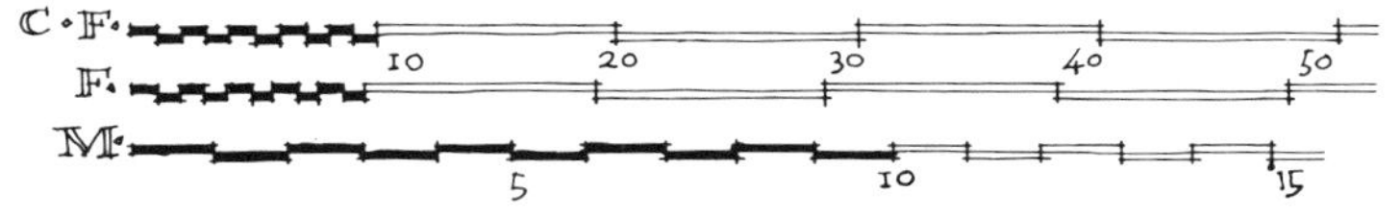

$\frac{1}{16}$ INCH = ONE FOOT
1:192

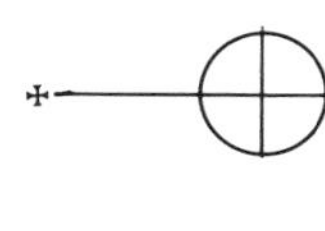

PLAN

PLAN OF ST. GALL. HEN HOUSE. Authors' reconstruction

The installation of the monastery's poultry in circular enclosures indicates that this kind of structure was not only in use at the time the Plan was made, but was sufficiently well known to be proposed as an exemplary solution for a monastic community of some 250–270 people. The enclosure provided for maximum flock size with greatest economy of space. With eggs a chief source of protein in the monks' diet, the more haphazard methods of raising poultry—i.e., letting birds run and nest at will all over the farmyard—were inappropriate; there was no time in so well-regulated a community to search each morning for the eggs of perhaps several hundreds of birds! Feeding, watering, sanitation, and doctoring were likewise attended to with ease through the architectural sophistication of circular fowl houses. A disadvantage of this type of enclosure is that it cannot readily be enlarged, and is thus most appropriate for a community of planned population.

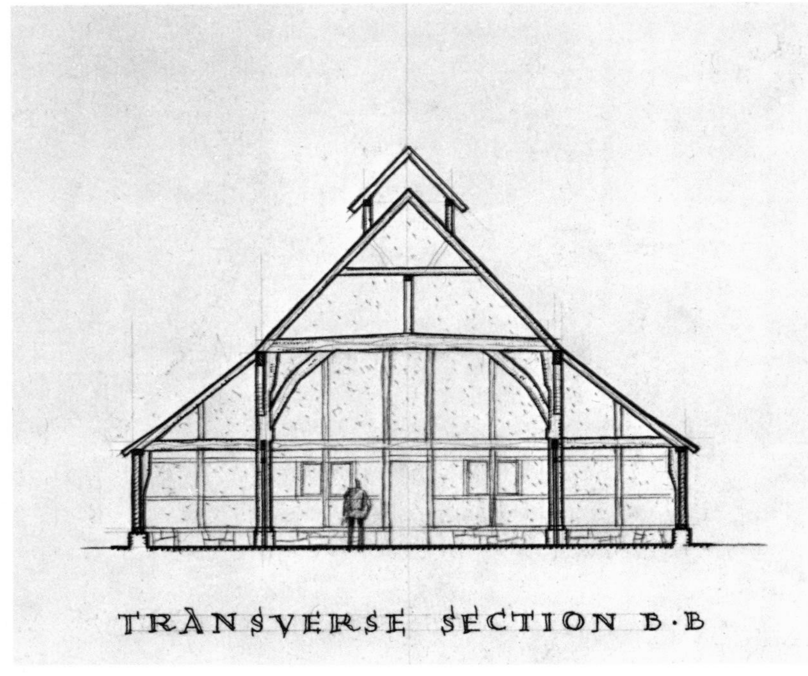

TRANSVERSE SECTION

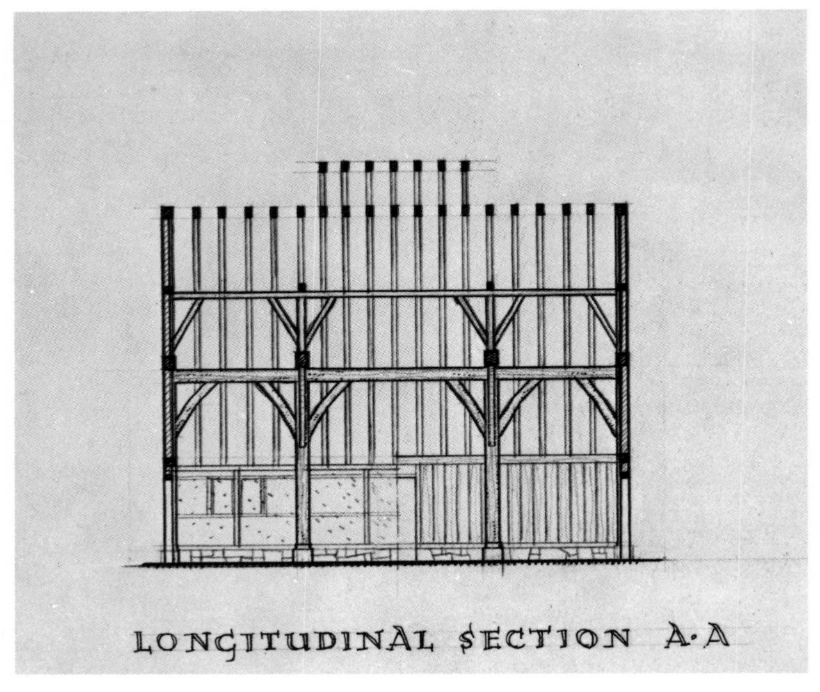

LONGITUDINAL SECTION

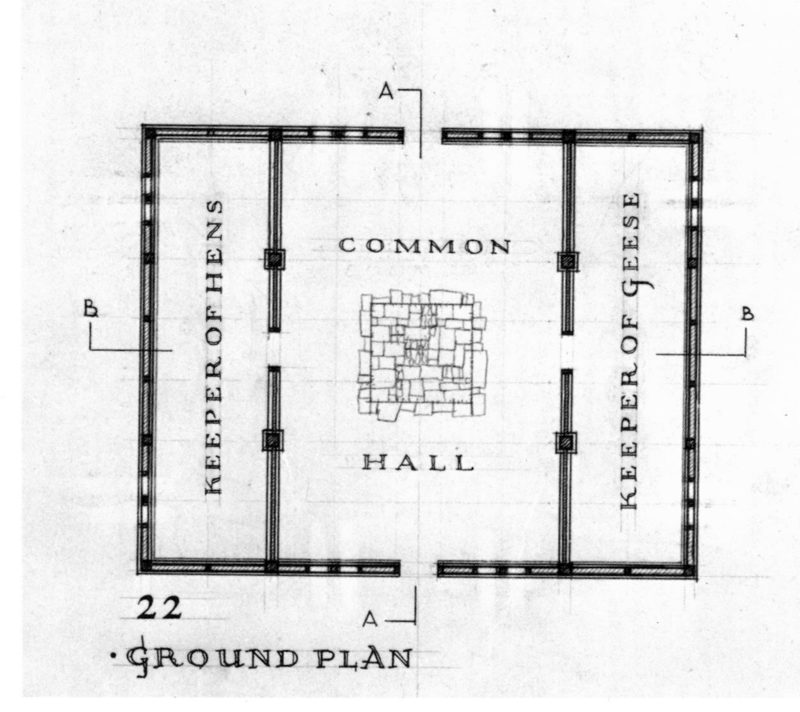

GROUND PLAN

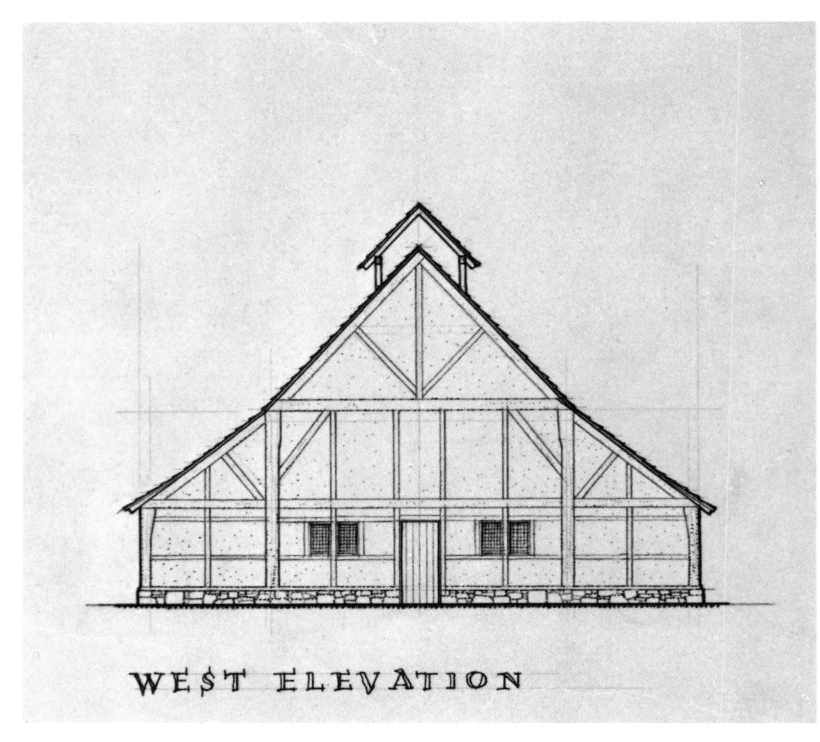

WEST ELEVATION

22

1:192

HOUSE OF THE FOWLKEEPERS

AUTHORS' RECONSTRUCTION

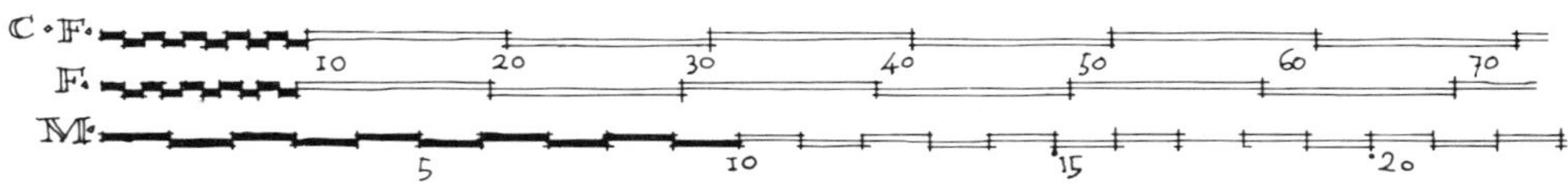

Among the guest and service buildings of the Plan, this house is the sole example in which the communal inner hall is flanked by aisles only on its two long sides. The hall is divided into three bays—a center bay 15 feet deep and two gable bays 10 feet deep. A division into four bays of equal width would have brought the center truss into conflict with the fireplace and doors leading from hall into aisles.

HOUSE FOR SHEEP & SHEPHERDS
STANDARD HOUSE & VARIANTS

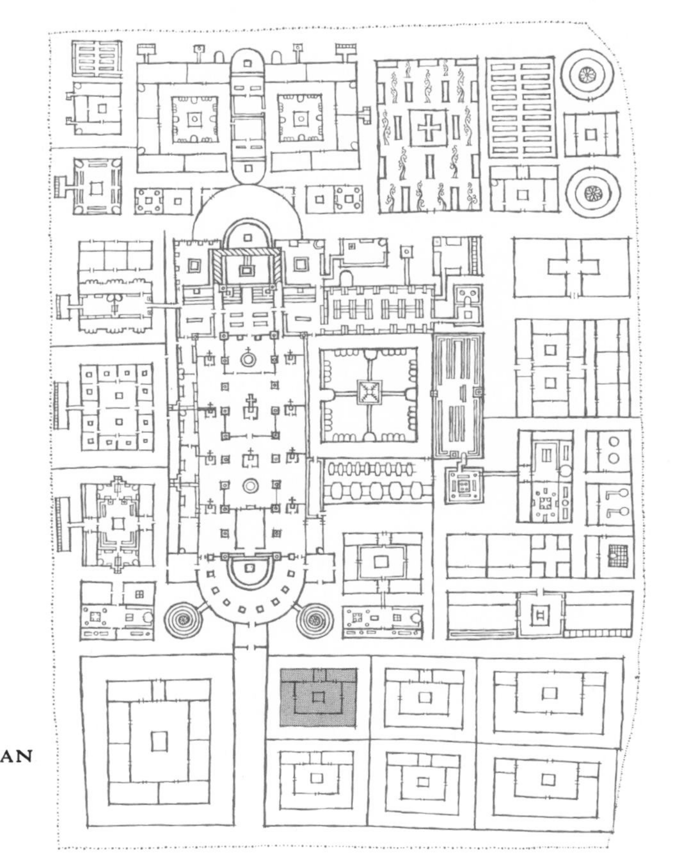

Site plan

ANIMAL HUSBANDRY WAS A PRIMARY OCCUPATION OF daily Benedictine life. Although serfs, guests, and the ill required meat, livestock by-products were more important to the community: cheese from milk of cows, sheep, goats; leather from tanned hides; animal skins for parchment; wool for clothing. Oxen and horses were raised for plowing, cartage, transportation, and in time of war, to mount armed men. The buildings in the northwest tract of the Plan housed livestock. Each had a central common living space with an open fireplace. Above it at the ridge of the roof a lantern allowed smoke to escape and admitted light. Peripheral spaces provided herdsmen's living quarters and animal stalls. The plan type is identical with that of the houses for distinguished guests, and pilgrims and paupers (pp. 42f, 48f). Earlier students of the Plan interpreted the large inner spaces of these buildings incorrectly as being open courts with living quarters ranged around them, as

continued on page 76

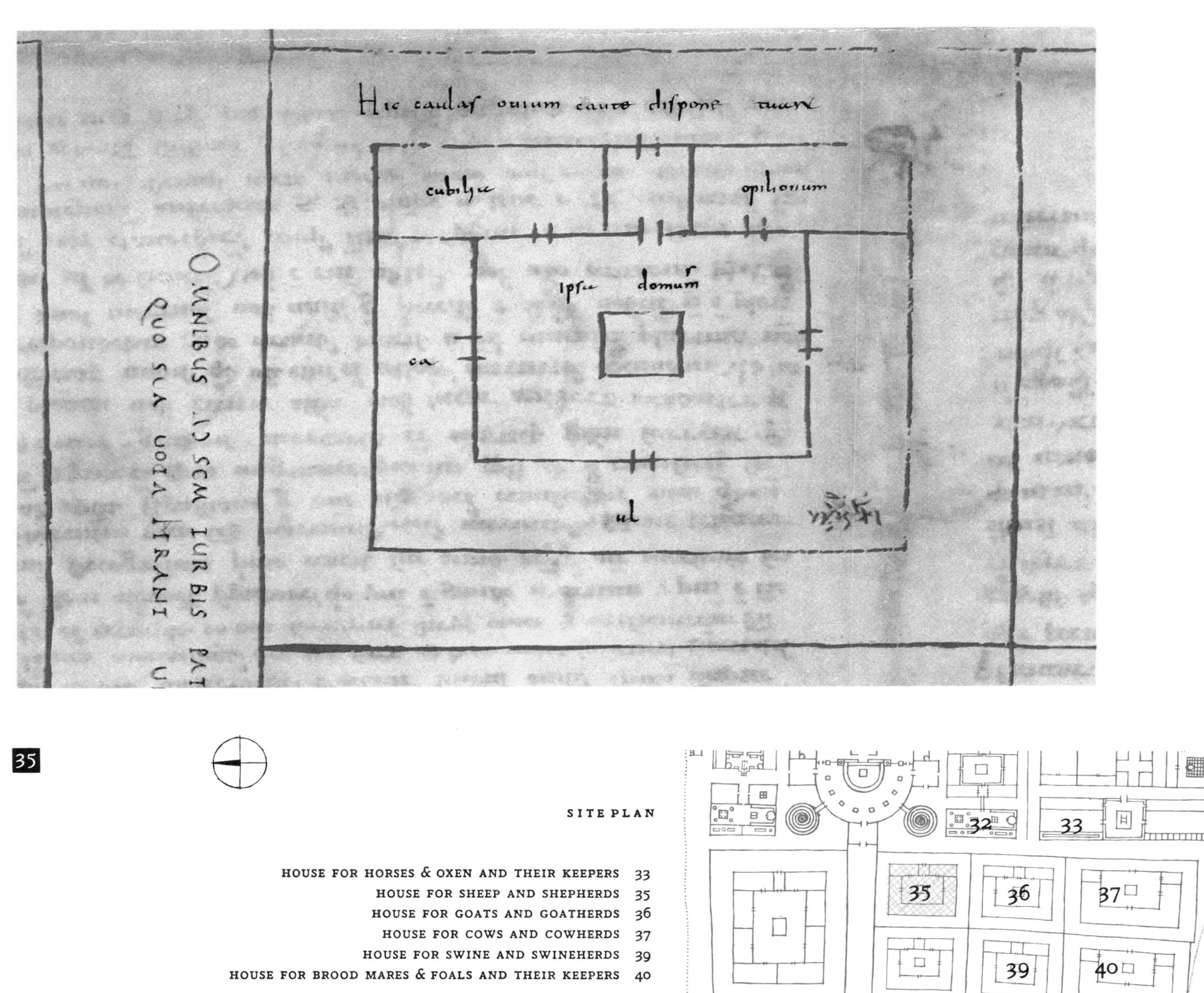

35

SITE PLAN

HOUSE FOR HORSES & OXEN AND THEIR KEEPERS 33
HOUSE FOR SHEEP AND SHEPHERDS 35
HOUSE FOR GOATS AND GOATHERDS 36
HOUSE FOR COWS AND COWHERDS 37
HOUSE FOR SWINE AND SWINEHERDS 39
HOUSE FOR BROOD MARES & FOALS AND THEIR KEEPERS 40

PLAN OF ST. GALL. HOUSE FOR SHEEP AND SHEPHERDS

continued from page 74

in the Roman atrium house. Careful analysis of inner and outer spaces later disclosed that these buildings are unrelated to Greco-Roman architecture. Rather, they descend from a house type common in Northern territories settled by Germanic peoples.

Such houses are found in numerous archaeological sites; some date to the Iron Age (3rd cent. B.C.). Like the houses of the Plan, they have multiple functions and were adaptable to human habitation, animal shelter, or storage. Their chief architectural feature was the large rectangular center space with hearth. All are ground floor plans with a single

continued on page 78

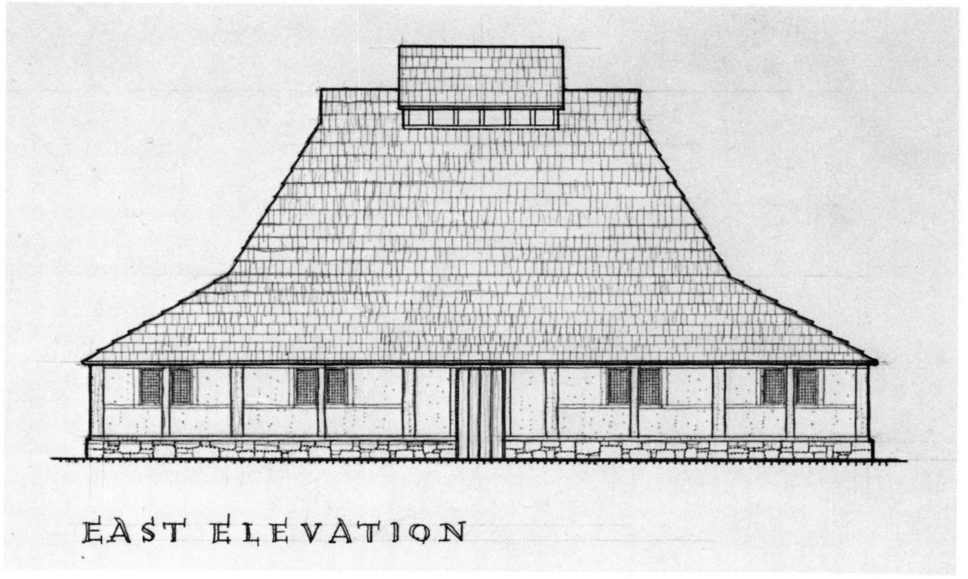

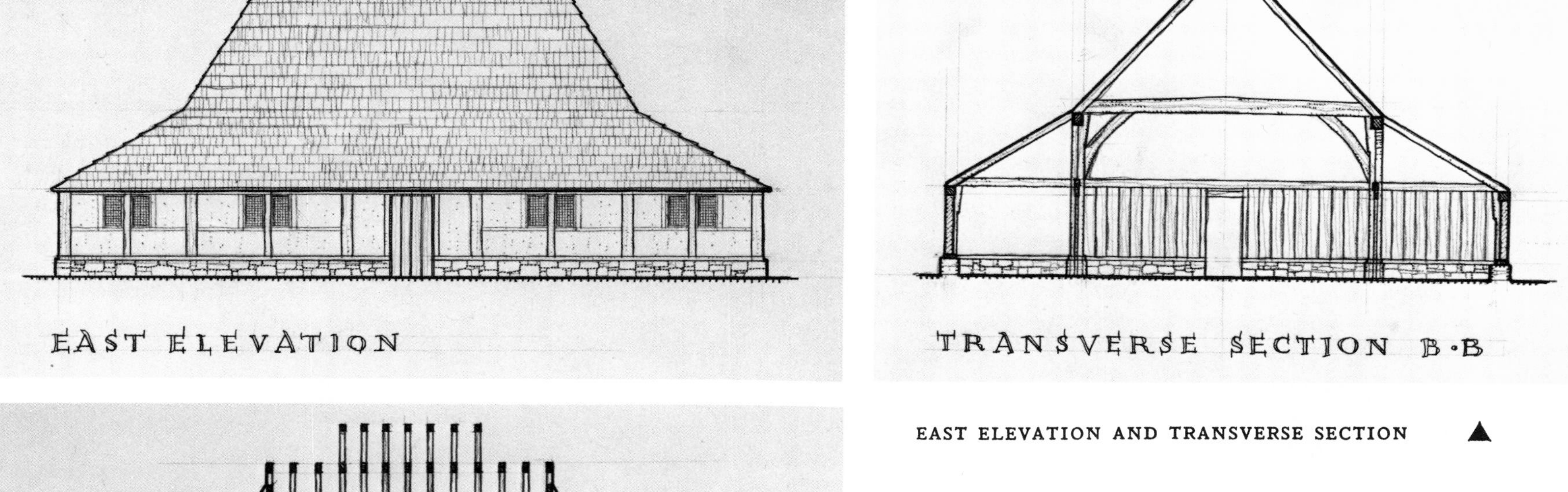

EAST ELEVATION AND TRANSVERSE SECTION ▲

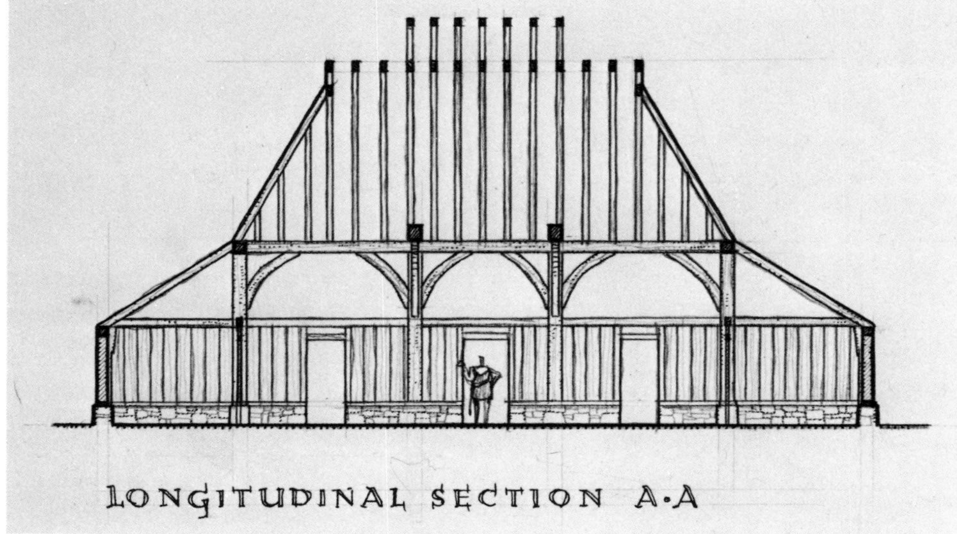

LONGITUDINAL SECTION

Archaeological evidence shows that the traditional building material for this type of house was timber for all its structural members, wattle and daub for the walls, and shingles or shakes for the roof. Criteria for reconstruction are identical with those that guided that of the House for Distinguished Guests (p. 45) and the Hospice for Pilgrims and Paupers (p. 50). Being smaller and of more modest purpose, there is no reason to assume that any part of this house was of masonry, beyond (as sound construction would suggest) a shallow stone plinth to protect the roof-supporting timbers from damp earth.

FOR GRAPHIC SCALE SEE PAGE 74

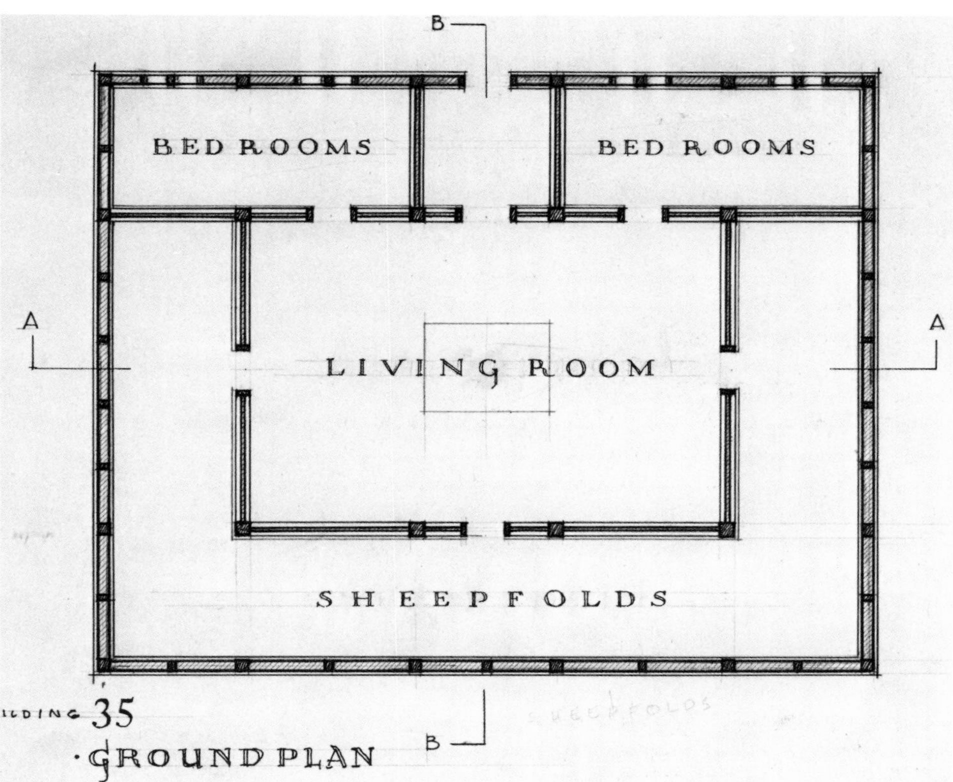

HOUSE FOR SHEEP AND SHEPHARDS. AUTHORS' INTERPRETATION

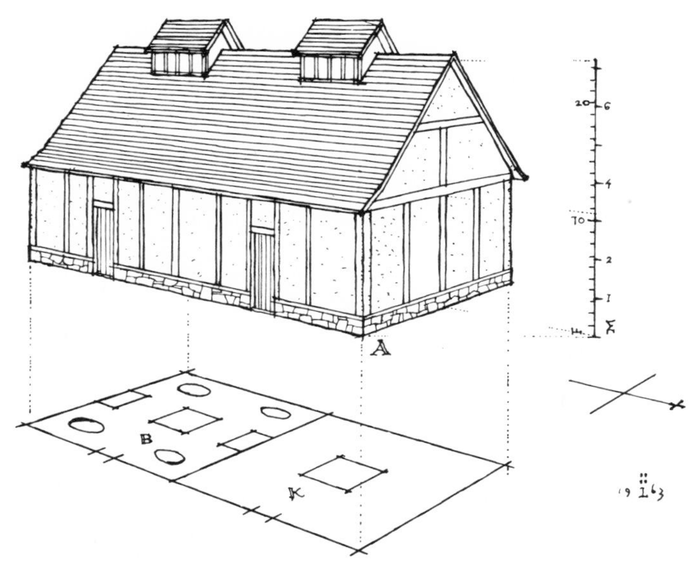

BATH AND KITCHEN FOR THE NOVITIATES

SCALE 1/16 INCH = 1 FOOT [1:192] ON VERTICAL EDGE A

PLAN OF ST. GALL

HOUSE WITH BASIC FORM: MAIN SPACE WITH NO PERIPHERAL SPACES

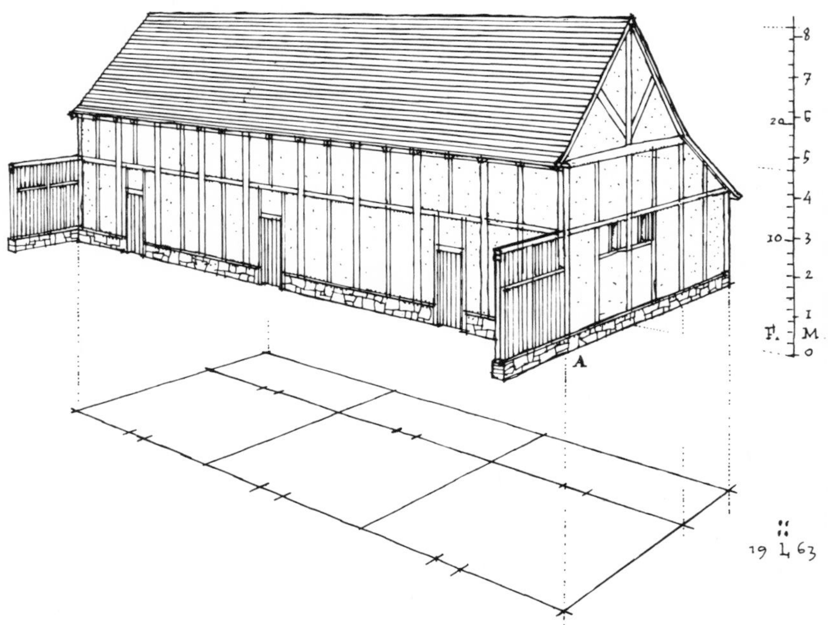

ANNEX TO THE GENERAL WORKSHOP; GOLDSMITHS, BLACKSMITHS AND FULLERS

PLAN OF ST. GALL. HOUSE VARIANT I

MAIN SPACE WITH AISLE ADDED TO ONE SIDE

THE STANDARD HOUSE. ITS BASIC FORM AND EXPANSION BY ADDITION OF LEAN-TO AISLES.

continued from page 76

broadside entrance, typical of Plan buildings occupied by animals with keepers. Excavations at the Ezinge site (p. 80) reveal remains of houses startlingly similar to the standard St Gall house in length-to-width proportion.

The basic house form of the Plan has no lean-to on any side. Additional space was gained by adding aisles (Variants 1, 2, 3A-3B), which also provided greater structural stability. Variant 4, the most advanced type, with aisles on 4 sides, represents the standard house of the Plan. Nine of its 37 buildings are of this type or an adaptation of it.* Elongation of this plan (by adding bays to extend one axis) into the Northern Germanic longhouse tended to occur in order to provide additional shelter exclusively for animals‡ (p. 81), or else to meet dwelling needs in a hierarchical society that recognized social differences between chieftains and persons of lesser rank.

The most significant construction feature of this house was the post-and-beam framework that divided the interior into nave and aisles, and carried the light timber frame of

continued on page 80

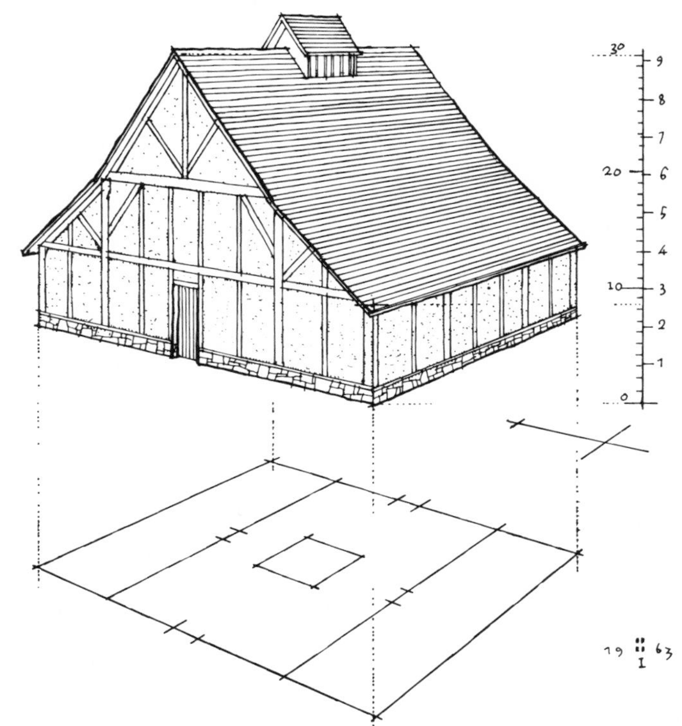

PLAN OF ST. GALL. HOUSE, VARIANT 2

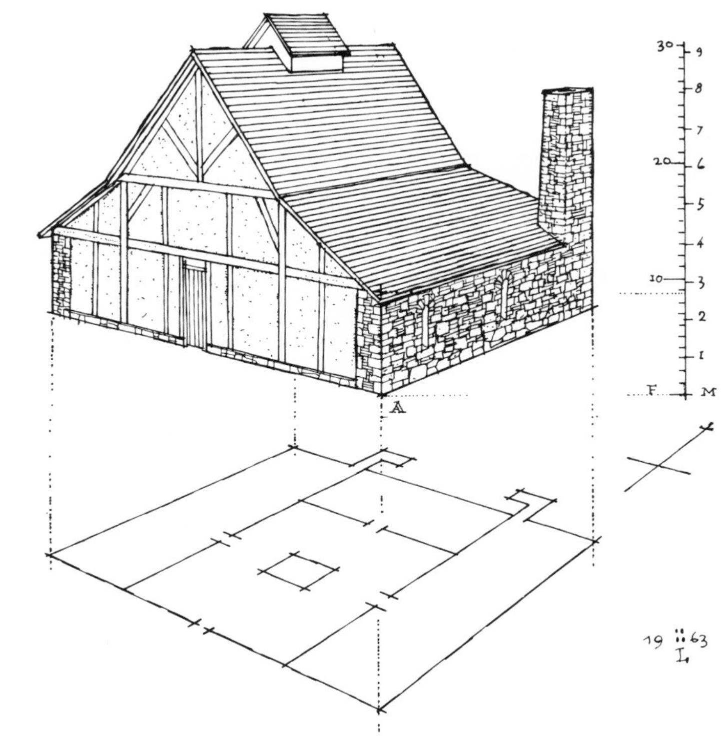

VARIANT 3A

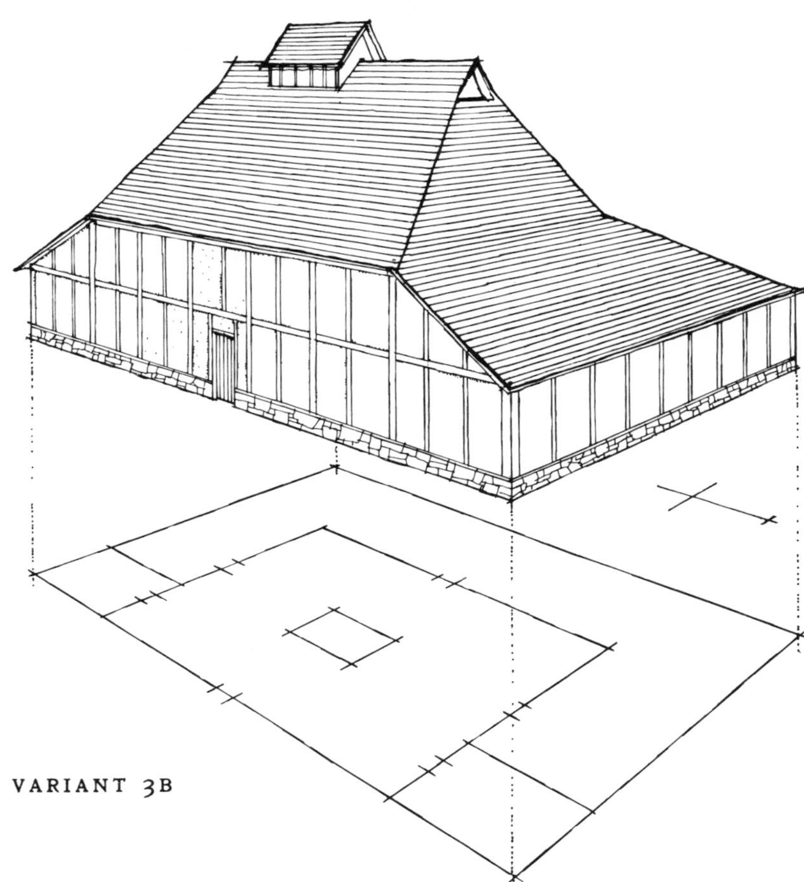
VARIANT 3B

HOUSE FOR BROODMARES, THEIR FOALS AND KEEPERS
HOUSE FOR COWS AND COWHERDS

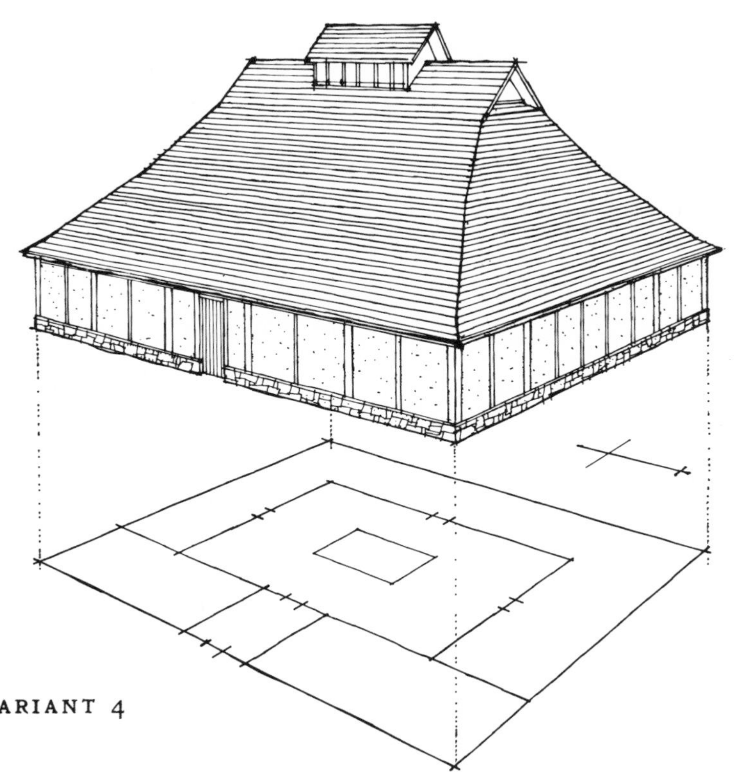
VARIANT 4

HOUSE (TYPE) FOR SHEEP & SHEPHERDS / COWS & COWHERDS /
SWINE & SWINEHERDS / SERVANTS OF EMPEROR OR NOBLES

* These include: outer school, house for distinguished guests (p. 47f), pilgrims and paupers (p. 50f), workshop for the abbey craftsmen (p. 55f), livestock buildings for mares, sheep, and swine, house for visiting servants (bldg. 38) and for the emperor's retinue (bldg. 34), the largest service building of the Plan.

‡ The house for horses and oxen (bldg. 33) is of longhouse form.

PREHISTORIC PROTOTYPES

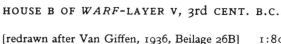

EZINGE (GRONINGEN), THE NETHERLANDS

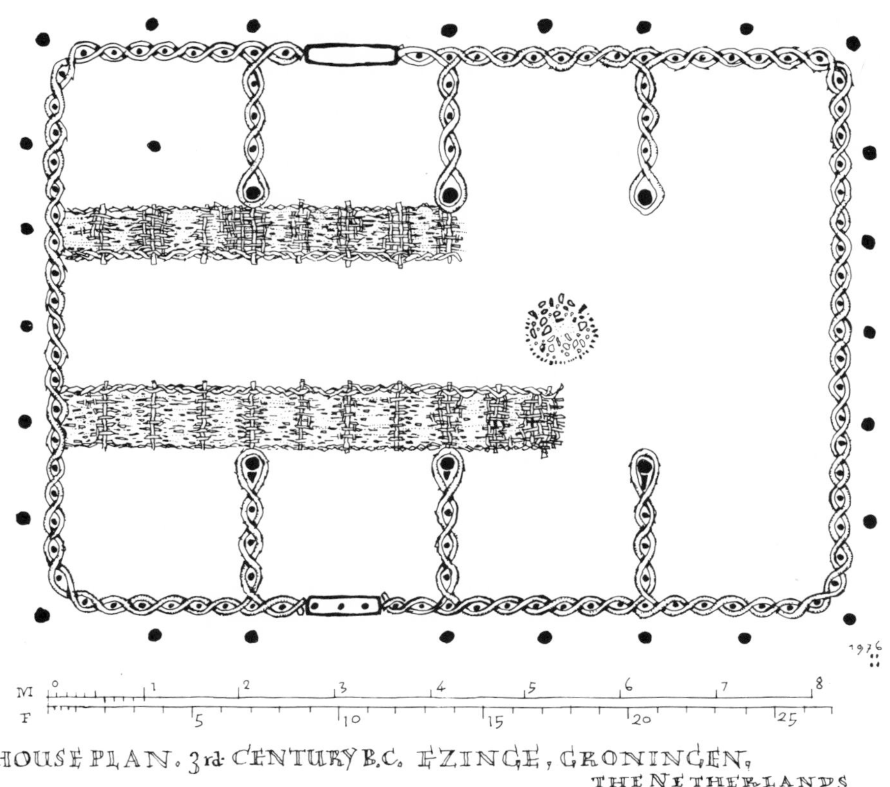

HOUSE PLAN. 3rd CENTURY B.C. EZINGE, GRONINGEN,
THE NETHERLANDS

HOUSE B OF *WARF*-LAYER V, 3rd CENT. B.C.

[redrawn after Van Giffen, 1936, Beilage 26B] 1:80

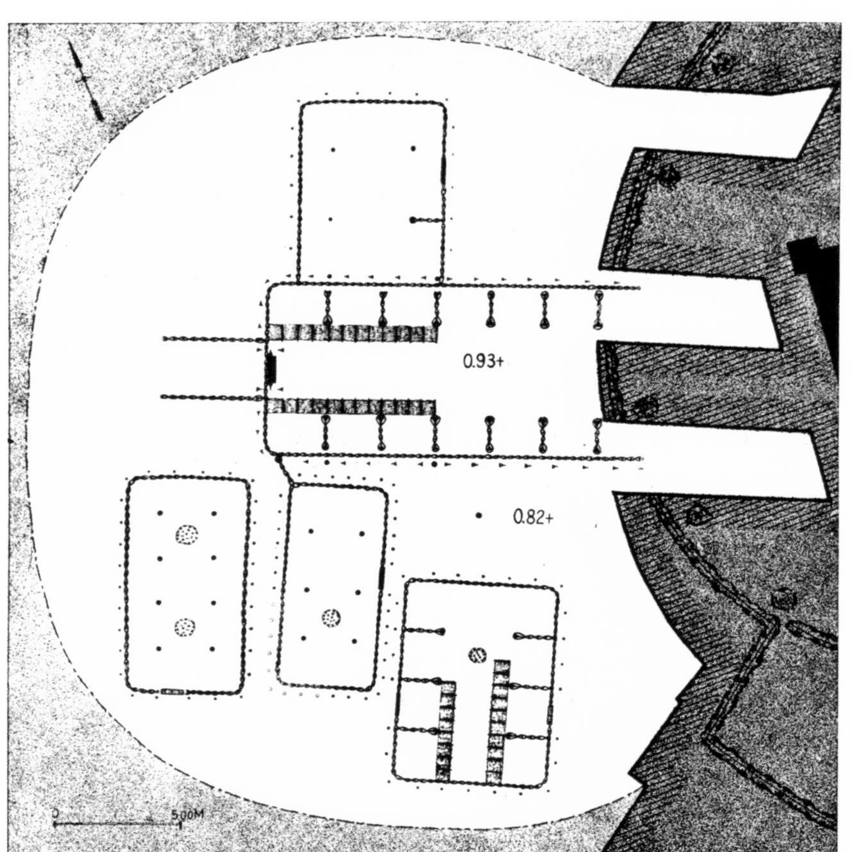

PLAN. CLUSTER SETTLEMENT, *Warf*-layer V, 4th–3rd cent. B.C.

[after Van Giffen, 1936, Beilage I, fig. 4]

continued from page 78

the roof. Nave and periphery posts carried a timber-framed roof system. In the Northern house persistence of its frame type and two later kinds of roof construction—one of rafters *(Sparrendach)*, the other of trusses with rafters, beams and purlins *(Pfettendach)*—reveals in its descendants (p. 83) an impression of the strength, versatility, and beauty of this ancient structural form.

Arranged in a rectangular gridlike plan, the timber posting of these early houses evoked a powerful geometry through its construction system of successive bays. This produced a rigorous modularity which, enduring 2000 years, emerged in the masonry construction of bay-divided churches of Romanesque and Gothic architecture. This preponderant modularity, prefigured in the church of the Plan of St Gall (pp. 12f, 22), when carried into the elevations by a pervasive system of bay-framing shafts and arches roofed by masonry vaults, attained a soaring aesthetic effectiveness.

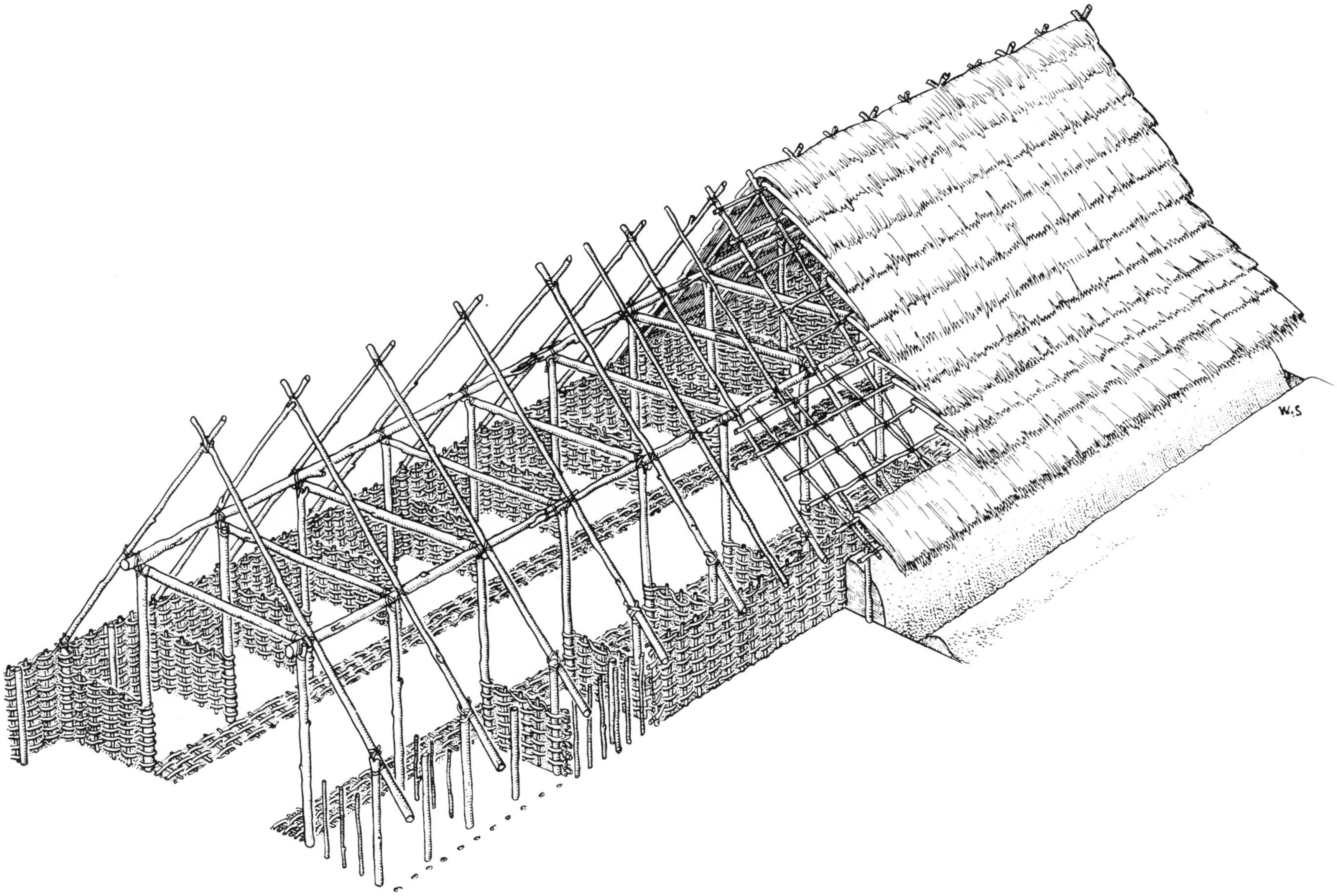

EZINGE (GRONINGEN), THE NETHERLANDS. CATTLE BARN OF *Warf*-LAYER IV, 2nd CENTURY B.C.

[author's reconstruction, drawn by Walter Schwarz]

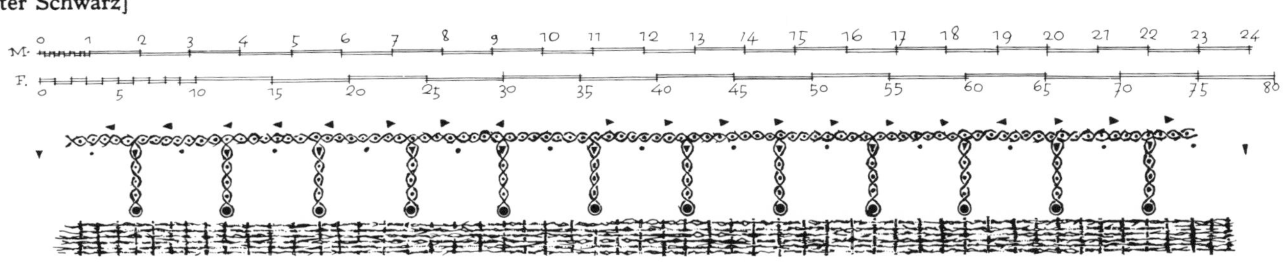

PLAN

REDRAWN FROM VAN GIFFEN

1:150

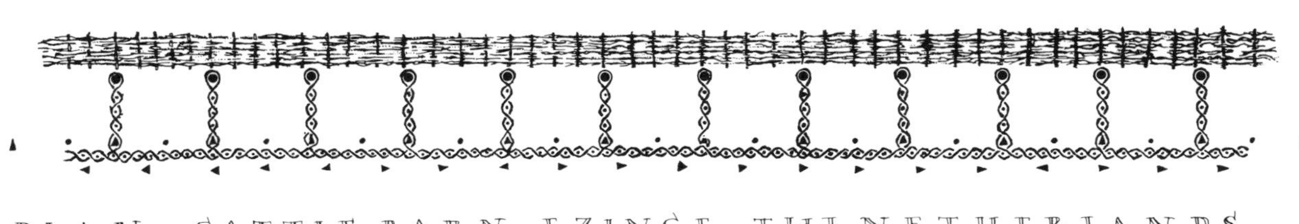

EZINGE (GRONINGEN), THE NETHERLANDS

INTERIOR, HOUSE B, CLUSTER SETTLEMENT, *Warf*-layer v, 4th-3rd centuries B.C.

[author's reconstruction drawn by Walter Schwarz]

House B of Warf-layer V played a dominant role in our attempt to identify the constructional features of the guest and service buildings of the Plan of St Gall. Like the majority of the latter, it is entered broadside through a long wall, and in layout consists of a spacious inner hall with open fireplace in the axis of the house, and a peripheral suite of outer spaces accessible only from the center floor and used for more specialized functions such as sleeping, or the stabling of livestock.

This is a reconstruction of the interior of House B, which appears at the bottom right of the plan of Warf-layer V. The drawing was made before the excavator realized that the animals stood with their heads not inward, but toward the outer walls of the dwelling. The braided wattle mats running along the posts on either side of the center aisle were found to be manure mats, not fodder mats as previously supposed. Since the artist is no longer alive, and since his handsome drawing portrays quite persuasively the general character of the space in the dwelling, we decided against trying to retouch the drawing; the animals remain incorrectly positioned.

GREAT COXWELL, BERKSHIRE, ENGLAND. BARN OF THE ABBEY GRANGE

In the northern stretches of the Whitehorse Vale rises the medieval barn of the abbey grange of Great Coxwell. William Morris, who lived at Kelmscott House within walking distance of this barn, loved it so passionately that he proclaimed it "the finest piece of architecture in England." In no other surviving structure of this kind are the basic architectural capabilities of wood so forcibly and convincingly expressed. Radiocarbon dating of its timbers indicates it was constructed in the mid-thirteenth century.*

From THE BARNS OF THE ABBEY OF BEAULIEU AT ITS GRANGES OF GREAT COXWELL AND BEAULIEU ST. LEONARD'S, *by Walter Horn and Ernest Born, University of California Press, 1965. Drawing reproduced with permission.*

* Rainer Berger, *Scientific Methods in Medieval Archeology,* pp. 108, 110, University of California Press 1970.

ENSUING EVENTS

TIME ALTERED PROFOUNDLY THE LIFE OF THE ABBEY & the town that through its influence had grown up around it over the centuries. Political change, fixed national boundaries, renewal of an urban society, and religious dissent eventually sundered the ancient ties between them. In 1475 the City of St Gall purchased independence from the abbey for 7000 guilders. This act terminated the feudal relationship; events leading to the Protestant Reformation of 1524 ended the religious one. Gozbert dedicated his church in 837 A.D. Later abbots added chapels, enlarged the choir; fires in 937, 1314, and 1418 claimed the church roof and portions of claustral buildings. Each time the Carolingian stonework was restored. So far as records and excavations can reveal, siting of the church, cloister, dormitory, refectory, outer school, abbot's house, and monks' cemetery largely followed the layout of the Plan of St Gall.

In 1712 Protestants sacked the monastery, damaging it badly. In 1719, 900 years after Gozbert first assessed its restoration, Father Gabriel Hecht began to study the site to develop a proposal for its complete refurbishment. In 1922 August Hardegger brilliantly analyzed Hecht's drawings of Gozbert's church, using a scale based on the Carolingian foot. He discovered that Gozbert had made drastic changes in transept and choir spaces, set his nave columns at intervals of 12 feet clear span, and built a church 200 feet long, in conformity with the Plan's direction to revise the design embodied in the drawing. To this structure Hecht had proposed adding a dome-surmounted pseudotransept, two rows of chapels, and a higher nave, retaining Gozbert's 12-foot column spacing—a scheme never implemented. In 1755 all extant monastic buildings were razed. The magnificent Baroque church that is the pride of modern St Gall now rises upon Gozbert's foundations. No stone of Carolingian origin stands today above ground level.

ST. GALL. VIEW OF THE CITY FROM THE WEST, IN 1545

HEINRICH VOGTHERR. WOOD ENGRAVING (29.6 × 42cm)

The rendering shows the town and its surroundings from an imagined perspective in the air. Not yet separated, abbey and town are enclosed by a common masonry wall elaborated by towers, houses, and two main gates. A glimpse of the Bodensee (Lake Constance) orients the view to the northeast.

Dominating the countryside are meadows cleared for bleaching linen, a local industry. The view is crowded with dwellings, farms and outbuildings, an inn, a fort, barracks and parade ground, an exercise and training yard. The main access road appears smooth and well paved approaching the city's crenellated gate; down the other, rougher road a carter gallops three span of horses hitched to a drey, laden perhaps with baled linen. A group of buildings amid trees (center, right) suggesting modest dwellings is situated outside the city walls. By mid-16th century, St. Gall clearly consisted of URBS and SUBURBS, a dichotomy that attested the arrival of modern times.

The four largest meadows are bisected by the Irabach; its water-course, now underground, formed a natural boundary between town and monastery in the early Middle Ages. Two mills locate the cascade of the Steinach; its course deflects sharply westward, broken by the escarpment of the monastery site. The abbey church lies slightly south of the east-west axis of this rise of land, its staggered roofs indicating various steps of construction. Similar views from different angles confirm the veracity of the rendering.

Photo: Courtesy of Zentralbibliothek, Zürich, Department of Prints and Drawings. Each of the two extant prints of this subject is somewhat damaged; this image is made from a photographic composite of them, in order to obtain the best possible reconstruction.

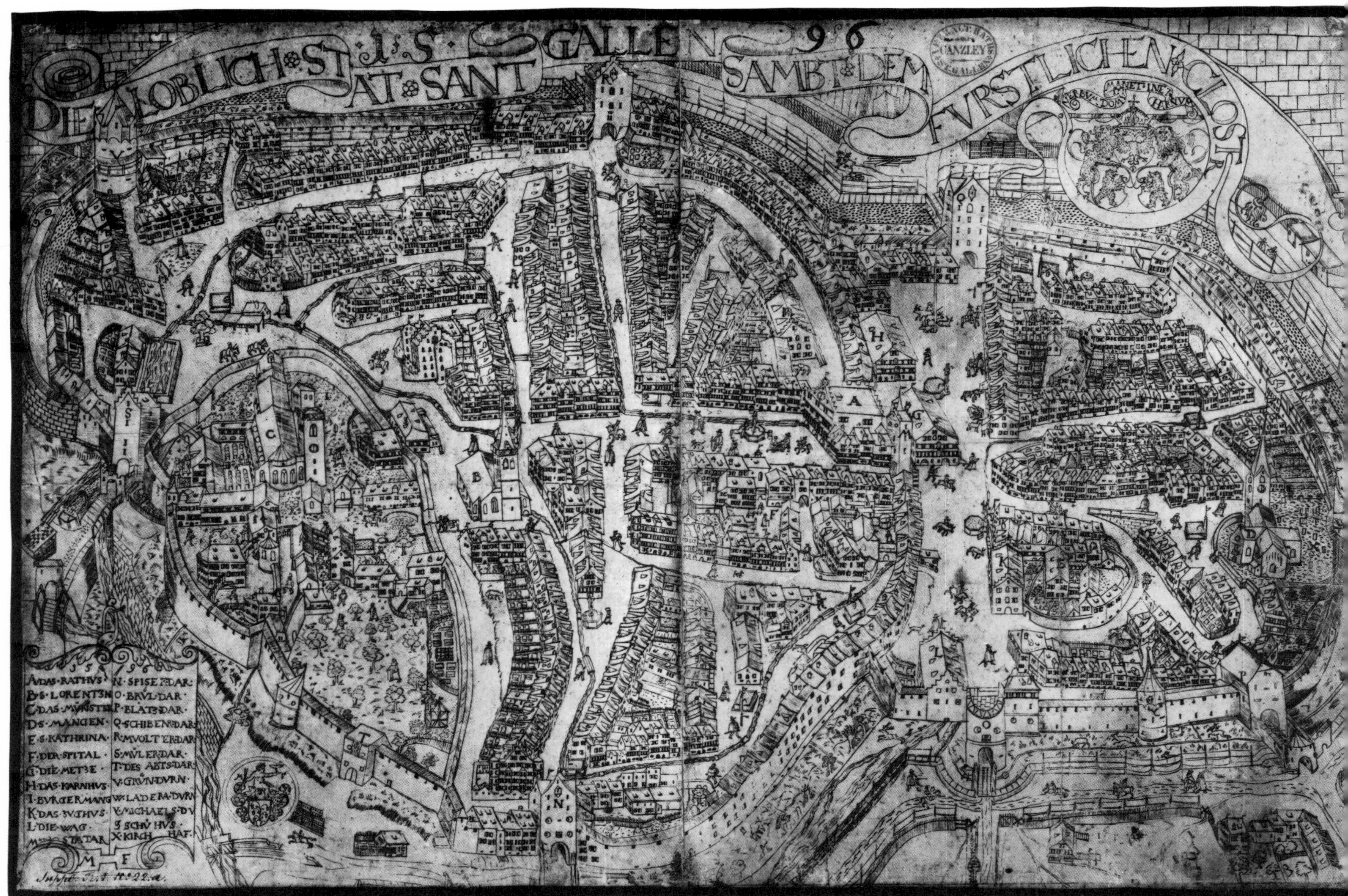

MELCHIOR FRANK.
1596 DIE LOBLICH * STAT * SANT GALLEN * SAMBT * DEM FURSTLICHEN * CLOSTR
ST. GALL. VIEW OF THE CITY FROM THE EAST. ETCHING ON IRON (40×61cm)
[Courtesy of the St. Gall Historical Museum]

The etching portrays with great precision the wedge-shaped boundaries of the elevated site (lower left quadrant) on which St. Gall founded his original cell. The site owed its distinctive shape to the courses of two converging streams, the Steinach, skirting the monastery to the south, and the Irabach, forming its northern boundary. The river escarpments not only sharply delineated the boundaries of the monastery site, but also afforded, at least initially, a good measure of natural protection. Even in Abbot Gozbert's day (816–836) the monastery appears to have been enclosed only by wattle fences.

The earliest settlement of serfs and tenants grew up on the north side of the monastery where the ground was level. Its dependence on the abbey is permanently engraved into the architecture of the city by the semicircular course of its streets, that even today hug the contours of the monastery grounds. Search for urban freedom strained the relationship of abbey and city throughout the entire Middle Ages and reached a first climax in 1475 when the city purchased its independence from the abbey at a cost of 7000 guilders. During the Reformation (commencing in 1524), abbot and monks were forced into exile but were allowed to return when the power of the citizens was temporarily weakened by warfare with Kapel.

Increasing conflicts culminated, in 1567, in the erection of a separation wall that segregated the territory of the city from that of the abbey, and thereby froze into permanency the confessional division brought about by the Reformation. Henceforward, city and abbey led their separate lives politically, culturally, and economically. In 1798 the abbey was divested of all its temporal possessions. Total supression came in 1805. In 1847 the church became the seat of a bishopric.

Melchior Frank's etching is a so-called Planprospekt, a perspective from the air based on measurements taken on the ground. The plate is lost; the only known print is held in the Historiches Museum, St. Gall.

Flugbild Photo Grosse, St. Gall

ST. GALL SITE OF THE FORMER MONASTERY WITH ITS PRESENT BUILDINGS

AIR VIEW FROM NORTHWEST LOOKING SOUTHEAST

The Carolingian church and virtually all other monastic buildings were completely rebuilt between 1755 and 1767/68, but the street pattern and alignment of houses clustering around the church even today reflect, with amazing accuracy, the boundaries of the original monastery site. The Baroque church is co-axial with the three preceding medieval churches and almost identical with them in width and overall length. Double-apsed like the church of the Plan of St. Gall, it is, like the latter, without façade. By contrast its towers, flanking the apse at the eastern end of the building, do not guard the western entrances to the church, but rather signal to the outside world the location of the high altar and the relics of St. Gall.

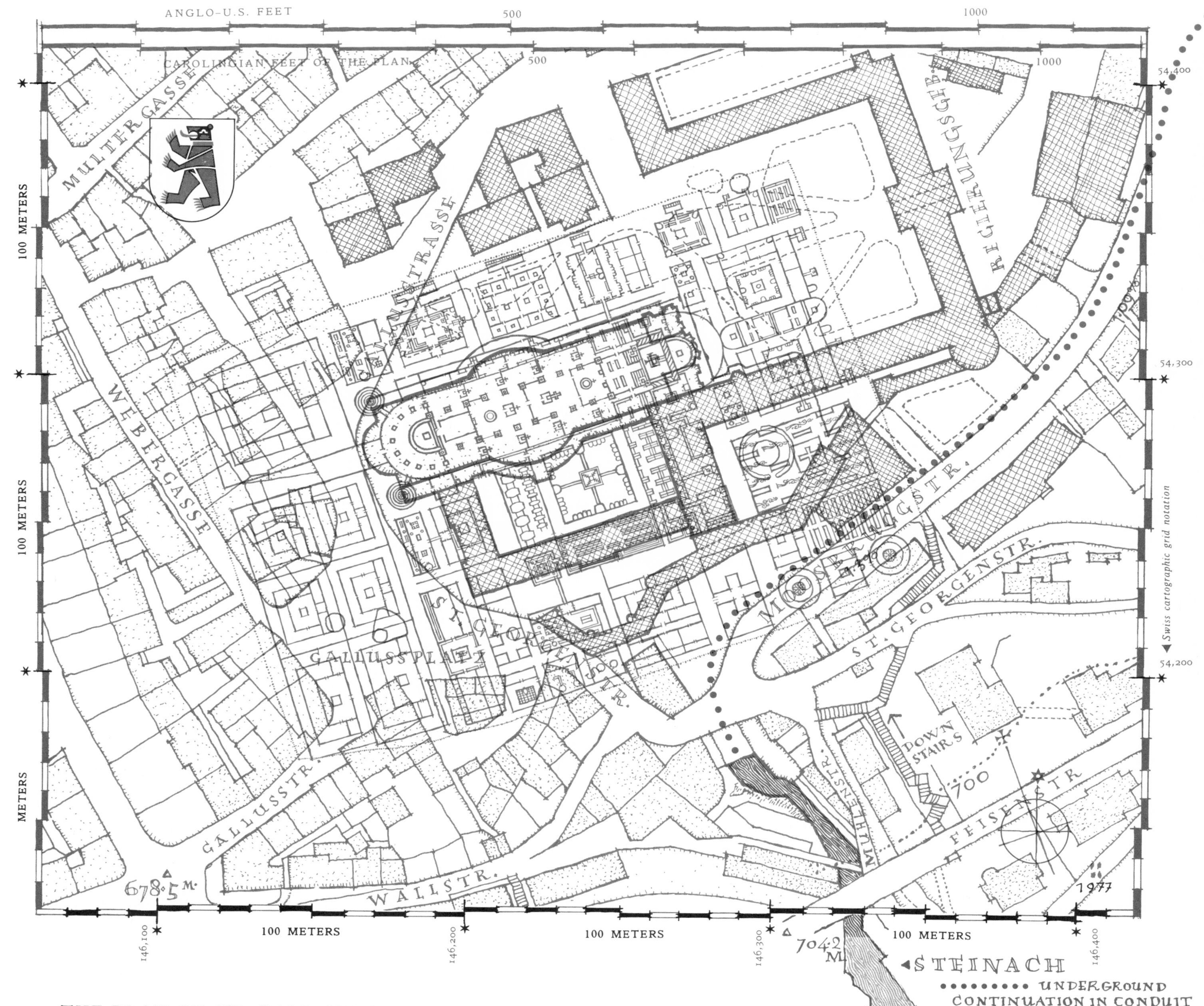

THE PLAN OF ST. GALL IMPOSED ON A CADASTRAL PLAN OF ST. GALL OF 1965

RED DRAWING, PLAN OF ST. GALL, SHOWN 1/8 ORIGINAL SIZE (1:1536) IMPOSED ON CADASTRAL PLAN AT SAME SCALE

Even a cursory glance at the shape of the site to which the monastery was confined discloses that it could not have been an easy task to attempt literally to superimpose the rectangular scheme of the Plan of St. Gall upon so irregular a plot. The superimposition emphazises the ideal character of the Plan and foreshadows adjustments that, in ensuing centuries, were to be made in many other places where the topography of a particular site prevented complete realization of the ideal monastery of the Plan.

In order to be built on this particular site, as foreseen on the Plan, the Great Collective Workshop, the Granary, the houses for fowl and their keepers, the Gardener's House, most of the Monks' Vegetable Garden, and even a corner of the cemetery, would have had to lie across the gorge of the Steinach, that at its lowest point lay some 50 feet lower than the monastery ground level.

This drawing also shows that the ground area of the Baroque church of St. Gall is congruent not only with that of the church as originally conceived on the Plan but also with the surface area the entire aggregate the medieval churches had attained after Otmar's church had been added to Gozbert's church.

A GENEALOGY OF THE EARLY CAROLINGIAN KINGS AND OF ADALHARD'S FAMILY

for caption see next page

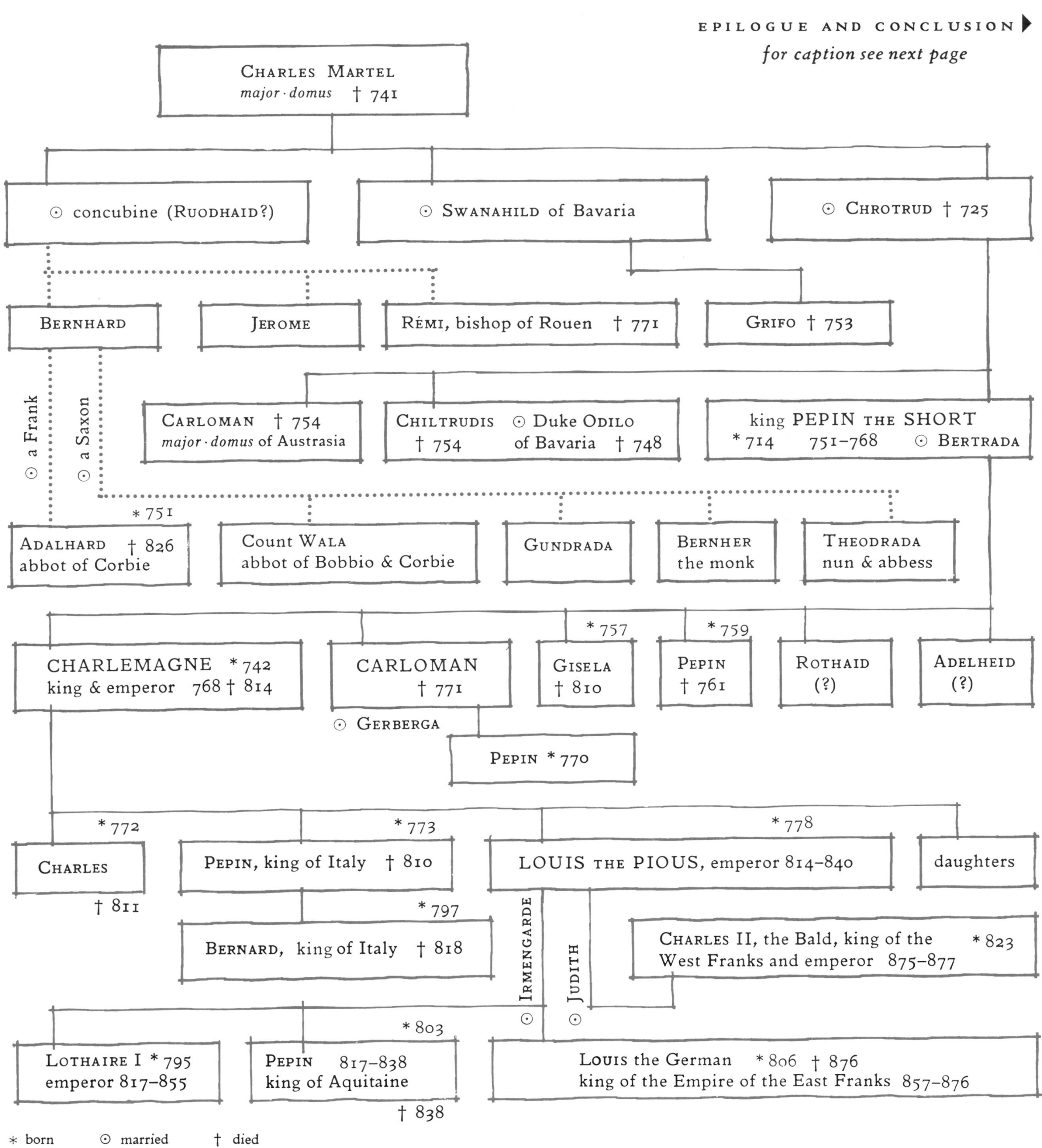

* born ⊙ married † died

ABCDEFG

THE CIVILIZING ACHIEVEMENTS OF THE CAROLINGIAN DYNASTY CANNOT OBSCURE THE FACT THAT ITS POWER RESTED ON PROWESS IN WAR: IT LOST THAT POWER WHEN IT CEASED TO BE CAPABLE OF ANSWERING VIOLENCE WITH VIOLENCE. ‡

◀ *See* GENEALOGY *page* 89

Dissolution of an imperial presence in the West did not arise solely from rivalries among father and sons. Louis' reign was complicated by the politics and influence of his two powerful cousins, the half-brothers Adalhard, Abbot of Corbie, and Wala, Abbot of Bobbio. These men, like his father Charlemagne, were grandsons of Charles Martel. First cousins Charlemagne and Adalhard, drawn closer by virtue of intellectual powers, worked together as king and councillor within a framework of kinship ties inseparable from Frankish polity. Adalhard was also regent for his young kinsman Bernhard of Italy, Charlemagne's grandson. Upon Charlemagne's death, Louis the Pious promptly banished Adalhard to the island of Noirmoutier, for unknown reasons; one may surmise the new emperor feared Adalhard's Italian followers, or reflected a dislike his own advisor, Benedict of Aniane, may have held for Adalhard, or had his own plans for disposition of the Italian territories. Bereft of Adalhard's protection Bernhard revolted, unsuccessfully. Louis ordered him blinded; he died of his wounds in 818. In the year 821, Benedict of Aniane also died. Loss of both friend and nephew caused Louis intense remorse. In 821 he summoned Adalhard from exile, then made public penance for his misdeeds, and for the rest of his reign was wholly influenced by the churchmen Adalhard and Wala.

BY THE GERMANIC MODE OF INHERITANCE & BY THE WHIM OF THE FATES IT HAPPENED THAT the power and authority of the line of Charles Martel resided for a time in a man of remarkable genius and charismatic presence. Charlemagne and his father before him were sole heirs; Louis the Pious the same. But Louis had 3 living sons. In 843 his quarreling heirs resolved what portion of the realm each would inherit, according to Frankish custom. The instrument of agreement, the Treaty of Verdun, dissipated Charlemagne's imperial legacy.

Charlemagne's political empire had existed in the loose coalition of his magnates, landholders independent of central authority and one another. Like their Benedictine counterparts they prospered through agrarian self-sufficiency. Whether for love of battle, self-interest, or loyalty, they consented to serve Charles who rewarded them with land which enabled them to support armed, mounted, stirruped, and provisioned soldiers for his frequent campaigns. This military feudalism sufficed to content the magnates. But ironically their autonomy and strength eventually shattered the empire that came to be fragmented among Charles's weak and willful descendants.

Charlemagne's 44-year reign and the dynasty's vigorous first 9 decades evince compelling accomplishment. While a model for social feudalism evolved in the realm, a freehold of intellect emerged in Charles's court;

‡ JEAN HUBERT
The Carolingian Renaissance, p. 4, 1970

CONCLUSION

HIKLMNO ✡

he provided a generous patronage and formidable intelligence. He made himself, his children, his administrators literate. He summoned Alcuin of York, a man of letters and gentle manners, to oversee educational programs. Backed by Charles, Alcuin enlisted royal abbeys in the quest for literacy, inducing them to establish schools to educate young nobles. By written statute Charles laid down a comprehensive body of civil law, reformed coinage, regulated measure, established systematic communication between his seat at Aachen and the borders of the realm. In a matrix of confused and shifting values he fostered an ambience of brilliant innovation. By providing the Benedictine Order land and protection Charles assured that monastic learning and technologies would enter common usage, however slowly. The dynasty vanished; stirrup, heavy iron plowshare, Caroline script, reverence for learning, the 3-field rotation system, remained.

No more than a modicum of these far-reaching programs had continuous effect. The empire was too broad, self-interest too prevalent, illiteracy and fear of change too endemic. After Charles a thousand years passed before any European nation possessed codified universal civil law. But in its brevity the Carolingian renaissance was a well of light between darknesses. It held a rich succession of ideals and events which, defying final evaluation, live on in Western life to stir imagination and spirit.

See TABLE I *next page* ▶

ORGANIZATION OF A BENEDICTINE MONASTERY IN CHARLEMAGNE'S TIME

Adalhard of Corbie assumed authority from a long line of abbots who enjoyed royal favor. Corbie had been founded on royal demesne between 657 and 661 by the English queen Balthilde, wife of Clovis II. Subsequent rulers including Charlemagne steadily enriched its holdings.

Located about 70 miles north of Paris, Corbie lay on the main road from Britain to Italy; it became a model of Carolingian culture. An important classical library was assembled; the 7th-century Maurdramnus Bible, called the first dated example of Carolingian minuscule, was copied there.

Like Adalhard, many of Corbie's residents were nobles. Experience of the world was needed to manage the abbey's extensive holdings, including 27 villas within a day's journey, and extending to Saxony, Alsace, and the Rhineland.

Adalhard's metier was administration; he drew up a set of directives to manage these wealthy and diverse holdings. His program focussed upon the cloister, the compound (equivalent to the community of the Plan of St Gall), the domain of 27 villas, and extensive, more distant feudal holdings.

Corbie, like St Gall, was an arm of theocracy. A complex interaction of secular and ecclesiastical offices reflected the vision of an ideal state, joined in the person of the king, in which each secular act had its religious counterpart.

✡ CALCULUS VICTORII AQUITANI MODEL ALPHABET (CA. 836)
Model alphabet included with a book on arithmetic. Employed chiefly for titling of manuscripts, these monumental capitals, descendants of letter forms used in Roman inscriptions, are executed with utmost precision in a style established in use during Charlemagne's reign.

BERNE, BURGERBIBLIOTHEK MS 250 fol. 11v *Redrawn and enlarged two times original.*

◄ see caption previous page

TOP ADMINISTRATION

ABBOT *ABBAS*

*

Head of monastery & lord of a vast web of memorial estates. Accountable to God for the physical & spiritual welfare of the community.

*

PROVOST (PRIOR) *PRAEPOSITUS*

First after the Abbot inside and outside the monastery enclosure
Head of the monastery in the Abbot's absence. Under his special jurisdiction: administration of outlying estates, all work in the fields, vineyards, buildings: all work and personnel involved in rearing of livestock.

*

SENIOR DEAN *DECANUS SENIOR*

*

In charge of spiritual conduct and monastic discipline.
Third in command of the monastery as a whole in the absence of Abbot and Provost.

*

SPIRITUAL SERVICES * * * * * * * EDUCATIONAL SERVICES

JUNIOR DEAN
DECANI JUNIORES
In charge of enforcement of monastic discipline through numerous roundsmen & seniors

SACRISTAN
CUSTOS ECCLESIAE
Custodian of church responsible for observance of liturgical timetable and care of liturgical equipment.

CHOIR MASTER
CANTOR
In charge of everything pertaining to chants.
PRAECENTOR‡
SUCCENTOR
CONCENTOR

HEAD of NOVITIATE
MAGISTER PULSANTIUM
Teacher in charge of training future monks.

HEAD of the OUTER SCHOOL
MAGISTER SCOLAE EXTERIORIS
Teacher in charge of training secular clergy & noblemen.

LIBRARIAN
BIBLIOTHECARIUS
In charge of all books, readings & writing.
WRITERS
ANTIQUARII
*
ILLUMINATORS
MINIATORES
*
CHARTER CUSTODIAN
CUSTOS CARTARUM

RECEPTION OF VISITORS * * * * * * * MEDICAL SERVICES

PORTER *PORTARIUS*
Receive, feed, & shelter all visitors, rich and poor, drawing for that purpose on one-tenth of all revenues from outlying estates.

MASTER of the PILGRIMS & PAUPERS
PROCURATOR PAUPUERUM

MASTER of the INFIRMARY
MAGISTER INFIRMORUM

PHYSICIANS
MEDICI

BLOOD LETTER
SANGUINATORES

*

MATERIAL SUSTENANCE

FIRST CELLARER
CELLARARIUS PRIMUS
In charge of everything pertaining to kitchen, food, drink. Supervises the work of cooks & appoints the weekly servers.

*

FIRST CHAMBERLAIN
CAMERARIUS PRIMUS
Responsible for clothing, bedding, furnishings, tools & equipment; in this capacity supervisor of all craftsmen and workmen in the monastic enclosure & workmen in villas tributary to the monastery.

JUNIOR CELLARER
CELLARARIUS JUNIOR
Assigns and issues the daily measure of wine or beer to monks.

KEEPER OF BREAD
CUSTOS PANIS
Responsible for storage of grain after delivery to monastery, for correct amount of bread to be baked & for all baking operations.

CELLARER of SERVANTS
CELLARARIUS FAMILIAE
Assigns & issues daily measure of wine or beer to all laymen residing in the monastery.

ABBOT'S CHAMBERLAIN
CAMERARIUS ABBAS
In charge of goldsmiths, silversmiths and blacksmiths, sword grinders, furbishers, saddlers, turners, parchment makers.

KEEPER of CLOTHES
VESTIARIUS
In charge of fullers, garment makers, shoe makers.

GARDENER
HORTOLANUS
ORCHARD KEEPER
CUSTOS POMORUM
In charge of vegetable garden operation and in charge of orchard operation.

✡

TABLE I

ADMINISTRATIVE AND EXECUTIVE ORGANIZATION OF A BENEDICTINE MONASTERY IN THE TIME OF CHARLEMAGNE AND LOUIS THE PIOUS

"The Abbot is believed to be the representative of Christ in the monastery and his order should be received as a divine command and not suffer any delay in execution." St. Benedict, who wrote these lines, was wary of the office of Provost, preferring instead to divide power among deans rather than centralize authority in a second in command, whose presence "might lead to rivalries and dissention." But the growing managerial complexities of the medieval monastery, with its vast web of outlying estates, and with serfs and workmen living within the monastic enclosure itself, made inevitable the existence of such an executive.

‡ Latin words lacking English equivalents are set in roman type, an exception to normal editorial style.

A SHORT LIST OF DATES

4 B.C. Birth of Christ
1st c. A.D. Apostles found the Christian community
2nd-3rd c. Roman persecution of Christians a state policy
250-76 Germanic tribes invade & pillage Roman Gaul
3rd c. Latin uncial script evolves
310-30 Sts Anthony, Macarios & Amun found eremetic settlements in Egypt
313 Edict of Milan makes Christianity a legal religion
325 Constantine convenes the Council of Nicaea to combat Arianism
350s Arian & Donatist heresies revive
361 Julian the Apostate re-adopts paganism
380 Theodosius reinstates Christianity & bans pagan worship
ca. 400 (?) Visigoths adopt Arianism
5th-6th c. Barbarians invade the West & sack Rome
432 St Patrick establishes Irish monasticism
476 End of Roman Empire in the West
*476 -†543 St Benedict of Nursia
486-751 Merovingian Dynasty in Gaul
496 Clovis, king of the Franks, converts to Christianity
520-60 Growth of Irish monastic schools
529 St Benedict founds Monte Cassino
ca. 550 Birth of St Gall
563 St Columba founds Iona
568 Lombards return Arianism to Italy
*570 -†632 Mohammed
6th-7th c. Technical advances in agriculture & crafts slowly enter Western usage (crop rotation, pooled labor, waterpower, iron plowshare); Irish monks develop Insular script
602 St Columban quarrels with Frankish bishops; leaves for Breganz
612 St Gall (†*ca.* 640) leaves Columban's mission & with 12 others founds a monastic settlement on the Steinach
639-732 Moslems conquer lands ringing the Mediterranean
664 Synod of Whitby adopts the Roman calendar
*673 -†735 The Venerable Bede
680 Pepin of Heristal is mayor of Frankish palace & sole ruler by 687
680-98 Irish manuscript illumination flourishes
714 Charles Martel is mayor of the Frankish palace
720 Otmar is abbot at St Gall
723 Boniface founds Benedicine settlements in Germanic territories
**ca.* 730 -†804 Alcuin of York
732 Martel defeats Moslems near Poitiers
741 Death of Charles Martel
742 Birth of Charlemagne
744 Synod of Estinnes establishes Benedictine Rule among Franks
747 Pepin the Younger is mayor of the Frankish palace
751 Pepin deposes Childeric III & is king of the Franks
751/2 Lombards capture Vienna & threaten Rome
754 Pope Stephen II annoints Pepin & sons Charlemagne and Carloman
Carolingian Dynasty Begins
769 Charlemagne crowned king of northern Franks & at Carloman's death (771) is sole ruler of all Franks
772-90 Charlemagne campaigns in Saxony, Pavia, Benevento, Bavaria, Istria
781-96 Alcuin heads palace school at Aachen
787-89 Charlemagne supports Alcuin's translation of the Vulgate, Roman liturgy, Gregorian chant, & establishes monastic & cathedral schools
791-806 Charlemagne campaigns against Avarii, Bohemians; converts Pannonia
800 Charlemagne crowned emperor in Rome
800-810 The Court School of manuscript illumination flourishes; the Book of Kells is written, possibly at Iona
801-12 Charlemagne campaigns in Spain, Dalmatia, Venetia
814 Death of Charlemagne
814-40 Reign of Louis the Pious
816-17 Synods of Aachen
816-36 Gozbert is abbot of St Gall
817 Louis arranges division of his realm among his three sons
830-31 Louis' sons revolt; he regains power
840 Death of Louis the Pious; his son Lothair (†855) inherits his office
End, Golden Age of the Carolingian Dynasty
843 Treaty of Verdun divides the empire in 3 "realms". Lothair receives middle realm
857-75 Norse raid Gaul annually
875-77 Reign of Charles the Bald (western realm)
881 Coronation of Charles the Fat, son of Louis the German (eastern realm)
888 Death of Charles the Fat: virtual end of the Carolingian Dynasty
Louis the Sluggard, last Caroline king of the western realm, dies childless in 987, marking the technical end of the Dynasty. Hugh Capet, founding the House of Capet (957-1328), succeeds him

ARCHITECTURAL MODELS

A NOTE: *by* Lorna Price and Ernest Born

SCALE MODELS HAVE LONG BEEN A TOOL OF THE ARTS, CRAFTS, AND PROFESSIONS IN which study and development of forms is aided by making small-scale three-dimensional renderings of proposed objects or structures. Accurate scale models can be put to a variety of uses, and may serve both theoretical and practical ends. Truss and bridge models not only provide a visual mode that is an adjunct to working drawings, but also, under special controlled laboratory conditions, can yield informative data relevant to the proposed structure at full scale. In certain technical applications, such as design of ships' hulls, scale models are indispensable. They have also been made since at least the Renaissance to help visualize paintings, sculpture, and architecture. A model may enable an architect to communicate an impression of how a building will eventually appear on its site to a client unversed in skills or ungifted in the ability to read drawings. Whatever the reason for making them, scale models can be an important step in the process that begins with formation of an intellectual concept, and logically ends in the execution of a three-dimenisonal object or structure at full scale.

Architectural models are primarily instruments of study. They reveal certain aspects of space, volume, and proportion in a proposed structure, as well as relationships between structures and groups of structures. But in employing a model as a device to visually evaluate the concept of a building, it is necessary to understand that as a means of visual communication, the model has distinct limitations. It is but one kind of idea-form, rising from abstraction, of an altogether different object or structure. Possessed of its own reality, the architect's model may serve to guide the imagination toward comprehension of essential principles that will attain reality only when embodied in a structure at full scale. The model is not an instrument of literal interpretation. Therefore is must never be regarded as the "small" form, or as a miniature, of what it represents. Although a virtually universal human fascination with miniature objects tends to beguile this recognition, a scale model remains a thing apart, with its own identity; a viewer will acquire a specific and unique visual relationship to it.

For example, an architectural model can readily be examined externally from many more perspectives than can a building already erected on its site. Only a few steps are required to walk all around it, or to look down on it; from across the room a building model can be seen unencumbered by the context of other buildings that will rise in the foreground, background, or alongside. Even if a scale model of a proposed building is presented in the context of a site model, the condition of relative scale, viewer to model, creates what is akin to theatrical illusion—an abstraction. But in the vastly enlarged theater of the structure at full scale, the physical relativity of viewer to object or building will have altered so radically that the earlier perception of the model may seem to bear no relationship to the structure it purported to represent. Thus, in practice, a model can be disastrously deceptive. But on the contrary, if studied with awareness of its use as a guide to the imagination and recognition of its limitations, a model may be a vital participant in discovering fine solutions to many architectural problems.

The word "model" may refer to drawings or a set of drawings of exemplary intent (or may even consist of a written memo) in which a proposed structure is depicted. In that sense, the Plan of St Gall is itself a model—a composition consisting of a scale drawing of ground plans for an ensemble of buildings, supported by numerous explanatory and informational inscriptions that concern the function of parts of the Plan. Therefore, to make an architectural model in order to give three-dimensional expression to the buildings of the model that is the Plan, is an appropriate as well as a rational exercise.

Representation of the buildings of the Plan of St Gall always involves a degree of conjecture or supposition. The red delineation hints at but few building features of elevation in a plane normal to the Plan, that is, in vertical section or elevation. From the drawing we know, for example, of the fenestration of the scriptorium and arcading of the cloister, while specific mention of second stories occurs in inscriptions that supplement the orthographic projection of the Plan.

Just over 100 years ago the sculptor Jules Leemann of Geneva built a scale model of the Plan's buildings based on drawings furnished him by Georg Lasius in 1876.* This model, which can be seen today at the museum of the Historical Society of St Gall, incorporates as part of an exercise in architectural history numerous details suggesting kinds of wall construction, roof types and coverings, and extending to interior furnishings (visible when the removable roofs are lifted). It also demonstrates the scholar's theory that the Plan's guest and service structures were predicated on classical, rather than vernacular prototypes.

In 1965 a model of the Plan's buildings was commissioned by the Council of Europe through its director, Prof. Wolfgang Braunfels, for display in Aachen as part of the exhibition "Charlemagne". Constructed at twice the scale of the Plan (1:96 or 1/8 inch = 1 foot = 12 inches), it was made by Siegfried Karschunke from more than forty reconstruction drawings by Ernest Born and Carl Bertil Lund, working in close collaboration with Walter Horn.‡ In it the Plan's guest and service buildings are

* We have been unable to determine the scale of this model.

‡ Generous support for these drawings was provided by the Office of the Chancellor, University of California, Berkeley, and the Committtee for Research.

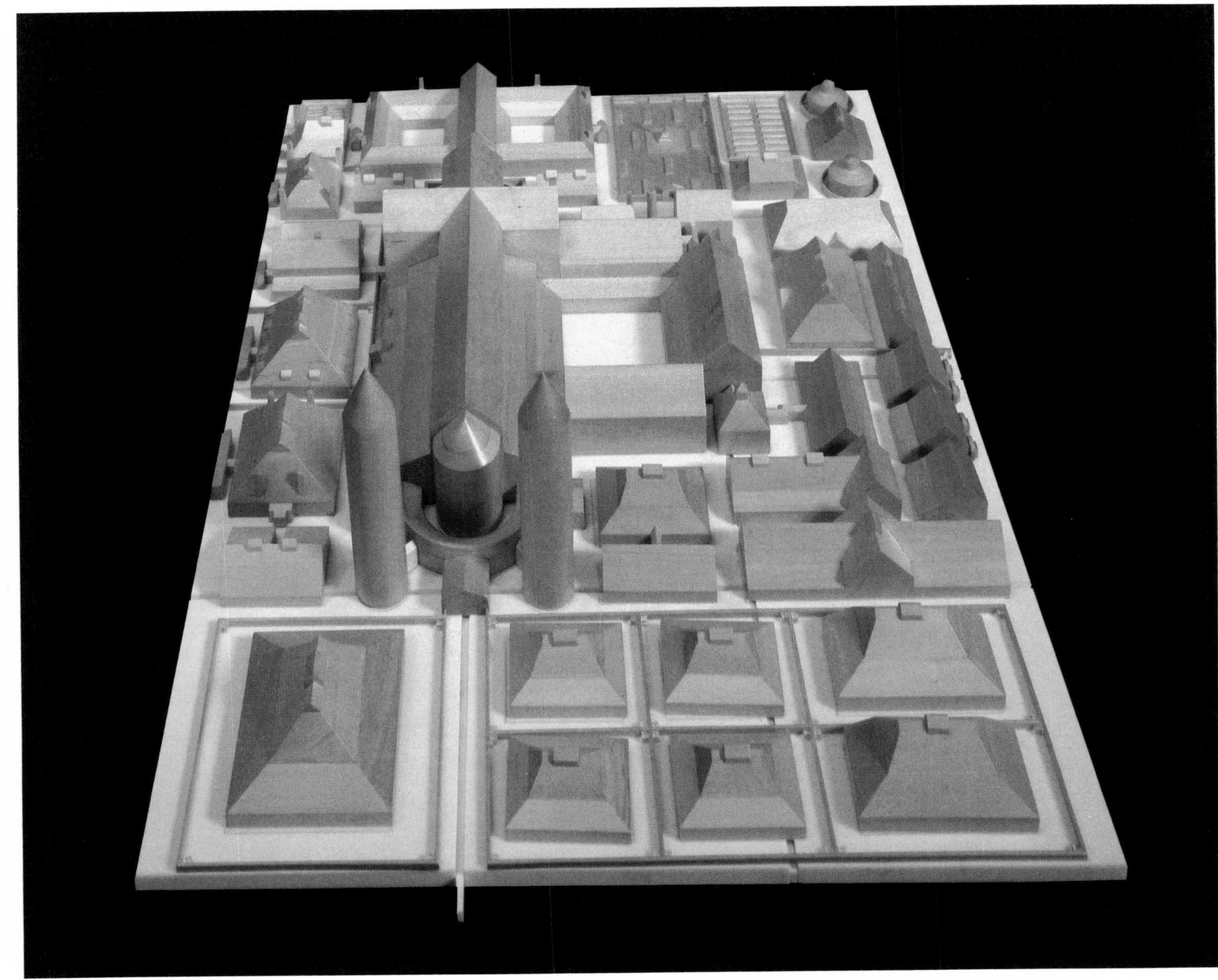

PLAN OF ST GALL: AIR VIEW WEST TO EAST

▲

The reconstruction model of the site aspires to portray with reasonable authenticity the monastic complex delineated on the Plan of St Gall. Buildings are composed on twelve white squares arranged in a pattern three squares wide and four long; each represents a module of 160′ x 160′, largest of the Plan's organizing spatial units (see p. 17). The divider strip protruding beyond the model base establishes the east-west axis of the church, a key reference line in the Plan's organization.*

Foreground buildings chiefly shelter livestock. Arrangement of service structures in the tract's western and southern periphery gives primary architectural emphasis to the imposing mass of the church and its dependencies.

constructed in the traditions of Northern vernacular architecture. The scale of this model permitted inclusion, in certain buildings, of proposals for timber framing and roof structure; even many details such as fenestration and masonry projections are rendered schematically.

In contrast, the model illustrated in these pages is conceptually of an entirely separate order, presenting a visual interpretation of the Plan's buildings differing radically in purpose and technique of execution from the two that preceded it. First, it is constructed to the same scale as the Plan of St Gall, 1:192 (1/16 inch = 1 foot). Second, it is an abstract creation without details of timbering, miniscule indications of wall surface, or scheme of fenestration. This model derives, as much as possible, from in-

* Color photography, pages 95-98 by Raymond Frayne, San Francisco

NORTH

WEST

EAST

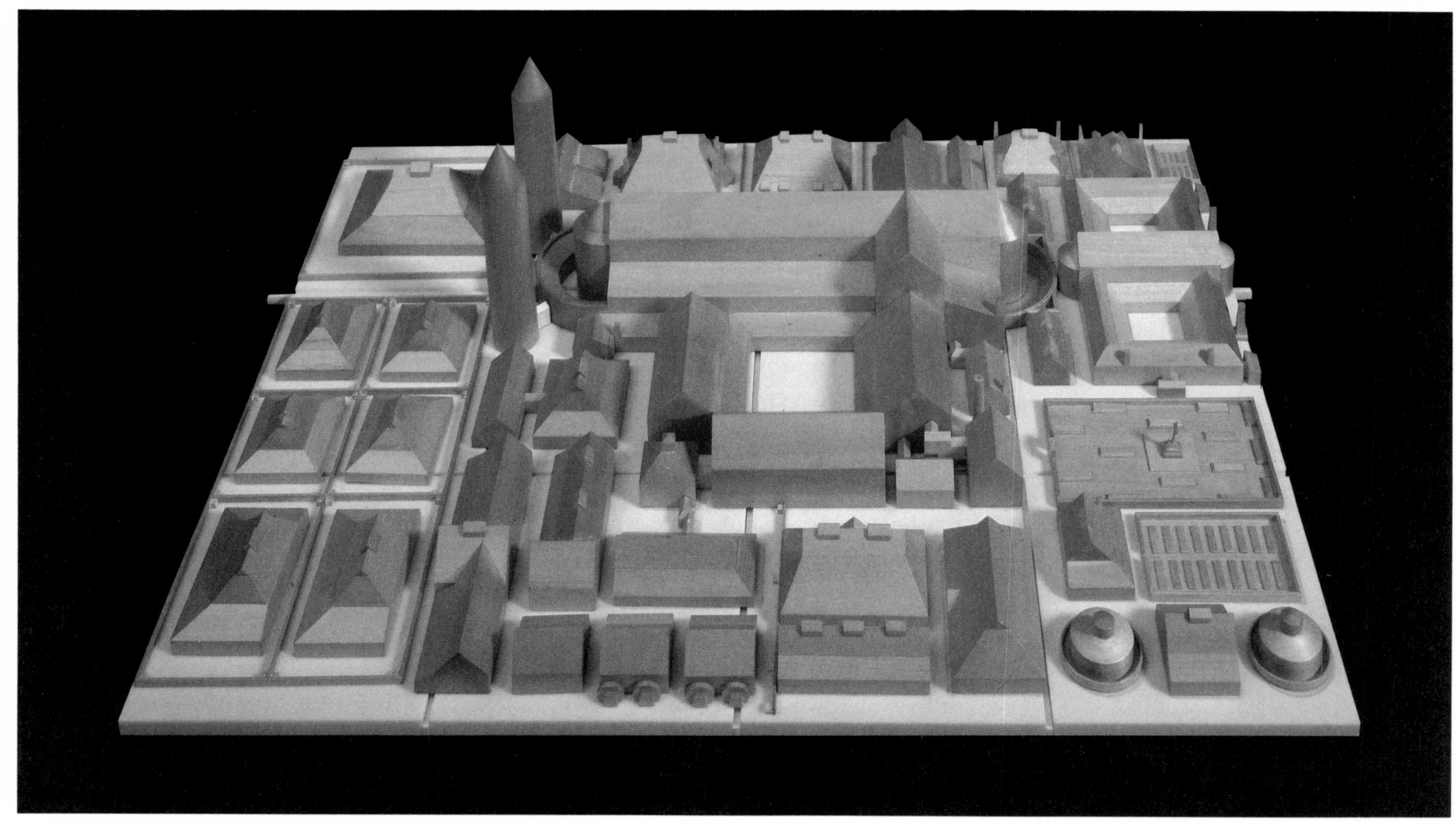

SOUTH

PLAN OF ST GALL: AIR VIEW SOUTH TO NORTH

▲

This view, in central position, vividly presents the required containment of claustral buildings and church within the architectural surround of the Plan's service buildings. Twin cloisters of novitiate and infirmary (upper right) flank a smaller church (over 100 feet long), axially aligned with the main church, that repeats the architectural theme of double apses. Lower right are poultry houses (circular) to the east and west of the keeper's house.
Three smaller square buildings (foreground, center left) house grain processing for flour and brewing. Immediately behind them are the brewer's granary and the monks' bake and brewhouse. Careful planning for proximity of preparation and usage is evident throughout the entire layout of the Plan.

formation contained within the red delineation of the ground plan drawings and scholarly examination and interpretation of the Plan's explanatory legends. Abstraction execution of the model in block form reduces to a minimum conjecture and subjective inventiveness in projecting a two-dimensional delineation, such as the Plan of St Gall, into a three-dimensional interpretation. Third, the model also preserves an essential visual characteristic of the drawing. By adhering to the scale of the Plan, it retains and reflects the same sense of scale that existed between the drafter of the Plan and his creation. Hence it is possible to see the entire visual ensemble of the Plan's buildings from any perspective—a visual and conceptual quality sacrificed in models of large scale. In effect, the abstract model can be viewed in the same visual mode

SOUTH

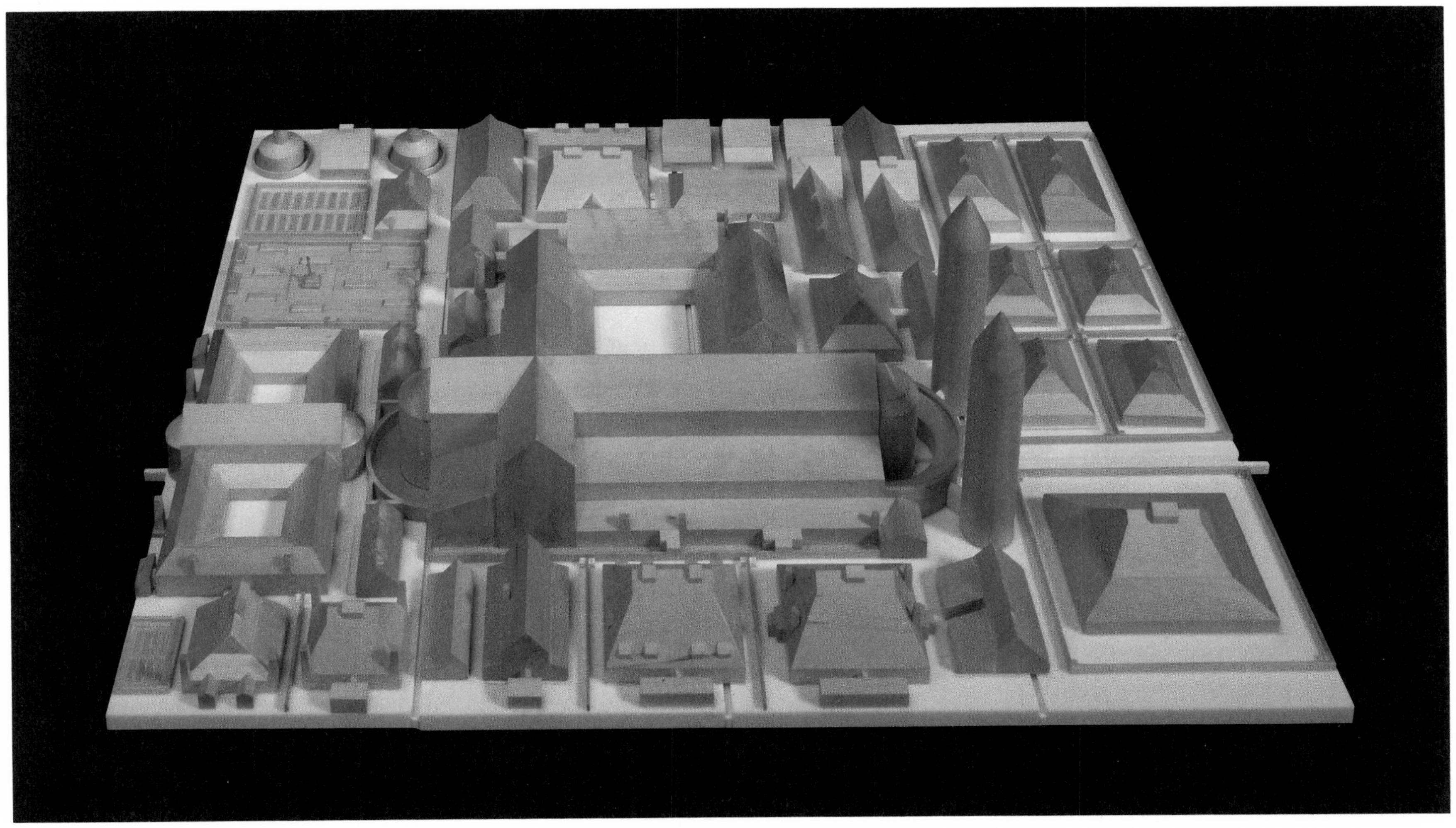

EAST

WEST

NORTH

PLAN OF ST GALL: AIR VIEW NORTH TO SOUTH

▲

The monastic community, charged to care for the ill, educate the young, and shelter travelers, did so in facilities ranged along the north edge of the monastery site. Infirmary cloister, physicians' house, house for bloodletting lay east (left) of the abbot's house; west of it (right) are the outer school and house for distinguished guests with its kitchen, bake and brewhouse.
Lower right is the house for the emperor's following; after the church, this is the largest structure in the monastery complex.
Segregation of monastic life from worldly and necessary activities that supported it is a striking accomplishment of the planner's genius in reconciling the monastery's spiritual goals within an architecturally diverse, yet coherent community.

as the Plan itself. Unaugmented by minutiae of surface enrichment or detail, this model seeks to provide a powerful substantiation of the drawing from which it is derived: a dominating visual statement that communicates both evidence of a reasoned intelligence at work, and a profound coherence as "an architectural entity whose outer order most nearly reflects its inner order, and whose laws govern the aesthetic organization of even the smallest buildings and gardens" (see p. ix, Foreword).

To claim more for this or any architectural model is hazardous. The Benedictine makers of the Plan drew upon long experience and profound thinking to frame it. They then employed a drawing technique to postulate a new conception in architecture for a monastic community. This conception is embodied in the Plan of

WEST

SOUTH

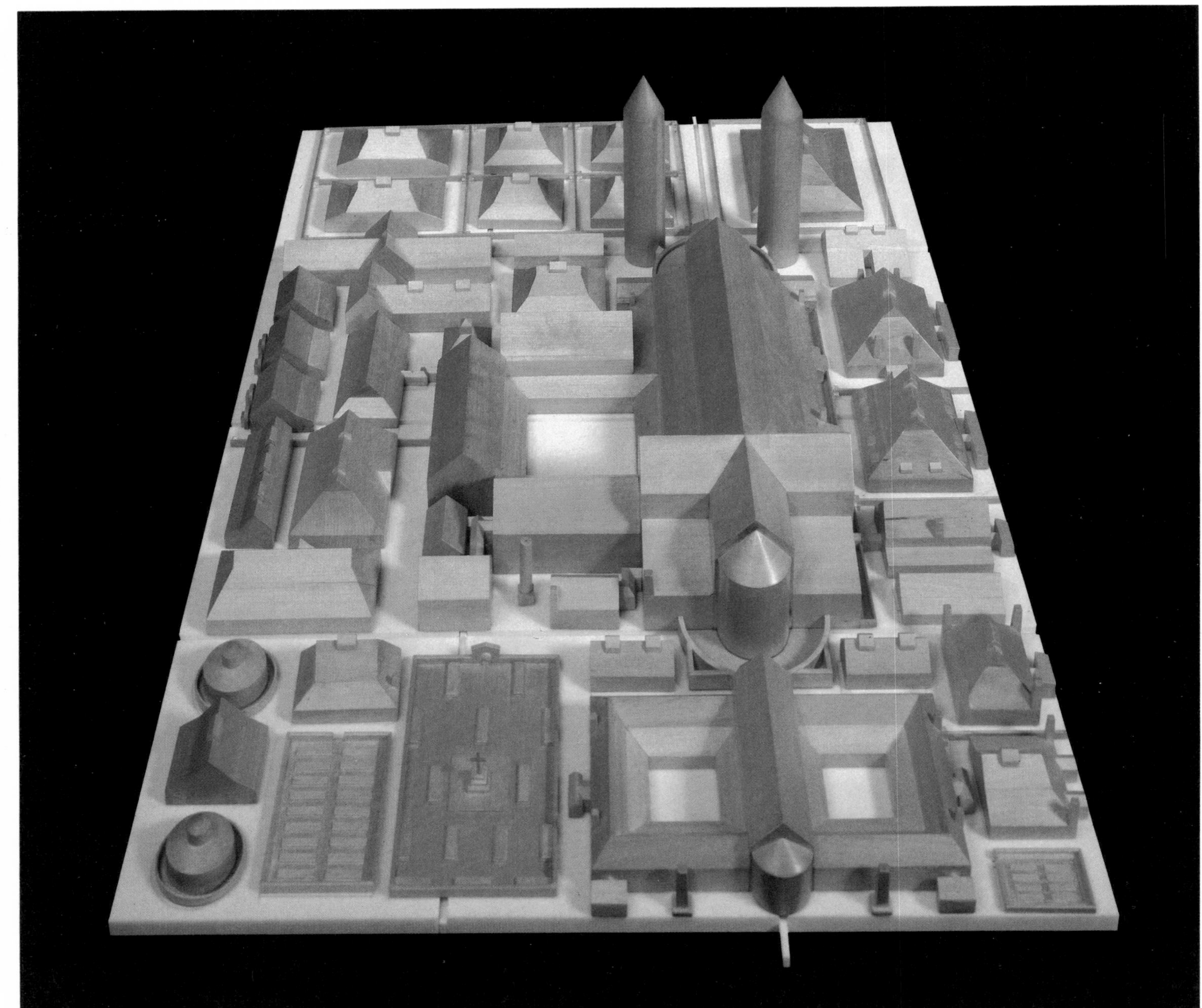

NORTH

EAST

PLAN OF ST GALL: AIR VIEW EAST TO WEST

St Gall, a graphic image that arises from intellectual sources lying between empirical and *a priori* reasoning, and partakes of both. Drawing and model are different modes of expression, two elements in a vocabulary of communication techniques that also includes verbal language and alphabetic writing. The realization of the Plan of St Gall as drawn in a fully executed work of architectural construction, never fulfilled, will always be immanent, eternally stimulating to the imagination. A model of the Plan's buildings can succeed only imperfectly; but in some small degree it can translate and reflect the depth of the document's conceptual sources to offer an exhilirating interpretation of one of the most innovative architectural programs ever created. L.P. E.B.

A NOTE ON THE MAKER OF THE ARCHITECTURAL MODELS

CARL BERTIL LUND's long and distinguished career began in San Francisco under architect Lewis Hobart. Lund spent a lengthy period in New York in the office of John Russell Pope as close assistant to Otto Eggers, Pope's famous designer and one of the greatest architectural draftsmen of this country.

Lund returned to San Francisco late in the 1930s, and was Ernest Born's assistant until retirement. In addition to rare talents in architectural draftsmanship, Mr. Lund possesses remarkable skill in woodcraft, including uncanny expertise in fashioning small objects that demand a high degree of exactness essential to making models accurately to scale. His unique combination of training and special endowments, a passionate attachment to architecture, and an intense zeal for perfection, impart to this work a vibrance and feeling rarely found in abstraction-representation that the model of the Plan buildings typifies.

A MASTER PLAN FOR THE BUILDINGS OF A BENEDICTINE MONASTERY WORKED OUT IN SYNODS OF AACHEN A.D. 816-817. INTERPRETATION DRAWN TO SCALE OF THE DIMENSIONS OF A COPY MADE FOR ABBOT GOZBERT AND KEPT IN THE LIBRARY OF ST GALL. ▶